Class Clowns

CLASS CLOWNS

How the Smartest Investors
Lost Billions in Education

JONATHAN
A. KNEE

Columbia Business School
Publishing

Columbia University Press
Publishers Since 1893
New York   Chichester, West Sussex
cup.columbia.edu

Library of Congress Cataloging-in-Publication Data
Names: Knee, Jonathan A., author.
Title: Class clowns : how the smartest investors lost billions in education /
Jonathan A. Knee.
Description: New York : Columbia University Press, [2017] | Series: Columbia
Business School publishing | Includes bibliographical references and index.
Identifiers: LCCN 2016027438 | ISBN 9780231179287 (cloth : alk. paper)
Subjects: LCSH: Education—Economic aspects—Case studies. |
Education—Finance—Case studies. | Investments—Case studies.
Classification: LCC LC65 .K59 2016 | DDC 338.4/337—dc23
LC record available at https://lccn.loc.gov/2016027438

∞

Columbia University Press books are printed on permanent
and durable acid-free paper.

Printed in the United States of America

c 10 9 8 7 6 5 4 3 2 1

Cover design: Fifth Letter

For Roger C. Altman
who gave me a job when I needed one
and didn't fire me no matter how I tempted him

Contents

Acknowledgments

THIS BOOK BEGAN long ago and far from where it ended up. Shortly after the publication of my last book, *Curse of the Mogul*, I had an idea for an extended essay about American culture. I was deeply influenced by my undergraduate thesis adviser, moral philosopher Alasdair MacIntyre. I had the good fortune of studying under MacIntyre when he was working on his masterpiece, *After Virtue*,[1] which argues that long-held social practices and beliefs can become untethered from their original justifications over time. As a result, the practices and beliefs persist long after the conditions that were the basis for their legitimacy have disappeared.

After Virtue is preoccupied with the roots of the moral virtues generally accepted in Western civilization. I was interested in specifically examining those characteristics that Americans believe make them unique. My hypothesis was that many of these beliefs—grounded either in historical reality or a mythology that emerged over time—are strongly held but contrary to clear empirical evidence. My plan was to explore the genesis and impact of a wide range of these peculiarly American conceits.

Whatever its merits, the project never really got off the ground. Both of my previous books were based on subjects about which I already knew a fair amount. *The Accidental Investment Banker*, a history of investment banking, used my personal experiences to tell the story of the dramatic changes in the industry during the most recent decade. *The Curse of the Mogul* came out of a course I and my coauthors had been teaching for years. Although each book required extensive additional research, a deep foundation of data and information was already in place when I began.

This newer literary enterprise, provisionally titled *American Lies*, would need to be undertaken from a standing start. What's more, my background as a long-time media investment banker and some-time business school professor didn't make me the most logical chronicler of contemporary cultural peccadillos, no matter how potentially interesting the framework. So I gradually lost my enthusiasm—or maybe just my nerve.

A number of the topics I had planned to tackle in *American Lies* related to fundamentally misguided beliefs that Americans hold about education. For instance, most Americans embrace our anachronistic—from an international perspective, in any case—method of choosing first-year university students. Admissions decisions in the United States rely, in part, on essays, recommendations, and extracurricular activities, and there is a broad consensus that these criteria constitute laudable and effective devices to build diverse student bodies. In fact, the historic origin of this approach was the realization by our most selective universities that any of the more objective mechanisms, whether based on test scores or grades and still used almost everywhere else in the world today, would yield too many Jewish students for their taste.[2] Similarly, relatively few are aware of the eugenicist philosophy of those who initially promoted the SAT exams that continue to play a central role in admissions decisions.[3]

As a media investment banker, I had noted a certain irrationality, particularly in deals undertaken by empire-building moguls in the entertainment industry. Some of these observations had informed the analysis of *Curse of the Mogul*. Separately, however, I was struck by the fact that in education—a media subsector in which I had been active for more than twenty years—deals ended up being as bad as or worse for the buyer but the animating ethos often seemed quite different from that of the entertainment moguls. Quite often the investors actually seemed driven, at least in part, by a genuine desire to improve education, although they were operating under deeply flawed assumptions about the nature of the education business.

It occurred to me that a closer look at how and why otherwise successful investors had failed so spectacularly in education would allow me to pursue some of the questions that had interested me in *American Lies* while writing about a topic on which I already had some expertise and credibility. I decided to radically shift the book's focus accordingly, and this is the result.

My experience as an investment banker since the 1990s introduced me, directly or indirectly, to many of the individuals and transactions highlighted in the book. For instance, I was part of the team that represented the special committee of the board that approved the go-private transaction of Edison Schools. I also represented the seller or the buyer—or tried to—in many of the other transactions discussed. In all cases, the information contained in the book is based on public information or interviews conducted and materials provided explicitly for this purpose.

In writing *Class Clowns*, I am particularly appreciative of the dozens of individuals who agreed to talk with me (whether on the record or, more often, on background) and to provide documents relating to the businesses and transactions covered. Even when I was directly involved with a company or situation covered, my focus was not on this book's topic. These supplemental conversations accordingly provided me with nuance and perspective that I could not have otherwise obtained.

My greatest debt is to those who slogged through a draft of the entire manuscript and provided detailed feedback. Myra Kogen, the long-time director of the Brooklyn College Learning Center, is always my first and most patient reader. She manages to be supportive and enthusiastic, even as she provides incisive criticism. Darren Carter, a portfolio manager at Neuberger Berman, is a friend and former colleague who combines investing and writing prowess in equal measure. Dr. John Edward Murphy, my oldest friend, is a brilliant scientist, elegant writer, and merciless critic. Fiona Hollands, associate director and senior researcher at Teacher College's Center for Benefit-Cost Studies of Education, did what she could to remedy my lack of foundation in educational policy and research, all with remarkable good humor. Professor Bruce Greenwald's contribution to my intellectual and personal well-being extends far beyond this book; it is not an exaggeration to say that this book would not have been possible without him.

Two colleagues at Evercore, where I have been a banker since 2003, merit special thanks. Jason Sobol and Nathan Graf have borne the thankless job of protecting me from myself (with admittedly an uneven track record through no fault of their own) for many years and in many contexts, with their substantive criticism of my first draft representing only the latest example. Jason has been my professional partner for a dozen years, and, in the absence of his breathtaking ability and tireless support, I could never have been able to operate with one foot in investment banking and the other in academia for as long as I have. Nathan, in addition to being responsible for the book's title, is a constant source of sharp insights that have always made me stronger, though sometimes I admit that I worry they could kill me. Together, by virtue of their talent and generosity, they have allowed me to transition to being a full-time professor at Columbia. They are even nice enough to pretend to still benefit from my occasional input as a senior advisor at Evercore.

Others at Evercore have taken time out of their otherwise highly demanding jobs to perform research and analysis that underpins much of this work. In particular, Alexander Foster, Adam Frankel, Stephen Hannan, Melody Koh, Helen Li, Michele Luchejko, Austin Settle, Katherine Xu, and Emily Zhou all lent their time and their judgment to improve the final product. I am also appreciative of the help from Nadine Jackson and Christine Sycz, my executive assistants at Evercore over the period of the book's long gestation.

At Columbia, I benefited from the comments and suggestions of several of my colleagues—Professors Malia Mason and Miklos Sarvary at the Business School, James Stewart and Nicholas Lemann at the Journalism School, and Tim Wu at the Law School. Ankit Shah, from Columbia College, served as my research assistant and pressed ahead even over the holidays. More generally, I rely relentlessly on Hollis O'Rorke and Jamie Chandler at the Business School's Media and Technology Program; they help me keep all the balls in the air at the same time. And at Columbia University Press, I owe Myles Thompson and Stephen Wesley deep thanks for their help and their advocacy of this somewhat unconventional academic tome.

Finally I want to thank a longer list of friends, colleagues, and industry participants who provided encouragement, commented on some part of the manuscript, or just shared their perspective on some aspect of the book's thesis. In light of the more controversial aspects of the narrative, some of these people requested not to be thanked in print. Those still willing to be publicly associated with me include Ethan Berman, Paul Ingrassia, Judith Kaye, David Knee, Chaille Maddox, Nick Pearson, Clare Reihill, Andrew Rosen, and Patrick Tierney.

Needless to say, none of the people mentioned above should be blamed for the final product. That said, you cannot imagine what it would have looked like if I hadn't had their input.

Class Clowns

Introduction

"Education is not preparation for life; education is life itself."[1]
—JOHN DEWEY (SORT OF)

THE FINAL YEARS of the twentieth century witnessed a surge of interest from a veritable who's who of investors, entrepreneurs, academics, and policy makers who all had the idea that education could be dramatically improved by implementing radical new business models. Some of this euphoria coincided with the first Internet boom, during which many traditional ways of doing things were thought to face imminent obsolescence. In the case of education, however, the intensity of conviction was bolstered by a belief in the power of applying market disciplines to a sector that often seemed to shun them on principle. Technology might accelerate the coming revolution, but it was new big ideas about education that fueled it.

And money. Lots of money.

The billions of dollars that had and would continue to flow into education were unsurprising given the stakes involved. The overarching objective, according to the *New York Times*, which closely chronicled these developments, was no less than to "turn the $700 billion education sector into 'the next health care'—that is, transform large portions of a fragmented, cottage industry of independent, nonprofit institutions into a consolidated, professionally managed, money-making set of businesses that include all levels of education."[2]

In this environment, the initial public offering (IPO) of Edison Schools on November 11, 1999, was a signal event. Edison represented the powerful proposition that a private company could deliver better public schools for less money, leaving taxpayers, investors, and children better off. With ambitions to operate a thousand public schools, Edison would represent less than 1 percent of all public schools, but its impact could be far broader. If successful, Edison could establish a standard of excellence by which all schools would then be judged and to which they would aspire. As founder Chris Whittle predicted, "Ten years from now, when you think about who does the best schools, we want there to be only one word that quickly comes to mind."[3]

It wasn't that the offering was particularly successful by traditional criteria. The shares were priced at $18, below the original proposed range, and they barely budged once trading began. By contrast, many of the eighteen other NASDAQ IPOs of that week experienced the kind of explosive value bump typical of the era's technology offerings. But Edison was definitively not a technology stock. It did, however, have one important characteristic in common with many high-flying technology offerings of the era: it did not and had never made money. In fact Edison, founded in 1991, around the time the first webpage was created and well before the Internet was commercialized, had managed to lose money for far longer than any of these public market darlings.

The Edison IPO represented the establishment's embrace of the notion that education was poised to be revolutionized for the better. Merrill Lynch, a long-time leader in equity underwritings, managed the offering.[4] The investors represented the best in breed of individual and institutional investors. Paul Allen, who had recently invested $30 million, was not just the legendary cofounder of Microsoft but also a leading Silicon Valley venture capitalist. Just that week, he had been involved in two other successful IPOs—Expedia and Charter Communications.[5] The leading commercial bank, J.P. Morgan, and the leading bank to growth companies of its day, Donaldson, Lufkin & Jenrette, were also investors.[6] John W. Childs, who had engineered the wildly successful leveraged buyout (LBO) of Snapple as a senior executive of Thomas H. Lee Partners before founding his own buyout firm, was an early backer, as was the Wallenberg family investment vehicle, Investor AB. The company had also attracted the president of one of the oldest and most prestigious educational institutions in the United States, Yale University, to serve as its chief executive officer (CEO).

On November 12, 2003, shareholders voted overwhelmingly to sell the company for less than a tenth of the $18 per share paid in the IPO four years earlier. The very public collapse of Edison did not, however, dampen otherwise sophisticated investors' enthusiasm for transformational educational concepts. Indeed, if anything, the flow of capital into the education sector has accelerated in the decade since the first Edison debacle, though often with similar results. As the activity level has increased, the high caliber of the backers for these enterprises has held steady—encompassing the top echelon of financial institutions, wealthy individuals, corporate sponsors, private equity, sovereign wealth, venture capital, and even hedge funds—as have the dismal financial outcomes.

The stories of financial failure that follow are filled with the names of individuals and organizations whose successful financial exploits in other domains have defined the era. The strategic vision of billionaire moguls Rupert Murdoch and Ron Perelman shaped both the structure of the global media industry and the art of deal making. John Paulson's hedge funds made $15 billion in 2007, predicting the coming financial collapse. Michael Milken may still be controversial, but few question the transformative impact to the economy of the financial instruments he popularized and the markets he developed. The world's leading investment banks—not just J.P. Morgan, but also Goldman Sachs, Credit Suisse, and many others—certainly generated fees from the sector but also lost hundreds of millions from a combination of bad investments, loan defaults, and ill-conceived underwritings. And the long list of multibillion-dollar private equity and sovereign wealth funds that have continued to fare poorly in education represent some of the most storied names in a sector whose influence on global financial markets is unprecedented. Might their collective fate provide clues to the seemingly intractable challenges facing education more broadly?

Introducing the subject of education is like administering a political Rorschach test. Questions of educational policy elicit intense reactions on a wide range of emotional hot-button issues, from unions to affirmative action to the gap between rich and poor. More than thirty years after the publication of the landmark *A Nation at Risk*[7] report by the National Commission on Excellence in Education, education has seemed to remain in perpetual crisis. Warring constituencies find little common ground on the nature of the problems, much less their solutions. If there is any consensus, it is that things are not getting better. Whether it's school children's falling rankings internationally in math, reading, and science proficiency or the lack of preparedness of our college graduates to enter the workforce, these fundamental deficiencies have only become more pronounced. From time to time, a shining example of isolated success—whether a student, an educator, a program, or an institution—is held up, only to be contrasted with the inadequacy of everything else.

The persistence of these disagreements reflects the extent to which our approach to education as a nation implicates how we think of ourselves as a people. At the most basic level, the American identity as the land of opportunity is deeply intertwined with how educational opportunity is made available.

American exceptionalism, in education at least, is not a myth; rather, it is grounded in the reality of how the country came to be. American's peculiar attitude toward education was central to Alexis de Toqueville's coining of the concept of "exceptionalism" in *Democracy in America*. "From the beginning," wrote de Toqueville, "the originality of American civilization was most clearly apparent in the provisions made for public education."[8] Providing basic education to all was viewed as an essential element to building the anti-aristocratic society the early settlers envisioned. In fact, these fiercely independent Puritans were happy not only to collect taxes for this purpose but also to enforce payment and actual attendance through fines and even the potential deprivation of parental rights.

The ideological tinge to the current educational debates reflects this combination of historical and contemporary controversies that lie just beneath the surface. Into this witch's brew of themes and concerns are inevitably added deeply personal considerations. The formative experiences of being educated leave an indelible mark. Every successful person has at least one oft-replayed story about that teacher or that course or that administrator or that institution that made a difference—whether good and bad—in his or her life.

These education-related turning points in individuals' lives may have very little to do with pedagogy or policy. The teacher who took a lonely and isolated child seriously. The book that spoke to a long-held secret. The class in which you met your first true love. The psychological lives of young people grappling for a sense of identity in the face of a vast menu of new experiences and emotions are complicated. What actually serves as a transformational catalyst in a particular case is impossible to predict in advance and almost as hard to accurately diagnose after the fact. It is unavoidable, however, that these epiphanic moments are, to some extent, generalized and incorporated into one's views on education.

These multiple sources of interest explain only in part the intensity, ubiquity, and nature of the various ongoing political and intellectual debates on educational matters.[9] The rest of the explanation is just how much money is now involved. Roughly $1 trillion annually in the United States alone, the sheer volume of public expenditure on education ensures that it will be the subject of heated combat among and between groups focused on minimizing taxes, getting funds, and using the services.

The massive pool of government largesse flowing to education takes the form of everything from teacher salaries and capital investment to student loans, veterans' benefits, tax deductions, Head Start, and school nutrition programs. With this much at stake, education cannot

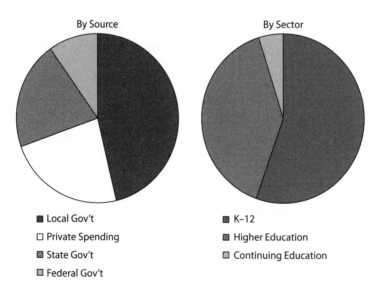

Figure I.1 2015 U.S. education spending. *Sources:* U.S. Census; U.S. Department of Education; BMO Capital Markets.

help but be a high-profile issue. There is a political multiplier effect, however, when matters of money—particularly enormous quantities of money—also implicate matters of principle and personal identity.

Outside the government sphere, the flow of private funds has grown dramatically. The Bill and Melinda Gates Foundation is the most well known of a cadre of foundations that have become major consistent sources of educational funding. For the past decade, a combination of established funds like the Ford Foundation and the Carnegie Corporation have joined newer organizations like the Broad Foundation and Lumina Foundation, along with multiple locally oriented education foundations, to invest $4–$5 billion dollars annually into a mix of public, nonprofit, and for-profit educational ventures.[10] In addition to private institutional funding, rich individuals have increasingly become enamored of the idea of making a difference in education. Having a building or a program named at one's alma mater is a long-established practice, but recently, charter schools and education policy advocacy groups have become the charity of choice among a large swath of hedge fund billionaires.[11]

If education is failing, it is not for lack of money or attention. Our greatest minds and our deepest pocketbooks seem committed to making it better. How can we reconcile this depth of commitment to improve things with the apparent inability to do so?

The passions elicited by educational topics have proven a double-edged sword. Passion ensures enduring focus, but can also color perspective and generate a level of conviction that the facts do not support. Passion can lead to an embrace of simplistic, all-encompassing explanations, whereas the reality is all nuance. Passion can take the well meaning down dark alleys paved by less-well-meaning suitors who exploit emotional weakness.

When brilliant, rich, passionate people disagree, reaching quiet resolution is an unlikely outcome. In educational matters, where the debate is on matters of principle and the data are often ambiguous and subject to multiple interpretations, progress is even harder to come by. There is no agreed measure of success, except at the very highest level of abstraction—that is, "improved student outcomes," which becomes the subject of intense debate when actually defined. The frequent lack of consistent, transparent, timely data on educational effectiveness exacerbates the structural obstacles to consensus. Even the policy implications of widely available basic metrics, such as test scores (are the right things being tested?) or graduation rates (are the graduates actually prepared?), are the subject of heated controversy.

The story of Edison Schools reminds us that, outside of academia, the public sector, and the nonprofit world, there is a thriving marketplace for educational ideas, where success and failure are not subject to debate and can be measured quite precisely—in dollars and cents. Some of the most respected minds of our generation have invested many billions of dollars in for-profit education enterprises. And, with surprising regularity, they have lost their shirts.

No less a personage than Steve Jobs spent most of the time between his two stints at Apple trying to transform education with Ross Perot's money (and when that ran out, with Canon Corporation's money). After more than a decade, the company (NeXT) created some interesting software, but it was a disaster commercially and had no appreciable impact on the education market.[12]

The simple idea of this book is that by highlighting where these otherwise accomplished individuals went demonstrably wrong, we can identify a number of common errors that have undermined progress in education. These mistakes have often flowed from a basic misunderstanding of the education ecosystem specifically and the importance of industry structure more generally. Collectively, the lessons drawn provide guardrails that can help not just investors and businesspeople but also policy makers and administrators avoid some of the more treacherous and persistent pitfalls.

The book is organized around four extended case studies from which the core lessons emerge. The ability of Chris Whittle to repeatedly raise money for questionable business propositions more than a decade after the unambiguous failure of Edison reflects a self-destructive tendency of education investors to cling to misguided convictions in the face of contrary evidence. The good intentions of Rupert Murdoch and Joel Klein in trying to revolutionize how our children learn led them to irrationally discount the increasingly high probability of disappointment as their plans soured. The failure of a string of investors to appreciate the costs and risks of creating educational content, as well as of the need to continually refresh it, is a key factor in the serial insolvencies undergone by storied publisher Houghton Mifflin. The fate of the vast array of unconnected educational ventures backed by Michael Milken was sealed by his lack of appreciation for the critical role of specialization in building financially robust educational businesses.

These four case studies are followed by a number of contrasting profiles of successful educational ventures. The book's final chapter explores in more detail the recurring themes embedded in the recounted tales of financial success and folly, including those lessons just noted and many others.

There are disadvantages to using cases from the for-profit sector. Although it is true that it is relatively easy to identify whether someone made or lost money, this is different from determining whether their pedagogic objectives were achieved. We all know that "bad" products sometimes seem to make lots of money. That said, every educational business plan is built on assumptions about how students learn, how teachers teach, and how decisions are made about what products and services to use. They also rely on a view of the education ecosystem's structure and on locating a position within it that permits the establishment of a sustainable competitive advantage. When those plans miss the mark, particularly on a grand scale, important lessons can be learned about which specific underlying assumptions were misplaced.

More important, even when an enterprise is nonprofit in nature, it is necessary to appreciate its place in the overall industry structure in order to assess its long-term viability. Nonprofit businesses often rely on the ability to continue to attract government and private funding. A miscalculation of the capital needed can be as deadly to its survival as running out of money is to a for-profit educational business. Understanding the key drivers that enable the development of sustainable educational business models is as critical to building enduring nonprofit enterprises as it is for building enduring for-profit enterprises. So although the case studies employed here are all from the for-profit sector, in which the bottom line can be clearly assessed, they are designed to enable both for-profit and nonprofit enterprises to better identify the structural imperatives that will facilitate their survival—a necessary, if not sufficient, condition for making a positive contribution to education.

There are other, more fundamental objections to using financial profit or loss as a relevant metric for education. Some express deep ideological hostility to the very existence of for-profit educational institutions. For-profit primary and secondary schools have always faced opposition from those concerned with the historic equalizing role of public schools, the impact on teacher unions, and the increasing gap between rich and poor. For-profit universities have been viewed with similar derision by those who view these institutions as opportunistically exploiting government's abandonment of its responsibility to support a strong network of public community colleges. The recent scandals around widely publicized abuses of the federal loan programs by for-profit universities have provided compelling fodder for those who hold these views.

Even the loudest proponents of public education, however, do not object to the for-profit nature of the educational enterprises that make up the majority of the sector. For-profit schools represent an increasingly small percentage of the total revenues of the vast web of private enterprises engaged in educational endeavors. These enterprises produce everything from the textbooks and software that provide the teaching materials to the testing and assessment products that monitor the results to the technologies that assist communication and decision making across every element of the learning cycle. Literally thousands of businesses big and small exist only to support the activities of not just educational institutions but also the training and development efforts of the corporate sector. In any case, philosophical hostility toward for-profit education should not extend to the possibility of gaining insight from the ashes of their efforts.

An altogether different and more practical objection to focusing on for-profit education is that it just doesn't matter that much in the scheme of things. Educational spending overall is overwhelmingly dominated by and directed toward public entities. Of the estimated $1.3 trillion expected to be spent on U.S. education in 2015, mostly from government sources, less than 10 percent will go to the for-profit education sector.[13] That said, the $125 billion in revenues expected to be generated by for-profit education is still an awful lot of money. Furthermore, as noted, understanding the key structural, strategic, and operational considerations that make the difference between successful and unsuccessful education businesses is equally relevant to nonprofit education businesses. Most important, however, is the central role played by the pervasive government regulation of the sector. Without an understanding of the key drivers of private-sector behavior, the public sector cannot hope to structure an effective regulatory regime for whatever objectives it is pursuing. A partnership between the public and private sectors in education based on mutual understanding could create a virtuous circle in which both are strengthened. In practice, however, that interaction has yielded a vicious cycle in which regulations have resulted in outcomes contrary to those intended, precisely because of confusion regarding underlying industry dynamics—only to prompt yet more regulations that only exacerbate the problem.

In addition to highlighting the key structural attributes of educational business, the cases used for this exercise were selected, in part, to reinforce an overarching theme: educating students presents a diverse and complex set of challenges that do not lend themselves to a single set of easy solutions. Like all "big" social questions, such as crime and poverty, the gravity of the issues involved cry out for a simple comprehensive strategy that quickly yields meaningful improvements. Yet, this idea lends itself to grand-sounding initiatives—whether a "War on Poverty" or "No Child Left Behind"—that inevitably fall short.

The historical evidence is that, time and again, the greatest successes come from a series of targeted incremental steps forward that confront, one by one, the full variety of problems to be addressed.[14] This book's objective is for the lessons outlined to provide such incremental benefits, rather than an overarching "solution." Conversely, based on the evidence presented here, the biggest failures in education come from trying to do too much, too soon. Pursuing "revolution" or "transformation" by blindly applying insights gained from a particular context across a broad range of only tangentially related situations is likely to do more damage than good.

This book examines three broad domains of education (Table I.1): (1) education through high school (generally called K–12 education, but also encompassing prekindergarten and early childhood learning[15]), (2) colleges and universities (called higher education), and (3) continuing adult learning (whether independently undertaken or as part of corporate training efforts). Some of the case studies focus on a single domain: Both Whittle and Murdoch, for instance, were preoccupied exclusively with K–12 education. Michael Milken, by contrast, had multiple investments in each of the three domains.

Within each segment, there remain critically important distinctions—for example, the challenges of teaching advanced placement calculus to gifted high school students is very different from selecting the best manipulatives for a kindergarten class. However, there are two important reasons to treat K–12, higher, and continuing education separately.

First, from an economic perspective, the nature of who businesses sell to in each of these arenas is fundamentally different. This, in turn, has a profound impact on the most effective organization of the

TABLE I.1
Summary of education sectors ($ in billions)

Sectors	Total Spending 2015	For-Profit Revenue 2015	Estimated Annual Sector Growth 2015–2020	Key For-Profit Subsectors
K–12	$745	$45	2.7%	Childcare/early learning; For-profit schools; Textbooks/supplemental publishers; Testing and assessment; Professional development; Learning management system; Enterprise management system
Higher Education	$530	$65	3.4%	For-profit universities; Curriculum/textbook developers; Student lifecycle services (e.g., admissions, retention, placement); Learning management system; Enterprise management system
Continuing Education	$65	$15	3.9%	Instruction-led training; E-learning training/certification; Content developers; Platform/infrastructure developers
Total	$1,340	$125	3.3%	

Source: BMO Capital Markets

businesses and their basic business model. K–12 sales are generally made to governmental entities, school districts, or sometimes even states that formally "adopt" particular products, often on a long-established, multiyear schedule. Higher-education sales are more ad hoc and are generally made either to individual institutions or to individual teachers who are typically free to decide what products to use in their classes. Continuing education is often sold directly to consumers or to the corporate human resources divisions of for-profit enterprises. Given these important distinctions, it is not surprising that many of even the largest educational companies operate primarily or exclusively in only one of these education realms.

Second, from a public policy perspective, the most contentious issues are also quite different in different domains—as are the nature of the resulting regulations that constrain the operations of these businesses. This, in part, relates to where the money comes from—K–12 funding is predominantly a state and local matter, whereas higher-education funding comes primarily from a combination of federal, state, and private sources. Continuing education has less direct funding but is sometimes the subject of various tax incentives. More fundamentally, however, the issues at stake in educating the very young, those preparing for a career, and those looking to upgrade their existing job are viewed very differently. Even when the same issue is raised, it would not be unusual or necessarily inconsistent for the same person to have a very different reaction depending on the context. For instance, many who are happy to have tenure at universities abhor it in their local public schools.

Just as K–12, higher, and continuing education broadly support different types of business models, so too do traditional publishing, software, and services businesses. The largest educational publishing businesses are multibillion-dollar enterprises that, in some cases, are more than a century old and have shown modest growth in the face of changing business models, though they often still generate prodigious cash flows. The software and technology businesses that have sprung up over the past decade have, in many cases, grown quickly and garnered outsized attention relative to their size and profitability. These include a wide range of digital content, analytics, learning and administrative management, and distribution businesses. The business of actually providing educational services in direct competition with incumbent public and nonprofit private institutions has proven, as noted, the most controversial of the for-profit enterprises.

Whatever one thinks of these endeavors, understanding their underlying economics is still useful. Many of the largest educational enterprises now encompass a portfolio of businesses that reflect most, if not all, of these potential modalities. In general, however, a single business model still predominates. All of the educational publishers have launched a variety of software businesses, and some actually now operate schools of their own. In addition, certain for-profit universities have purchased educational content businesses. Sometimes these expansions reflect a natural extension of the core, and sometimes they are just an effort to hedge the risk in the core. In selecting cases to examine, I chose examples of each of these types of businesses to high-light the key distinctions in both the underlying business models and the expansion strategies.

Each case explored in this book tries to tell a story. Sometimes the protagonist is a person—perhaps an investor or a business leader—and sometimes it is the product or business itself. The stories also represent a mix of fundamentally bad businesses, blindly pursued, and poten-tially good businesses that were poorly run or wrongly capitalized. In all cases, money was lost, sometimes quite a bit and sometimes repeat-edly. This kind of track record tends to elicit an instinctive search for villains. Readers may spot a few within these pages, but it is a sur-prisingly small number given the magnitude and circumstances of the losses. In most cases, despite the fact that these are for-profit ventures, the individuals involved appear to have been motivated, in part, by a genuine desire to improve education. That desire is often associated with a deep-seated belief about what is wrong with the current system. The moral of these tales is how the intensity of desire and belief can cloud the judgment of even the most sophisticated investor.

Brilliant, rich people with a passionate emotional commitment to an idea not only have trouble responding to rational debate, but they also, unfortunately, have a tendency to attract con artists, the best of which instinctively know what story to tell and what information to feed a mark so committed to an idea that they will fail to verify claims. It is sometimes hard to distinguish a crook from a true believer. The narratives presented here try to stick to facts and withhold judgment. I would suggest, however, that the most probative evidence is to what extent the money lost is one's own or others'.

At the end of the day, the underlying motivations of the various actors matter less than knowing how to avoid the mistakes detailed here. The trick is to retain the passion for education but lose the emotional or ideological commitments to particular solutions. When it comes to educating future generations, the stakes are indeed high. As investors and as citizens, the downside of letting ourselves be conned is substantial, regardless of whether we are being tricked or we are simply fooling ourselves.

CHAPTER ONE

The Wizard of Ed

LATE IN 2013 John Fisher, scion of the family that founded Gap, co-owner of the Oakland A's, and chairman of the well-regarded nonprofit charter school chain KIPP, purchased control of Avenues School. Avenues is a private elementary school that first opened its doors to students the previous year. The school is housed in a magnificent new building created on Manhattan's far West Side by the architecture firm Perkins Eastman and the interior design firm Bonetti/ Kozerski Studio, "best known for crafting Donna Karan's sensuous but scrupulously minimalist Manhattan apartment."[1] Unlike KIPP, which operates public schools for low-income families in underserved communities, Avenues set the high-water mark for private school tuition in New York City and fashioned itself "The World School" in anticipation of a network of comparable campuses in "20 or more" leading cities around the globe.

What was unusual about this high-profile deal is that there was no press release and no media coverage whatsoever. This is particularly strange given the entrepreneur who raised the cash to fund the original venture, legendary salesman and promoter H. Christopher "Chris" Whittle. Few others have succeeded in securing front page *New York Times* coverage for the launch of new ventures.[2]

The quiet sale to Fisher followed industry whispers that Whittle would fail to find backers to finance his global ambitions. Why would Whittle choose not to use the vote of confidence from a respected billionaire to trumpet his success? In fact, the transaction was a kind of hostile takeover that followed the collapse of frantic efforts by Whittle to find alternative financing that would leave him in control of Avenues.

The first public acknowledgment of the change of ownership was buried toward the back of Avenues's New Year annual letter in 2014. Whittle's letter mentioned only that Fisher was "an important new investor" who would add to Avenues's "financial strength and overall leadership."[3] Later, the letter noted that in addition to providing needed capital to the business, Fisher would be buying out one of the two original investors after less than three years. Finally, "an important new team member" was welcomed. Jeff Clark, Whittle said, would serve as president/COO where he would be responsible for "buildup of infrastructure, methods, and systems." Left unsaid was that no one would now report directly to Whittle and that all of the operating decisions would be made by Clark, the leader placed by Fisher.

Whittle's effective removal from any day-to-day responsibility for Avenues was not itself a surprise. Indeed, to a greater or lesser degree, that had happened at each of his previous ventures. Time and again, investors or senior executives insisted on Whittle relinquishing control as a condition of their continuing involvement. What is surprising, even shocking, is that for over twenty years, in the educational arena Chris Whittle has been able to continue to separate sophisticated investors from their money despite a plethora of red flags that in any other context might be viewed as disqualifying.

Whittle's durable fundraising success in the face of financial and operating failure can only in part be explained by his marketing prowess. By the time Whittle directed his full attention to the educational arena in the early 1990s, his previous exploits had already left a widely publicized trail of unhappy partners, tales of profligate corporate spending and personal excess, accounting irregularities, exaggerated claims, and charges of self-dealing, all culminating in financial collapse. A close examination of Whittle's track record reveals much about the faulty assumptions and predispositions that have made education investors particularly vulnerable to his unique talents.

> "Oh, no my dear. I'm a very good man.
> I'm just a very bad Wizard."[4]

The rise and fall of Chris Whittle's mini-media empire of specialty publication and video products that preceded his exclusive focus on education has been thoroughly documented over the years.[5] Backed by a

University of Tennessee professor, Whittle and some college friends launched what was called 13-30 Corporation in 1970 in an abandoned pillow factory in Knoxville. The original business created free publications underwritten by a single advertiser. These first targeted college students—*Knoxville in a Nutshell* was the maiden effort—and later expanded to serve other geographic and demographic niches. However, in 1979 with the help of money raised from the Swedish Bonnier publishing empire, 13-30 bought control of *Esquire* magazine.

The birth of Whittle Communications came in 1986 when Whittle and his founding partner, Philip Moffitt, agreed to go their separate ways—Moffitt keeping *Esquire* and Whittle keeping the the specialty publications. The break with Moffitt reflected the culmination of a long-running psychodrama in which Whittle struggled to emerge from the shadow of his one-time mentor.[6] But the tensions were aggravated by the extent to which the growth of the business and the introduction of serious outside money—which by this time included not only Bonnier but also Lord Rothemere's Associated Newspapers—had fed Whittle's weakness for lavish spending and self-promotion.

Whether the topic was expensive new hiring, a personal car and driver, or the need for either personal or corporate PR, Moffitt had consistently served as a constraint on Whittle's desires. Whittle had developed a close personal bond with architect-designer Peter Marino, a Warhol protégé who specialized in opulence and had become popular with celebrities. Together they spent four years putting the final touches on Whittle's apartment in the Dakota, complete with sock drawers lined with hand tooled leather. Whittle also purchased a Vermont farmhouse and adjoining land and supervised the complete relandscaping of the property. Even as he oversaw these projects, Whittle found time to travel the world amassing dozens of precious works of art of all types.

Untethered from Moffitt, Whittle's extravagance escalated, both in his outlays and in his claims about the performance of the business. Furthermore, without a day-to-day partner, there was no one to enforce boundaries between the personal and professional at close range. Immediately after the split, Whittle launched a massive project to construct a headquarters covering two square blocks in downtown Knoxville, Tennessee. Designed by Marino and modeled on an Ivy League campus, the project was dubbed "Historic Whittlesburg." This one project would ultimately cost over $50 million—even though the assets of 13-30 taken over by Whittle Communications had generated revenues of only $40 million the previous year.

On the business side, Whittle began to launch niche market media products beyond his historic focus on free single-advertiser magazines. An effort to extend the business model to book publishing, for instance, failed to catch fire. Whittle Direct Books paid large advances to famous authors to write books distributed free to select "opinion leaders" on behalf of a major advertiser.

Most fateful, however, were two initiatives that, unlike his various publishing launches, required massive start-up capital investment. Both Channel One, which programmed a network for elementary school classrooms, and later the Medical News Network (MNN), which programmed a national network of doctor's offices, relied on the same business model: install televisions to attract a customer base and hope to be able to sell enough advertising later to justify the upfront investment in equipment, programming, and sales.It was Channel One that first introduced Whittle to the K–12 education market. In anticipation of its launch he began giving speeches on the need to transform education arguing, for instance, that textbooks were an obsolete "technology straight from the Middle Ages."[7]

"If you build it they will come" business models like Channel One and MNN can succeed, but they require an appropriate capital structure to provide the funds to build the business to a scale that generates cash. The modest profits from Whittle's publishing business, particularly after the drain from the Knoxville construction project, did not come close to filling this gap. So in 1988, with the help of then-banker Richard Holbrooke, Whittle sought a major new strategic investor in Time Inc. Time, inexplicably, permitted all of the $175 million it paid for half of the company to go immediately out of the company to the shareholders. Whittle personally pocketed $40 million, leaving the company as financially constrained as before.[8]

By 1991, with construction of Whittlesburg just reaching completion, the company was running out of money and could not afford to pay bonuses. The top twenty executives held a two-day intervention of sorts with Whittle at a secluded (and of course expensive) Smoky Mountain resort. Viewed by many attendees as "the most crucial two days in the company's history,"[9] the team begged Whittle to scale back expenses and initiatives as the only way to avoid the inevitable implosion of the entire enterprise.

By this time, Whittle had already churned through a series of financial and operating executives who had departed after their similar advice had not been heeded. Hearing the same now in chorus from the collective executive team had little more impact. Instead, Whittle turned to what he did best: selling. This time the objective was a new investor who would fund both his personal appetites and the continuation of precisely the corporate behavior that the intervention had sought to restrain.

Whittle came tantalizingly close to securing an investment from private equity giant Teddy Forstmann, signing a letter of intent to obtain $350 million in return for a third of the company. Less than 10 percent of the investment would have gone to funding new projects, with the balance mostly going out again to equity holders and an increasingly important and wary constituent—the banks that had lent the company money. This dream transaction came to a screeching halt almost as soon as the Forstmann team landed in Knoxville and observed the disparity between the vision spun by Whittle and the reality reflected in the company's financial results. The company's own newsletter reported that Forstmann was too "stodgily substantive" for Whittle's taste and that when that "culture clash showed up in the numbers," they had decided to part ways.

Unfortunately for Whittle, even the most enthusiastic dreamers tend to get a little "stodgily substantive" before writing multihundred-million-dollar checks. Fortunately for Whittle, he found an investor with its own reasons for seeing the expensive new ventures thrive: much of the capital invested would be going to buy its products. Philips Electronics was already selling televisions to Channel One and wanted both to grow that business and to do the same for MNN. The net economics to Philips of funding Whittle's expansion accordingly were far superior to those of any unrelated party. Even with these structural advantages, Philips's 25 percent investment for $175 million, ultimately secured in early 1992, represented a devaluation of the company by one-third from what Forstmann had proposed only months earlier.

In the end, Philips got no bargain. In 1992, revenue actually declined as expenses and investments continued to mount. The banks became increasingly frantic. At a contentious meeting in the summer of 1993, the frustrated and skeptical board established a task force headed by Philips to get to the bottom of the company's results. It also insisted on the hiring of a CFO, which Whittle had resisted for two years even as the company's situation became more precarious.

The new CFO needed to negotiate a quick truce with the banks, who at this point would not even speak with Whittle directly, but needed new capital from the existing investors to do so. Only Associated Newspapers and Philips agreed to put in new money—Associated had benefited from a $100 million windfall from the Time investment and Philips could not let the company fail so soon after their investment. They both insisted that this $60 million would be the last. At a January 1994 board meeting, Whittle predicted that losses for the full fiscal year ending in June would be $25 million—even though the company had already lost $30 million halfway through the year. At the same board meeting, the CFO announced that the loss would likely be three to four times larger. The board replaced Whittle as CEO the following month with a Philips board representative who immediately began shutting money-losing businesses and radically cutting expenses.

Throughout this period, Whittle kept up a frenetic stream of activity and assurances—to the banks, to the board, to customers, to potential investors, to employees, and to the public. The activity was genuine, but the promises were not kept. Banks had negotiated covenants to require business lines to be shut down when targets weren't met, but these were ignored until Whittle was removed. Days before he was replaced, while the company was hemorrhaging cash and had inadequate advertising commitments to cover the cost, Whittle called a press conference to announce the $200 million rollout of MNN. And Whittle simply disregarded a board directive not to pursue any alternative transactions once an agreement with Goldman Sachs had been reached to avoid inevitable liquidation.

Whittle's decision to hire his own banker to contact a new buyer in the face of an explicit prohibition from the board was no doubt in part a function of his frustration with the unattractive terms offered by Goldman. But the real problem for Whittle was Goldman's refusal to make a side payment to address his personal financial straits. The other shareholders would not fund any further losses so were unwilling to run an auction or pursue any other alternatives that would put the Goldman deal at risk. But Whittle, despite all the cash he had pulled out of the business and from investors along the way, had by this time managed to rack up as much as $35 million in personal debt and could not afford to do any deal that did not provide him some relief.[10] Whittle in a sense would be no worse off if he pushed the company into bankruptcy, so he waited until someone—whether it was Goldman, his "partners," or an alternative buyer—was willing to pay him off.

In the summer of 1994, Whittle found a savior in K-III (later renamed Primedia), a portfolio company of private equity giant KKR that the new CFO had previously identified as potentially interested in buying just Channel One. The value K-III placed on the asset would satisfy the outstanding company debts even after a $10 million payment to Whittle.[11] The investors agreed once K-III committed to fund the losses until the deal closed. When it did, Philips lost its entire $175 million and Time lost well over half of its $185 million. Whittle Communications would forever be known at Time Warner as "Time Inc.'s Vietnam."[12]

In a final twist, a money-losing Channel One would ultimately be more or less given away by Primedia in 2007 to a small youth marketing and media company. When that company in turn was sold in 2012, the buyer, Time Warner, had only one condition—it would not take Channel One. The lessons of Vietnam were not lost on Time Warner.

Before the K-III transaction was finalized in October 1994, the price drifted downward as a number of accounting irregularities were discovered. Goldman had identified these same problems earlier. Revenues had been inflated by booking long term revenue deals up front. More concerning, the company had never bothered to file state tax returns despite the auditor insisting that it had told them to do so. The reported $300 million deal had become $240 million by the time it closed. The balance of the assets were sold off quickly at distressed prices or simply shut down.[13]

Interpreting Whittle's motives and behavior through the seemingly inevitable collapse of the business is a complex matter. Most damning, ironically, is a highly sympathetic biography by an author who agreed to let Whittle review the manuscript in advance as the price of cooperation. *An Empire Undone* contains many cringe-inducing passages by a biographer clearly smitten with his subject: "Designing a brilliant model for the Edison Schools was fairly easy. . . ."[14] This overarching perspective makes the sections most relevant to a prospective investor even more startling. Whittle routinely makes outlandish projections not embraced by the operating executives.

Those who counsel caution—particularly with respect to implementing needed operating disciplines—or predict financial disaster are disregarded or discarded. Even those most generous to Whittle speak of his alternate reality.

Whittle himself acknowledges his willingness to ignore the obvious in terms of financial risks but justifies it: "I call it robust naiveté or conscious innocence."[15] Whittle's choice of words is telling. In criminal law, securing a conviction requires "actual knowledge" showing an evil intent. A long-established line of cases, however, provides an exception to this general rule, condemning also those who merely "consciously avoid" becoming aware of the relevant facts.[16]

Even as his niche media empire started to crash down around him, Whittle had become enamored with the education market and begun to design what would become known as the Edison Project. The liquidation of Whittle Communications drew much unwanted attention as Whittle attempted to launch Edison as an independent venture. In October 1994, veteran journalist James Stewart wrote a wide-ranging article on Whittle in *The New Yorker* titled *Grand Illusion*.[17] Stewart, who had met Whittle during the *Esquire* years and expressed fondness for him, struggles in the piece with assessing Whittle personally. But with respect to the prospects of Edison in light of the Whittle Communications saga he is unambiguous:

> Irrespective of its educational merits, which have generated controversy and also garnered much praise, and its economic feasibility—a far shakier proposition—the likelihood at this juncture of major investors' trusting their capital to Whittle seems remote. . . . [O]nce the public school administrators of America have absorbed the magnitude of Whittle's failure with his other ventures they are hardly likely to trust him with their tax dollars, let alone their children.[18]

A large number of government entities did hand over both tax dollars and children. More incomprehensibly, major investors would continue to fund Whittle's ventures for years to come even after he repeated many of the worst excesses of Whittle Communications on a grander scale. In the case of the investments in Edison, what makes this particularly surprising, reputational issues aside, is just what a shaky proposition the economic feasibility represented on its own terms.

"If we walk far enough, we shall sometime come to someplace."

The basic idea of the Edison Project started morphing almost as soon as Whittle conceived of it in response to operational and financial realities, on the one hand, and political and investor pressures, on the other. Its modest current incarnation—EdisonLearning, on whose board Whittle still sat until recently—bears little resemblance to the initial formulations. These were developed first by Whittle himself and then in conjunction with a group of six "founding partners," whom he referred to as education's Mercury astronauts tasked with fundamentally redesigning how elementary education is delivered in the U.S.

Whittle had immersed himself in public policy ideas when he flirted with a Tennessee Senate run, even hiring Roger Ailes as a tutor at one point. In 1989 he gave a series of speeches followed by an article in one of his short-lived publications on creating something called the "New American School."[19] As first articulated, the idea was to have the federal government hand over $1 billion to the "one hundred best people you know." The goal was to inspire "visionary leaps of human consciousness" that would create "a new dynamic that will light the way to a transformed educational system." While not prejudging the outcome of this exercise, Whittle had plenty of ideas: year-round classes and no homework or tests; a teacher-student ratio of 5–1 achieved by enlisting millions of young and elderly volunteer assistant teachers; and on and on.

A year and a half later, in May 1991, Whittle came forward with the first formal presentation of the Edison Project. During this time, Whittle had directed a secret internal project to create a framework to achieve the "transformed educational system" of his earlier musings. Despite his friend Lamar Alexander becoming Secretary of Education, Whittle realized that the originally hoped-for $1 billion would not be forthcoming. In its place, the project relied on raising $2.5 billion from private corporate investors. In lieu of this money going to 100 visionaries, it would now be entrusted to a massive for-profit enterprise that would be part of Whittle Communications.

The plan was for that new business literally to build 1,000 new schools to serve two million students (around 10 percent of all elementary school students). These schools would be among the best in the world, based on a promised three-year $60 million project to design the optimal twenty-first century curriculum and overall delivery architecture. Although no formal research work had yet commenced and Edison had no dedicated employees, it was clear that the results would incorporate many of Whittle's earlier ideas like longer days and school year as well as additional technology resources. Whittle expressed confidence that such an enterprise would not only be profitable but that tuition could be held at the average cost per pupil of public schools—at the time, only $5,500.

All of this was announced at an elaborately orchestrated news conference in Washington, D.C. Publicity around the event was choreographed, with selected newspapers getting an advance look in exchange for prominent coverage. Yet it would be early 1992 before Whittle put in place his team of "astronauts" to begin to turn any of this into an operational design. Half of the six selected for this purpose came out of journalistic endeavors. Of the half with an educational background, one was an elementary school principal, one a Brookings Institution policy expert, and one a professor and former federal educational official. No one had any significant experience running a business, certainly not a multibillion-dollar one on the scale envisioned by Edison.

The team took until early 1993 to produce something that they felt was ready to present to potential funders. Whittle had, nonetheless, managed to keep interest in the venture high since the announcement almost two years earlier. On May 25, 1992, Yale President Benno C. Schmidt, Jr. informed the university trustees that he was resigning to join the project. Schmidt's announcement sent "shock waves" that "reached well beyond New Haven,"[20] provoking front page coverage from the *New York Times*.[21] The unexpected move had followed many months of intensive lobbying by Whittle.

The selection was vintage Whittle. At Edison and his previous ventures, he wooed a series of high-profile figures to play senior roles— journalist Michael Kinsley (who never ended up in a job) and former presidential chief of staff Hamilton Jordan (who did and was miserable[22]), among others. These expensive hires—known derisively within the company as Whittle's "million dollar men"[23]—reflected the founder's continuing obsession with image and brand. As the president of one of the oldest, most revered American educational institutions, Schmidt symbolized acceptance by the intellectual establishment, precisely the brand image required for this radical new venture. Given Whittle's deep disappointment at failing to get into Yale Law

School, then quickly dropping out of Columbia Law School, securing Schmidt—who had been Dean of Columbia Law School before his relatively short and unhappy tenure at Yale[24]—must have been particularly sweet.

Schmidt may have been a singularly powerful example of the potential marketing value of an investment in a "million dollar man." However, his selection shared an important common characteristic with many of the other celebrities from politics, journalism, and academia who had joined Whittle over the years—an absolute lack of domain expertise or meaningful experience in the function for which they were being hired. Schmidt, a First Amendment lawyer by training, had no relevant experience in any for-profit business or K–12 education generally.

Whittle and Schmidt spent the balance of 1992 on a road show of sorts—without the benefit of an actual completed operational design, much less a business plan—highlighting the need for educational reform, defending the potential role of the profit motive in the sector, and avoiding too much detail regarding what they actually proposed to do. The duo turned up everywhere from *Larry King Live* to the National Press Club and were sometimes treated skeptically but always respectfully. In the absence of specifics, the pair offered up the attractive promise of much more for less. Student spending had skyrocketed, but students' results had not: surely that meant that the problem wasn't money but "the system."[25] By reinventing the system, they argued, it would be possible to take back the presumably wasted spending, deliver the wanted outcomes, and still have money left over for investors.

Once the specifics of the Edison design became finalized in early 1993, the hard part started: finding investors. The design itself was a lot less radical than advertised. An Edison school ran longer hours, had shorter vacations, used more technology, and had more demanding curriculum requirements. The curriculum itself was largely not original—it used widely available, well-established course materials such as Success for All reading, developed at Johns Hopkins, and Everyday Mathematics, developed at the University of Chicago. In short, Edison looked like a very expensive private school that somehow charged very little but managed to be profitable.

Imagining anyone would underwrite this proposition—to the tune of $2.5 billion dollars—was fanciful. First, the amount of capital claimed to be required was cut in half, then cut in half again, and then by a factor of ten. By late 1994, as the balance of Whittle Communications was being liquidated, Whittle's pitch was simply to find $40 million to open twenty schools. Meanwhile, the entire business model changed from opening stand-alone private schools to managing schools for public systems.

But, as James Stewart had predicted, getting any outside money or any school districts to commit remained challenging, particularly once it became apparent that the overall Whittle Communications enterprise would be liquidated. Edison was spun out of the carcass of Whittle Communications, with Philips and Associated Newspapers continuing to own 40 percent each (Time Warner refused to have any continuing connection with the entity), and Whittle owning the balance. As compelling a salesman as Whittle was, the fact that neither of these owners—nor indeed any previous investor—would put another penny into the entity served as an unnerving "tell" to any potential new investors.

A senior K-III executive described Whittle's efforts to get them to fund Edison along with the side payment they made to him in connection with their acquisition of Channel One: "It sounded great but we saw how he was treating his partners from Whittle Communications," he said. "Whenever he was selling we felt like the oarsmen who had to block their ears from the siren's song to survive."[26] The former General Counsel of Time Warner used almost the same language to describe his role in being dispatched to attend any meetings that Time Inc. CEO Reginald Brack had with Whittle: to play Ulysses and provide the earwax whenever Whittle asked for money.[27]

An overenthusiastic entrepreneur, who plunges headlong into new projects even as previous ones falter, is not an unusual phenomenon in the venture world. Venture capitalists are also used to an early business model shifting, sometimes even radically, as market and product constraints are taken on board. But the trouble with Edison was that even radically scaled back, it required a far greater investment of capital than would be typical before a basic prototype had been proven out. In part this reflected Whittle's insistence on starting big. But it also reflected that Whittle's spending habits were inconsistent with a startup. And the perks demanded by Benno Schmidt were similarly unheard of in the venture world. In order to entice him to Edison, Whittle had provided him not only a $1 million salary but also a $1.8 million loan and access to a private jet.[28]

At the end of 1994, Edison was facing closure. A single potential lead investor, the Sprout Group, was still actively engaged in discussions with the venture. When they saw Edison's cost structure, Sprout executives were incredulous. The group had never had a CEO make over $200,000 in salary, and the $16 million in annual overhead was many times greater than what could be reasonably justified in an early-stage company. After the costs and ambitions were dramatically scaled back, an agreement was announced in March 1995.[29] Whittle, after selling enough art and residences to satisfy creditors, invested $15 million of his own money and Sprout invested $12 million.

The balance of the $30 million financing came from Benno Schmidt and two friends. By this time, Schmidt was having to explain the embarrassing collapse of Whittle Communications as he flew around the country trying to sign up customers for Edison. As a result, this critical piece of funding came only after Schmidt insisted that Whittle be denied the formal title of chairman at the company. Despite these early tensions, Schmidt would remain associated with all of Whittle's educational ventures for decades.

Sprout's investment was contingent on limiting the initial launch to four modest schools, serving around 2,000 students in total. In an interesting piece of revisionist history, Whittle argued that "the birth of Edison killed its mother, which was Whittle Communications, but the child survived." And despite these humble beginnings, in Whittle's view, this was going to be a very big baby. "Think of it, 30 percent of $260 billion rounds out to a new $75 billion category. . . . Edison should have a big piece of that market."[30]

"Pay no attention to the man behind the curtain!"

With the new investment, Whittle ceased to be an employee of Edison altogether—but was being paid as a consultant through the holding company for his shares. Although Schmidt did sign up additional schools, he obviously had no experience running any commercial enterprise, and Sprout had always insisted that a true chief operating officer be hired. When none materialized, Whittle reappeared two years later, first as president and then also CEO the following year. After that, Schmidt was given the honorific title of chief education officer for a few months, but then became simply chairman. When the company finally hired a COO a few months before the initial public offering (IPO) in November 1999, they chose a former lawyer, Chris Cerf, with no business or operating experience. When the company went public, the prospectus highlighted Cerf's background as a high school history teacher.

Although the business was growing quickly from new contracts, it was devouring increasing amounts of capital to open the actual schools. A new round of financing was required the following year, and then again every few months all the way to the hoped-for IPO. Throughout this period, as it actually began to run schools, the company refined its message and model, attracting capital from J.P. Morgan and the Wallenbergs in 1997 and from the Swiss bank UBS and Microsoft billionaire Paul Allen a few months before the IPO in 1999.

When the company published its prospectus in 1999, much of the critical public commentary was around the personal finances and compensation of Whittle and Schmidt.[31] Schmidt had borrowed money from the company and, even at the below-market interest being charged, he was in the hole to the tune of $2.5 million. As for Whittle, how often does the CEO and president need to pledge all of his stock to satisfy personal loans? This noise aside, the most important problem with the Edison Schools story is that it really didn't make much sense on its own terms and that story, whatever its virtues, was not consistent with the financials provided.

Whittle had consistently painted the portrait of Edison as a unique vision of education that came out of a multimillion-dollar, multiyear global study of how to design the optimal educational system. Suspiciously, most of the key elements of the design were present in the various presentations and talks Whittle gave before even putting together his much-vaunted design team in early 1992. The core design was created over the course of a year and only one of six designers remained past their two-year contracts, with the rest returning to jobs—like editor of *Mirabella* magazine—more suited to their backgrounds and skills.[32] In the prospectus under the heading "Research Behind the Edison Solution," it is asserted that the design and curriculum "grew out of a comprehensive three-year research project conducted by a team of approximately 30 full-time professional employees and numerous outside experts under the leadership of Benno C. Schmidt, Jr." In fact, Benno wasn't hired and the design team wasn't even aware he was being considered until they were halfway through their work.[33] In an interview with *60 Minutes* a few days after the offering, Whittle claimed the R&D underlying Edison was even more extensive. "Between 1991 and 1995, we spent $45 million," he told Morley Safer.[34]

Edison's core differentiator, according to the prospectus, is its ability to address what it views as the three main sources of the failure of public schools: the lack of consistent leadership, the inability to invest in the future, and the inability to exploit the advantages of scale. Yet if these are truly the correct diagnoses, Edison would on its face be an odd tool to correct them.

On the leadership front, none of the four members of Edison's "experienced management team" had previously run a single school and, with the exception of Whittle's own checkered experience, had not run a for-profit enterprise of any kind. It is hard to argue against the observation that "a sustained commitment to effective implementation over a lengthy period of time" is valuable in all things, but how can one then justify selecting individuals who had never implemented any commercial undertaking? On the investment front, the annual appropriations cycle of schools certainly is a constraint on long-term planning. But that hardly justifies replacing it with an unprofitable organization requiring regular new capital infusions to stay afloat and whose CEO's personal loan obligations could result in a sudden change of control to his banks.

The more fundamental business question, however, is whether this is a scale business and, to the extent it is, whether Edison would operate at a scale advantage or disadvantage. The structural competitive advantage known as economies of scale is easily misunderstood. Scale in this sense is a relative rather than an absolute concept for two important reasons.

First, scale refers to one's position relative to others in a relevant geographic and product market. This means that, even as one grows in an absolute sense, it is possible to diminish "scale." For instance, an operator who dominates a region and decides to compete nationally, where there are multiple larger competitors, moves from having a scale advantage to a scale disadvantage. The question of whether a market is primarily local, regional, national, or global is a function of the extent that the specific fixed cost investments can be leveraged. In the school context, most of the fixed cost infrastructure required to manage day-to-day school operations—hiring, building management, customer relations, new client development, and the like—all are locally or regionally based. So, for example, Edison organized its "business development" function under twelve regional vice presidents. Fixed cost categories that seem more national in nature, like curriculum development, also have a significant local component as curriculum must be modified to comply with specific state standards. Even the vaunted standard Edison "design" was modified locally wherever union agreements required that in order to secure contracts.

Second, the economic relevance of scale is greatest in business models where these fixed cost elements are relatively important. Where costs are purely variable, profitability will not significantly improve with scale. Average total unit costs start to fall dramatically as sales grow only where the central costs that do not increase with output predominate. The advantages of scale, then, will be most apparent in businesses with high so-called gross margins—the difference between revenue and direct costs before fixed expenses. From the Edison prospectus, it is not clear whether Edison schools were even profitable at the gross margin level. The company presents a term called "direct site contribution" that manages to eke out some margin, but it excludes a laundry list of site-level expenses from computers to teacher training to building improvements. In the two years leading up to the IPO, Edison losses grew faster than revenue, exactly the opposite of what one would expect in a scale business.

A number of additional "tells" in the company's filings and elsewhere suggest either that Edison is not intrinsically a scale business or that those running the enterprise don't understand scale—or possibly both.

In making his case for scale, Whittle frequently points out that the vast majority of school districts "tend to be small, independent and localized operations."[35] But the business plan, initially at least, called for a focus on the largest districts. These tend to be huge—there are over one million New York City public school students, and dozens of districts around the country serve at least 100,000 children—and have the additional administrative advantage of being tightly clustered. The seventy-nine Edison schools, by contrast, were randomly scattered around the country, in thirty-five cities across sixteen states, with only eight school districts using Edison for more than two schools. Although Edison boasted enrollment of 38,000 nationally, within any of the twelve regions into which it organized itself, even assuming stunning continued growth, Edison would continue to be among the very smallest players. The fact that Benno Schmidt spent an inordinate amount of time in the early days of Edison on his private plane making sales calls to Honolulu[36] (which still had not paid off by the time of the IPO[37]) reflects the team's failure to appreciate that regional density is the most powerful source of scale.

Local modifications aside, curriculum development intuitively seems like the area where benefits from a central infrastructure of scale could be realized. But even here, Edison often operated at a significant scale disadvantage. The business sought to operate in thirteen different grades, each of which require different curricula. Although Edison hoped ultimately to grow its elementary and middle school contracts into high school business, there was little evidence that the Edison solution had a viral quality—either to adjacent grades or adjacent communities. Less than 5 percent of Edison enrollment, representing just two schools, was in high school.

More broadly, Whittle's argument for the long-term economic viability of Edison seemed at times to be that it would allow governments to shrink the expensive and inefficient local education bureaucracies by leveraging the intellectual capital that would reside at Edison's more efficient scale center. Even if Edison were eventually capable of taking on these functions, the same political realities that made these bureaucracies lumbering in the first place made it hopelessly naïve to believe that they would downsize proportionally to their usage of Edison's schools. It would be far more likely that an incremental bureaucracy would need to be created to oversee the Edison contract implementation.

How, then, could the public and institutional investors be convinced to invest given the frightening financial profile and tenuous narrative?

Before large investment banks agree to sponsor a company in the public markets, it must be reviewed by each firm's "commitments committee." Central to the commitments committee process for an IPO underwriting is support from the bank's equity research analyst who oversees the sector. Equity research is supposed to operate completely independently of investment banking, and the analysts are meant to come to their own view of whether the company is of a quality that the bank should be associated with. Only then do they address the question of the value at which it should be offered to investors. During the IPO process, these research analysts share their views on the company's prospects generally, and valuation specifically, both with the internal trading sales force that is placing the stock and directly with the institutional investors considering participation.

The Edison IPO occurred before the imposition of stringent rules to ensure that research analysts were not unduly influenced by investment bankers. That said, there was no particular evidence of foul play here. Indeed, many of the research analysts who supported the offering were highly respected and went on to other positions of great responsibility. In some cases, they would themselves make investments in Whittle's future ventures, even after the collapse of Edison.

The fundamental methodology usually relied on by research analysts to support their recommendations is called a "discounted cash flow" or DCF analysis. Although stocks do not trade in line with DCF valuations and investors rarely use these as the primary basis of decision making, the apparent mathematical precision and intuitive appeal of the DCF leads not just research analysts, but courts, investment bankers, boards of directors, and others to lean heavily on this tool. The basic idea and math of the DCF is deceptively straightforward: estimate the future cash flows of the business and then, using an appropriate discount rate, crystallize a present value of all of those projected results.

The DCF can be a useful instrument, but it is an extremely blunt one. This is particularly true in instances where the company, like Edison, has no current cash flows and there is little basis for determining what "steady state" profitability might be achievable in the future.[38] Because it is not possible to project an infinite number of future year cash flows, the convention is to estimate the first five or ten years and then calculate a so-called terminal value to approximate the worth of the infinite number of years to follow. Although this terminal value concept sounds complicated, it ends up being just a function of how fast the cash flows are growing and the appropriate discount rate: 1/(discount rate–perpetual growth rate). This formula yields something called the "terminal multiple" which is simply multiplied by the last year's cash flow to produce the terminal value. That value is then discounted back and added to the other discounted cash flows of the interim years.

As an example, if a company has a discount rate of 10 percent and a perpetual growth rate of 5 percent the terminal multiple is 1/(10 percent–5 percent) or 1/5 percent, which is equal to 100/5 or a terminal multiple of 20 times. So, in addition to discounting back each of the projected first five or ten years of cash flows, in this case a complete DCF would require that you multiply a final year of cash flows by 20 and discount the resulting terminal value back as well.

Despite the elegance of this procedure, its precision is more apparent than real. The way the math works, the value of the terminal in such a DCF calculation almost always represents the vast majority of the total valuation. And remember that the terminal value is the result of multiplying two numbers: the terminal multiple and the estimated final year cash flow. Those two numbers are the source of the problem with the DCF.

The terminal multiple itself, we saw, is a function of the discount rate and the growth rate. Neither of these numbers, however, is very scientific. The right discount rate is something called "the weighted average cost of capital" or WACC for the company. The WACC is essentially the average cost, expressed as an interest rate, that the particular company needs to "pay" to raise capital.[39] This is a theoretical value, not something that can be empirically verified. If you asked a dozen bankers or economists about a given company's WACC, you are certain to get a scatter of responses that has a range of at least a few percentage points from high to low. Similarly, the growth rate required for the terminal multiple formula is not arrived at by calculating how fast cash flows have actually grown, but estimating how fast they will grow on average into infinity. Although most companies' growth over time converges toward the overall growth of GDP, there is always disagreement both about the long-term growth of GDP and the extent to which any given company's trajectory is likely to diverge from this.

The problem here is that even if the disagreements about both the growth rate and the discount rate are relatively small, the combined impact on the resulting terminal multiple are massive. Let's take our example of a 10 percent WACC and 5 percent perpetual growth rate. Assume we are confident that there is only a 1 percent possible variation in either number: 9–11 percent for WACC and 4–6 percent for growth. When we plug all these combinations into the formula for terminal multiple, it yields a range of terminal multiples from 14× to 33×—a variance of over 130 percent!

And what do we multiply this terminal multiple by to get the value which drives the DCF? A cash flow estimate for the year in which we have the lowest possible level of confidence. We know what last year's cash flow is and we have a good sense of what next year's will be, but with each passing year of projections our estimate becomes more speculative. The mathematical formula for terminal value relies on our estimate of the cash flows in the most distant year considered.

It is not too much hyperbole, then, to describe the terminal value that underpins the much-worshipped DCF methodology to be little more than a rough guess multiplied by a wild estimate.

In the case of a company like Edison, which has no current cash flows, the problems with the DCF methodologies are exacerbated. Instead of simply reflecting a *majority* of the valuation, the terminal actually represents over 100 percent because most of the interim cash flows are negative! The research analysts who would make stock recommendations built their models based on the level of profitability they believed ultimately achievable by a company with the business characteristics of Edison.

Let's look at the research report supporting a "buy" rating by respected analyst Greg Cappelli at Credit Suisse First Boston. Today, Cappelli is the CEO of the world's largest for-profit university, Apollo Education Group. At the time of the fifty-page report issued in December 1999, Edison shares had drifted down to $15 from its IPO price of $18 the previous month and had a public market value of barely $500 million. Based on his DCF, however, Cappelli concluded that Edison's intrinsic worth was more than double the current market value, giving the shares "60 percent price-appreciation potential" within the next year.

Cappelli's DCF projects that Edison would continue to eat over $200 million in cash flow over the next five years (2000–2004). To address the terminal value problem noted, however, he projects not just five or ten years of future results, but twenty-six years! The good news is that by pushing out the projections all the way to 2025, the terminal value actually represents just under half of the overall company valuation. The bad news is that the company that is imagined to exist at that future time—with over $8 billion in revenues and $1 billion in profits—bears no resemblance to the small money-losing entity being valued.

Cappelli justifies his approach by arguing that "our DCF analysis allows us to take a more sophisticated approach to identifying the intrinsic value embedded in Edison, because it explicitly incorporates more significant variables . . . than traditional methodologies."

In particular, Cappelli identifies a number of structural barriers to entry that he believes will allow Edison to achieve continuously improving profitability as it grows at an average compounded growth rate of over 17 percent for the twenty-six-year period. The two main competitive advantages highlighted on the cover of the report are "a clear first mover advantage . . . in the $300 billion-plus K–12 market" and "increas[ing] operating leverage through economies of scale."

The oft-uttered phrase "first mover advantage" suggests to many the idea that going first in itself represents a structural competitive advantage. In fact, a moment's reflection on various product categories—from cell phones to social networks to spreadsheet software—reveals that the clear winners are almost never the first or even second mover (VisiCalc or Lotus 123 anyone?). First mover advantage is a rare attribute available where product and marketplace characteristics facilitate quickly achieving scale. More often, the structure of marketplace demand or technology constraints imply a modest pace of adoption for entirely new product categories in the best of circumstances. In those circumstances, those who invest heavily early to test the contours of the possible are basically doing free market research for future competitors. Accordingly, going first where it is structurally impossible to gain scale quickly is more appropriately termed a "first mover disadvantage."

Is the marketplace Edison has chosen more likely to bestow a first mover advantage or disadvantage? Well, the fact that after almost a decade of work Edison represented less than 1 percent of the "$300 billion-plus" market wasn't a good sign. Even after the next five years of Cappelli's optimistic, projections during which Edison would continue to hemorrhage money, its market share was projected to be well under 5 percent. What would stop a new entrant during this extended period from closely observing Edison's successes and missteps in entering into and executing on school contracts? Would a fast follower need to spend the $50 million Edison claims to have invested in curriculum development (which resulted in mostly selecting widely available best of breed from third parties) and school design? Indeed, Whittle himself repeatedly bragged that Edison's success would allow others to replicate it easily.

Regardless of Whittle's claims, if Edison were a genuinely scale business with a primarily fixed cost infrastructure, replicating success would be no easy matter. Cappelli's model assumes that as much as 70 percent of all administration, curriculum, and development expenses would be fixed. This justifies the predicted continuous margin improvements over the twenty years following the point at which he hopes Edison would begin generating cash flow. As noted, however, the administration of schools is an intensely local activity, not only in lobbying and oversight activities but even in customizing the curriculum to address state standards and local concerns. Achieving the 15 percent margins Capelli assumes in the all-important "terminal" year of projections seems wildly optimistic. So does the implicit assumption that there would be no political backlash from generating anything like that kind of profitability.

In the first couple of years after the IPO, Whittle focused on growing the business quickly by signing up as many schools as possible. To achieve this result, he was willing to "customize" the Edison proposition to address union concerns here, political issues there. What the resulting contracts had in common, however, was that they were expensive. Pedagogy aside, all of the cash-strapped districts that signed on found the over $1 million per school Edison agreed to spend up front for facilities upgrades, computers, and educational materials highly attractive. Unfortunately for Whittle, before he was able to snag major contracts with the high-profile big cities like Philadelphia and New York that were his primary interest, the returns from the first wave of sign-ups started to roll in.

The problem wasn't that none of the Edison schools were good. With the significant upgrades in facilities and materials, many were far better than they had been previously and some were excellent in absolute terms. But quite a few still were not. Edison by this time had grown into essentially a mid-sized school system with the twin disadvantages of being spread all over the country and many of its contracts having slightly different requirements. Even if it had developed a deeper bench of seasoned operating executives, effectively managing the company would represent a challenge.

Complaints of high teacher turnover, enrollment declines, and poor student performance resulted in some cancellations and heightened the difficulty in signing up new schools.[40] And, as expected, any misstep was exploited by not just teacher unions, but other groups who were offended by the very notion of a for-profit running public schools. A particularly dramatic protest at the Las Vegas School Board featured the arrival of a community group dressed in black bearing a small white satin coffin filled with African American dolls.[41]

Financial results started to roll in as well. Of course, Edison had been projected to be unprofitable for its first several years. But the revenues were not growing as quickly as predicted. More concerning, the supposed benefits of scale did not appear to be manifesting. Indeed, administrative expenses as a percentage of revenues actually seemed to be increasing. The company cited the high cost of lobbying for major city contracts to explain the anomaly. But surely such activities would be an ongoing administrative cost of the Edison model as new cities were targeted and existing contracts came up for renewal.

In early 2002, another issue that had been endemic to Whittle entities from the start took on new urgency at Edison as a public company in the age of Enron: a lack of appropriate financial controls. In February, Bloomberg ran a story questioning the company's accounting policies and suggesting it might be overstating its revenues.[42] Edison stock had peaked at $36.75 in February 2001, and fallen steadily since then in the face of mixed news. By April 2001 it was below its original IPO. At the time of the Bloomberg story, the stock was around $13 and immediately fell another 10 percent.

Edison aggressively attacked the Bloomberg reports as "irresponsible" and never disclosed that the SEC launched an enforcement action on this and other accounting issues at the company until a settlement was reached in May. By then the stock was under $3, battered by the news that Philadelphia had awarded Edison less than half the schools expected. Reinforcing concerns about the underlying business model, Whittle's prescription for the ballooning administrative costs was to reverse course and intentionally slow the growth of new contracts.[43]

On top of the accounting issues, the mixed academic results, the failure to deliver a blockbuster big city contract, and the uncertain financial picture, the company was running out of money. It was only in August 2002 that the company came up with a complicated and expensive financing plan to provide the funds that would allow it to deliver on the modest Philadelphia contract. By then, Edison was a penny stock, having fallen below $1 per share in July.

The company also announced a management restructuring and four new independent board members. At the top, the restructuring did not add significant new industry or operational strength to the team. Instead, Chris Cerf added the title of president as well as COO, the general counsel also became an executive vice president, the controller was promoted to CFO and a board member, former UBS Capital executive Chip Delaney, was made "vice chairman." Delaney, the press release said, would lead a "re-engineering process designed to bring greater efficiency to the business" and join Whittle and Cerf in a newly created "Office of the Chief Executive."[44]

The addition of board members had been necessitated by the resignation of three previous members who had participated in the emergency financing and could no longer be considered independent.[45] What the new independent board members didn't know as they were elected in December 2002, and what the board would not be informed of for many months, was that Whittle and Cerf were already discussing with Cerf's brother, Monty Cerf, a banker at Bear Stearns ("Bear"), how to take the company private.

"The queerness doesn't matter, so long as they're friends."[46]

Although Bear was not formally hired until February 2003, Whittle and Cerf had begun planning the previous year. By engaging bankers personally, Whittle could ensure that so-called strategic buyers—companies with their own management teams and strategic perspective—would not be contacted and that his own personal employment and financial matters could be dealt with explicitly up front. In a company-run process under the oversight of the board, strategic buyers were much less likely to be excluded and the exclusive focus would be getting the highest value for shareholders. Any discussion of management would be meticulously avoided until a high bidder was identified.

Once engaged, Bear worked with Whittle to prepare a list of potential private equity firms with the money and likely inclination to back him in a buyout and a presentation to sell them on the idea. In late March, Whittle informed the independent board members what was going on. In the end, seventy-six private equity firms were contacted by Whittle and his advisors, of which nineteen were interested enough to take a pitch meeting. Nine of these agreed to undertake more detailed diligence of the company. When this was completed in early May, the stock was still trading at barely $1 and Whittle told them they would need to pay at least $1.40, which narrowed the field to four.

Whittle's personal financial situation continued to be precarious. Although he had sold 670,000 Edison shares in early 2001 when the stock approached $25, this was not nearly sufficient to cover his spending and outstanding obligations. He owed the company over $10 million, which he had borrowed to buy shares. These shares in turn were pledged to J.P. Morgan just as his equity holdings had been in Whittle Communications days.[47] Reflecting this situation, the final four interested parties were given an unusual term sheet that detailed Whittle's personal financial needs in any transaction. In addition to proposing employment and new equity requirements, he informed them that he planned to sell all of his existing equity in the company. Before selecting a middle-market private equity firm called Liberty Partners as the "winner" to be his preferred partner, Whittle negotiated these terms with the parties to determine where he could get the best deal for himself.

Generally a "management buyout" implies that, usually with the help of a partner, the management is actually using all or a substantial part of its equity in the company to help finance the transaction. Here, however, Whittle wasn't buying anything. He was looking to get completely cashed out and then provided a salary increase, new equity, new loans, and non-compete payments (as well, of course, as getting the expenses for his financial advisors paid for). Whittle ultimately negotiated that over the next several years he could make the company buy up to $10 million of that equity back from him plus another $7 million to cover the non-compete (held in escrow just in case).

While this was going on, the independent directors of the board were establishing a special committee and hiring their own financial and legal advisors to oversee what management was doing as well as assess whatever it might ultimately propose. This involved reviewing the private process run by Whittle and Bear as well as the company's prospects. Although Whittle informed the committee that he was considering making an offer with Liberty in the range of $1.58 to $1.65 per share, his advisors initially refused to share the actual proposals submitted by the finalists to Bear.

Whittle and his advisors ultimately shared the details of the proposals as well as Whittle's employment arrangements. A parallel negotiation ensued in which the committee sought a reduction in the more outlandish aspects of Whittle's personal deal—effective forgiveness of loans from the company, reimbursement of three years of almost $1 million of "business expenses"—while arguing for a better deal for public shareholders. On July 13, 2003, after Liberty had raised its price four times and Whittle acceded to the committee's demands regarding his employment agreement,[48] Edison announced that it had agreed to be sold for $1.76 per share.

"It is such an uncomfortable feeling
to know one is a fool."

Although Edison sold for a substantial premium to its recent trading price, this represented a tiny fraction of what the company had sold for to the public only a few years earlier. As the company's stock price had collapsed the previous year, the *New York Times* had reported that many finally had begun to "see déjà vu in Mr. Whittle's stewardship of Edison."[49] They pointed to the unrealistic expectations that had been encouraged, the financial regulatory problems, the high overhead costs, and hiring "smart, talented people who do not know enough about business and finance to keep Edison out of trouble," as all reminiscent of Whittle's previous ventures. In retrospect, some could be forgiven for wondering how they had been drawn in in the first place.

The fact that a presumably sophisticated financial buyer was interested in backing Whittle again, and that a number of such firms had been interested in doing so, created skepticism as to whether the public was getting the full story. Most major firms that had sponsored Edison had long before dropped research coverage and distanced themselves from the company. The few remaining research analysts—who had been enthusiastic about the stock at dramatically higher prices than where the newest group backing Whittle was buying it—smelled a rat. One ThinkEquity Partners analyst charged that the offer added "insult to injury"[50] and complained openly of the "shabby treatment of existing shareholders" and the "continued bad faith"[51] of management in withholding key operating information needed to evaluate the offer.

They needn't have worried. The public filings showed both the projections shared with buyers, and upside and downside sensitivities developed by the investment bankers who provided a fairness opinion in the transaction. In the most conservative case developed, Edison showed modest profit on revenues of $477 million in fiscal year 2008, the last of the five years projected. This was barely half of the $888 million revenues projected by Whittle for the "plan case" shared with buyers. In fact, in fiscal 2008, Edison was still unprofitable and had revenues of $264 million.

Although Edison continues to limp along to this day, amazingly with Whittle and Schmidt still on the board at least until quite recently, Liberty Partners was forced to write down its original investment years ago. Pieces of the business have been sold off[52] and what remains is now run by the former general counsel who, according to the company website, ascended to that position in 2014 when he "brokered the acquisition and directed the restructuring of the company."

Who was Liberty Partners and what were they thinking? The fund had been created in 1992 by former Merrill Lynch buyout group executives to specialize in so-called middle market investments. What made the fund unusual was that the entire fund was financed by the Florida pension funds. Although this arrangement avoided the expense of fundraising and managing diverse limited partners in the fund, according to an independent firm hired by the state to review overall performance by Liberty, fees charged were actually higher than typical while returns were "unequivocally unacceptable" and contained "far too much risk for the returns involved."[53]

At the time of the buyout, Florida teachers were horrified to learn that their pension funds were being used to back Whittle.[54] Speculation circulated that the presence of politicians sympathetic to the school reform movement on the board that oversaw the pension fund—notably Jeb Bush—had played a role in the investing decision.[55] Bush denied this, saying that he had no role in investing decisions. And to be fair, at least one other fund had arrived at similar valuation views.

At the end of the day, private equity firms take a view on a business model and management team and don't always get it right. Despite the warning signs, they too can be seduced by management assurances that they are favored and come to believe that "this time will be different." Furthermore, conversations with those familiar with Liberty decision making at the time say they were genuinely influenced by the "mission orientation" of the enterprise.

What is harder to understand, however, is how the same firm, having lost money in such a venture, would then back Whittle in entirely new ones. One theory relates to the idiosyncratic structure of the arrangement between Liberty and Florida. Liberty received numerous fees above the traditional management fees for sitting on boards and making investments but "paid no penalty" for money-losing investments. Furthermore, rather than returning any cash from harvested investments, as would be typical, "Liberty's profits were recycled into the fund, guaranteeing the managers a continuous investment stream."[56]

"Going so soon? I wouldn't hear of it.
Why, my little party's just beginning."

Whittle tired of Edison within a few years after the deal with Liberty closed. Costly high-profile contract failures resulted in a retrenchment from what was once the central Edison proposition. As this core Edison concept morphed and atrophied, entirely new business lines were developed to take up the slack. A UK partnership was announced in 2003 before the sale, by which time Edison had launched summer and after-school programs and something called "achievement management solutions" for school systems.[57] Then, over time, dropout programs, school "turn-around" programs, online programs, and a variety of other outsourced services to charter schools and districts were added. Some of these initiatives involved high-profile marketing partners like Magic Johnson. Within five years, Edison Schools changed its name to EdisonLearning, a rebranding meant to emphasize that Edison was no longer in the business of taking over schools but instead now was all about creating "partnerships with schools, districts, organizations, and charter boards and authorizers" to "achieve lasting gains in performance."

Before then, however, Whittle was already focused on his next big idea—and on getting someone to pay for it. That big idea was in some ways as far from the original Edison idea as one could go: instead of contracting to take over the running of local public schools, Whittle now envisioned creating a global network of high-end private schools available primarily to the super-rich international set who could afford them. As originally formulated in 2006, these schools would "offer an internationally integrated, globally-focused education program."[58]

What this vision shared with Edison's, beyond its grandiosity, was that its basic economics seemed questionable. Whittle would assert that the New York school "would be competitive with the finest schools in the city," meaning the likes of Brearley and Dalton. But any parent who sends their children to elite private nonprofit schools in New York knows that in addition to the high tuition, which Whittle's new venture intended to match, they are treated to a constant barrage of fundraising solicitations that these institutions claim are needed to cover basic operating expenses. Given that some of these schools also benefit from a substantial endowment, it is not obvious how a for-profit competitor would achieve attractive margins.

In addition, as Whittle learned from the high cost of even upgrading the existing infrastructure, the capital costs of bricks and mortar schools can be daunting. The elite schools he was trying to compete with already had facilities, while Whittle needed to find a way to cover the cost of finding quarters that would attract the clientele he was now seeking. There was no question that Whittle had experience overseeing expensive construction projects. At issue was whether the envisaged business model could support it.

Whittle's explanation of how the numbers would add up was reminiscent of the original Edison pitch: finding efficiencies through "economies of scale through their chain of large schools."[59] But if it was difficult to find such economies within distant domestic geographies at Edison, achieving them globally among countries with diverse laws, cultures, market dynamics and industry structures seemed more unlikely.

Whittle nonetheless found a new investor to fund his new dream. Sunny Varkey, a mysterious entrepreneur and self-educated Dubai-based son of Indian expatriate teachers, agreed to provide initial funding of $6.85 million. Varkey had built his own largely Middle Eastern-based network of private elementary schools called Global Education Management Systems (GEMS). To attract Varkey, Whittle also somehow convinced Edison's new owners at Liberty to invest $3.33 million, despite the disappointing performance of the current investment. In addition to that $10 million, the continuously financially strapped Whittle contributed only twenty-five dollars[60]—hardly a ringing endorsement. For his nominal investment and promise of involvement, Whittle received almost 5 percent of the equity of the venture. In January 2007, Edison and GEMS announced their international alliance, ultimately called Nations Academy, to build schools in major cities around the world.

As the need for operational discipline at Edison became more obvious, Liberty had brought in Terry Stecz, a healthcare and consumer products executive, as COO shortly after the buyout closed in 2004. Stecz added the president title the following year with the departure of Chris Cerf. Now, with Whittle becoming CEO of Nations Academy,

Stecz replaced him as CEO at Edison. Whittle would remain associated with Edison—the vehicle through which the Liberty investment was being made—but now as chairman.

Whittle immediately began doing what he did best: selling. Reminiscent of his initial claim that Edison would require a $3 billion investment, Whittle now predicted that this venture would produce $3 billion in revenue across sixty campuses around the world by 2021. In the shorter term, he hoped to open the first two such schools— one in New York and one outside of Washington, D.C.—by 2010 and another ten in cities like London, Shanghai, Paris, Hong Kong, and Los Angeles in the subsequent couple of years. Whittle announced an agreement to buy the historic Bethesda estate of early National Geographic editor Gilbert Grosvenor[61] and then a deal with Douglas Durst to develop 240,000 square feet on West 57th Street.[62]

During Whittle's publicity tour for the venture, Nations Academy expressed confidence that there was "enough money in place for the initial work."[63] In fact, the ongoing operating costs of this venture would eat up all of the capital contributed before ground was broken on the first school. Indeed, according to private equity investor Lynn Tilton's complaint charging "brazen fraud," by early 2008 Nations Academy had gone through all of its initial funding and was facing a series of $10 million deposit installments to Durst.

Lynn Tilton is not someone you want to mess with. A colorful, self-described billionaire, her private equity firm, Patriarch Partners, owns seventy-five portfolio companies including defense contractor MD Helicopters.[64] According to Tilton's lawsuit, Whittle and Varkey tricked her into wiring them $5 million based on a wide range of false representations and concealed facts about the venture.[65] Buried in the complaint is an excerpt of a memo Tilton somehow obtained in which Whittle threatened to blow the whistle on the precarious nature of Nations Academy's prospects as part of his ongoing employment negotiations with Varkey. Just as in the Channel One sale and in the Edison go-private transaction, Whittle had managed to ensure that satisfying his personal needs was a requirement of any transaction.

Tilton had asked for written confirmation from Whittle of his continued employment at Nations Academy, and he provided that a few weeks after the threatening memo to Varkey. Tilton wired the money a few days later, on July 1, 2008. In August, the Durst project was abandoned before the next $10 million payment came due.

By September 1, Whittle was no longer CEO of Nations Academy; the Washington school plan was publicly dropped a few weeks later.[66]

A year later, however, Whittle somehow had found a new secret funder to entice Durst to go ahead with an even more grandiose construction project at the same West 57th Street location for the same purpose, albeit with an undisclosed new name.[67] That funder was global education publishing giant Pearson. Reminiscent of Philips's earlier investment in Channel One, Pearson's funding would have been contingent on a deal under which the school would commit to use Pearson materials and technology so that much of its "investment" would come back in the form of purchased goods and services. On closer inspection of the business plan, however, Pearson ultimately could not justify the arrangement as an economic matter even with these structural advantages. The project was again abandoned.

The next year, 2010, Whittle located a warehouse near the New York High Line owned by a different developer that could be renovated for a fraction of the envisaged $200+ million construction project on 57th Street. Rather than relying on the questionable availability of tax-exempt bonds from the city Industrial Development Authority as he had the last time around, as little as $75 million ($60 million of which was for the building) from investors would cover the start-up costs of the New York flagship school of his planned global network. Whittle poached administrators from brand-name private schools like Dalton and Hotchkiss, but installed a long-time associate from Whittle Communications with no education experience as president.

Given Whittle's own track record and the lack of any proven for-profit education operating executive, who would underwrite the rechristened Avenues School, now described with typical Whittlesque hyperbole as "the first global school"? The answer was in part the same people who had lost money in Whittle's last two ventures, Liberty Partners. In January 2011, they and another private equity firm, LLR Partners, announced that they had split the $75 million investment required.[68] What were they thinking?

LLR is a mid-market Philadelphia-based firm for which "consumer and education" is one of six identified investment focus sectors. The partners had developed an investment thesis around an apparent market imbalance between the emerging wealthy in major metropolitan areas and the educational opportunities available to fulfill their aspirations for their progeny. Somehow they became convinced that the power of this idea combined with Whittle's prodigious marketing skills more than counterbalanced any concerns about Whittle's past performance.

Liberty is a more complicated situation given their long unhappy history with Whittle. The fund is currently in wind-down mode and declined to provide any perspective on their decision making. The unusual structure of their original investment vehicle has already been described and could provide part of the explanation. In addition, however, some have speculated that, because the Avenues investment was initially made through the shell of the failed Edison venture, it was viewed by Liberty as a "Hail Mary" pass to salvage the returns from the overall Whittle relationship.[69]

Within a few months, the Whittle marketing machine was in full swing in anticipation of a fall 2012 opening: a "spectacular" launch luncheon "attended by a who's who of New York educators,"[70] profiles and interviews across major media, a slick ad campaign including glossy full-page ads in the *Wall Street Journal* and *New York Times*, and over 100 elegantly catered informational sessions for prospective parents at the Harvard and Core Clubs and posh hotels mostly in New York but as far away as Beijing. These presentations were described as "masterly" by the *New York Times* and vintage Whittle: "packed with alarming figures and thoughtful reflections on so many different forces at work in the world and in education: the rise of China, the failure of American education, the importance of reading, the aspiration that our own children will not only embrace the world but also be fluent in it."[71]

A skeptic might be forgiven for finding Whittle's basic pitch a little reminiscent of Harold Hill's pitch to the residents of River City: your child is facing Trouble (with a capital T) if he or she goes into the newly global world without the otherwise unavailable tools that only "the first global school" can provide. Surprisingly, there was relatively little skepticism in much of the reporting on this newest venture. Most certainly made reference to Whittle's shaky track record. But even the *New York Observer*, traditionally the most skeptical of Whittle critics, somehow concluded that the Avenues venture had the hallmarks of the work of someone who had learned his lessons: "The difference, it seems, is that Avenues is eminently doable."[72] Although mentioning that the Nations Academy initiative had recently been scuttled, articles blamed this exclusively on the global downturn of 2008, and no reporter seemed to have noticed the by-then-public lawsuit brought by Tilton.

The aggressive marketing combined with the scarcity of space at the more established New York City private schools enabled Avenues to open its doors to an impressively large contingent of students in the fall of 2012. Since then, buzz about the school from parents has been largely positive. But amid the good feelings of the successful launch, basic unanswered questions remained about the underlying economics of the enterprise, the availability of continued funding, and even the product being delivered.

On economics, given the financial fate of Whittle's previous ventures, one might have expected a fully baked explanation of how the math would work. Instead, the explanations were reminiscent of those given at Edison's launch with talk of scale (this time globally) and efficiencies, buffeted largely with anecdotal evidence. For instance, when pressed on cost savings, Alan Greenberg, the former *Esquire* publisher selected to run the actual enterprise day-to-day, pointed to the fact that "there are some schools in town that teach 15 languages. We teach two. Huge efficiency."[73]

Unfortunately, language programs are not a big driver of a school's overall cost structure. Salaries are. In addition to a formidable central overhead of long-time cronies, Whittle was paying high-profile teachers and administrators as much as 20 percent higher than average to attract them to his untested venture.[74] In addition, Avenues made unprecedented technology start-up investments including the provision of both an iPad and MacBook Air to each student. This approach imposed costs not seen at any other school, private or public.[75] And, of course, significant development expenses are associated with the planned network of twenty global academies. The head of a competing Manhattan private school marveled at the outsized spending on salaries, marketing, capital, and development and concluded that "either Chris Whittle has lost his mind again or," in the alternative, "the investors have lost theirs."[76]

On the "positive" side, financial aid was much more limited than at a typical private school.[77] Whittle claimed that the New York campus had already "broken even" months before its doors first opened in 2012.[78] The problem is that this literally could not be true as, under generally accepted accounting principles, revenue cannot start to be recognized until services are actually delivered. Only a few months later, Benno Schmidt, who took the role of chairman at Avenues, told a reporter that the school would start turning a profit "in about five years' time."[79]

The $75 million Whittle had raised was largely spent on the building, but Whittle went to great lengths to assure his various constituents that there was minimal risk associated with future financing needs. The school, he said, would take on no debt and would fund future growth from the cash flows and a single round of additional funding.[80] The remaining nineteen schools, he said, will cost $500–600 million to establish, although it is not clear why these—some in locales with even higher real estate costs than New York—are projected to be less than half as expensive to create on average.[81] Although Whittle often touted the unique vision of Avenues, when it came to finances, he insisted that there was nothing unusual or complex about Avenues. "It's pretty simple," he told the *New York Times*, "there are thousands of examples worldwide to demonstrate it works."[82]

The question of whether a new school is any good takes many years to assess. Avenues graduated its first class in 2016. What is clear is that the venture is taking on a lot. Avenues is committed to an immersive curriculum in which half of all subjects, at least in the early grades, are not taught in English. Simultaneously developing a demanding new curriculum—one that integrates existing and new material consistent with its World School conceit—and opening all grades from nursery school to ninth, was a massive undertaking.

The idea of learning bilingually is not a new one, but its successful execution is complex and expensive. My own daughter goes to the Lycée Français in New York, which is part of a global network of almost 500 French government–subsidized institutions whose basic pedagogy was established by Napoleon over 200 years ago.[83] In addition to the historic track record, the Lycée usually requires that at least one parent supports the French language at home because of how demanding it is to learn bilingually. Avenues has no such requirement with respect to either its Spanish or Mandarin programs.[84] On a more practical level, the Lycée has a global network and home country from which to draw teachers qualified to teach all subjects in French. The challenge for Avenues in this regard is not trivial.

One key positive aspect of Avenues's financial model that Whittle did not speak about publicly is that it starts in nursery school. The cost of delivering education increases with student age. High school is by far the most expensive program, and the nursery and pre-K years cost a small fraction of this to administer. Tuition for these early years, however, in the prestige-obsessed New York market is usually not significantly less than for later years—and this holds true at Avenues. Most of the other high-end private schools that Avenues benchmarks against start at kindergarten despite the outsized "profitability" of the earlier years. The reason for this is the inability to meaningfully test at that age whether a child is likely to be able to meet the challenges of the later curriculum. In addition, a variety of cognitive disorders do not manifest themselves until after these years. It is because of such late-manifesting problems that the Lycée Français of New York eliminated its "petite section" several years ago, even though it is part of the French national curriculum. Whether Avenues's scholastic ambitions will ultimately clash with its desire to milk the cash flow potential of preschool will not be known for some time.

Some of Avenues's early investors didn't want to wait to find out whether a promising start would translate into a sustainable business and certainly didn't want to have to fund its global ambitions. Although the school opened at only half its capacity with around 725 students, it had attracted an unprecedented number of applications for a new school in New York. Avenues was poised to grow quickly to over 1,000 students with continued marketing and as high school grades started to open.

All the resulting early talk of "success" led Liberty to decide it was time to cash out after only a couple of years. Having lost money in both Edison and Nations Academy, no one knew better than Liberty the execution risks associated with staying too long in a Whittle venture. History had shown them that if there were a window of potential investor euphoria around one of Whittle's ideas, it was best to take advantage and move on before the actual financial results came in.

For once, Liberty had leverage with Whittle as it could block any new investor. But new cash was needed desperately as Avenues slowly grew into its full capacity a grade at a time. Relations between Whittle and both private equity investors had become poisonous by this time because of a recurring issue in Whittle ventures: a lack of internal expense controls. The marketing costs incurred to mount the impressive Avenues launch bore little resemblance to the approved budget. Furthermore, the promised international expansion would require significant new capital. Despite Whittle's public assurances that financing the international expansion would be simple, it seemed that every few months his timetable slipped. He had originally promised that Beijing and Sao Paolo schools would open in 2014. Then, Sao Paolo slipped to 2015. Then both did. Liberty stood firm and insisted that any new money that came in would also need to take them out.

An unlikely potential savior appeared in the form (again) of global education giant Pearson. Whittle had been apoplectic when Pearson had walked away from the earlier incarnation of Avenues on 57th Street. Now, Pearson had no interest in the school downtown but loved the idea of selling its software and content to a network of high-end global schools. A transaction was structured in which Pearson would invest only in the international operations in return for some cash and a long-term deal to be the soup-to-nuts supplier to these institutions. The New York school would remain in the hands of Whittle, LLR, and a new group of private equity investors including Providence Equity.

The transaction was moving forward, but Whittle's history and reputation came back to haunt him. Sitting on the Pearson board was Susan Fuhrman, the president of Teacher's College and an expert on educational policy and school reform. Fuhrman had followed Whittle's educational initiatives closely from inception. As dean of the University of Pennsylvania Graduate School of Education a decade earlier, Fuhrman observed Edison up close when she took over several of the failing Philadelphia schools not awarded to Whittle in 2002. Fuhrman was horrified to learn that Pearson was thinking of partnering with Whittle and strongly objected. The board declined to approve the investment.

For a second time, Pearson had left Whittle to start over. In this case, however, time was running out, limiting his options dramatically. John Fisher, the billionaire known for his interest in sports teams and educational philanthropy, had invested $5 million in the original $75 million Avenues financing (as did current Illinois Governor Bruce Rauner) and earlier expressed interest in an additional investment on very different terms and with very different governance. Whittle had waved him off, and the larger investors permitted him to do so as long as the Pearson deal that would have left Whittle in charge was a live option. Once the Pearson deal collapsed, Fisher began to deal with the other investors directly. Whittle's 2014 annual letter may have relegated his "important" new investor and new leadership team member to brief mentions following pages of details on the planned China expansion, but it was clear that Fisher's new team was now firmly in charge. Less obvious was whether this team had the same stomach for costly international initiatives—the letter also touches on plans and discussions in Sao Paulo, London, Shanghai, Hong Kong, Delhi, and "the Gulf region"—or whether they would focus closer to home.

When asked about his greatest fear regarding Avenues, Whittle said that he dreaded it becoming "just another fine private school."[85] Although no formal announcement would be made, it soon became clear that the new owners would indeed dramatically scale back Whittle's promise of twenty schools in ten years. The following year's annual letter from Whittle was unusual in two respects. First, it did not represent "an 'official' Avenues statement but rather" Whittle's "own opinions." Second, titled "A Beginner's Report on China," it was described as a "personal reflection more than a progress report." The almost 3,500-word musing on life and China was also notable for the fact that it said remarkably little about Avenues at all. Two months later, in March 2015, Whittle formally cut his remaining ties to Avenues.[86]

"A heart is not judged by how much you love,
but by how much you are loved by others."

Whittle, who will turn seventy in August 2017, has said of his ambitions for Avenues, "I view this as the last rodeo."[87] Such pronouncements from Whittle need to be taken with a grain of salt. As one incredulous research analyst remarked a dozen years earlier after Edison had been taken private: "If you look at his history, he's like a phoenix. Who knows what his next venture will be?"[88] Indeed, on announcing his resignation, Whittle already was singing a different tune. "It's in my blood," he said. "If there's anything an entrepreneur knows it's how to begin again."[89]

The more interesting question is whether sophisticated outside investors would ever back him again. There is a quarter century of evidence that the answer is probably yes. As compared to his other ventures, Avenues for now seems at least a relative success. Notwithstanding the lack of tangible financial or pedagogical proof of actual "success" and the continuing deferral of any international element to what was to be a "global" school chain, early enrollment numbers are genuinely impressive. And although this time the investor who saved the day could only be enticed by the promise of Whittle's exit from any further management role, the reality is that Liberty appears to have gotten out more than whole for a change.

Given his track record of raising money based on far less, it would be hard to believe that Whittle couldn't spin the Avenues story into something that would attract capital for his next venture or maybe even a fund to seek out new opportunities. Indeed, according to knowledgeable sources close to Whittle, he has already raised $20 million from rich individuals and international institutions to recreate his original broad vision of Avenues as a global network of schools. His non-compete with Avenues will apparently constrain exactly how he goes about this, but it appears that the effort will begin in Asia. The initial name for the new venture suggests that Whittle continues to believe that his own reputation is an asset rather than a liability: Whittle School and Studio.

More surprising at some level than Whittle's own ability to continue to move forward relatively unscathed by his track record is the ability of those connected with him to do the same. The Edison Schools saga was not just a monumental financial and operational failure, it represented a massive failure of appropriate corporate governance. Once informed of the ongoing work by Whittle and his team to find a partner amenable to their personal needs, the independent directors did everything they could to minimize Whittle's efforts to keep so much of the residual value of the business for himself. Even if future investors might convince themselves that they could put in place enough protections to get the benefits of Whittle's strategic vision without significant risk, why would anyone want to back those who both enabled his least savory personal proclivities and failed to execute on his big ideas? Yet many have found their association with Whittle to provide a more than satisfactory springboard to future opportunities in the private and public sectors.

Take Chris Cerf, the lawyer without any operating experience who was nonetheless chief operating officer of Edison. As the stock collapsed and performance faltered, the company had to hire a different executive to re-engineer the business for efficiency even as Cerf not only remained as COO but got the additional title of president. And Cerf brought in his investment banker brother, without informing the board, to prepare to market the company on behalf of the management team. One

Liberty executive involved in bringing on Terry Stecz as COO (notably not reporting to Cerf, who remained briefly as president) described Cerf as a "nice guy" but said that he had "nothing in his background to prepare him to be COO of an organization of that complexity."

This track record has yielded increasingly high-profile positions. On the public side, he served first as Deputy Schools Chancellor in New York City and then Governor Christie's Commissioner of the New Jersey Department of Education.[90] On the private side, he set up a series of consulting firms in his home but was ultimately briefly hired to lead the U.S. business of an obscure private Brazilian company called Sangari Global Education.[91] After his stint working for Christie, however, Cerf was tapped to run a division of Rupert Murdoch's unprofitable educational business before it collapsed. From there he was made superintendent of Newark's public schools.

Benno Schmidt has never worked for any for-profit business not affiliated with Whittle. But he has secured a number of high-profile appointments in the nonprofit and public sectors that suggest a lack of concern regarding his leadership as chairman of the board of Edison. Most notably, he has served as chairman of the board of trustees of the City University of New York. The late John Chubb was the Brookings Institution researcher who was a member of "Mercury astronauts" who produced the Edison School design. This association did not impede his being appointed president of the most influential national trade association of private schools or being sought for public policy advice by presidents and presidential candidates.[92]

Part of why alumni of the failed Edison adventure fared so well is that they have positioned themselves as early "leaders" of the so-called school reform movement. Although Edison was much more focused on getting contracts to operate entire school systems, some of their schools were operated under early charter school legislation—when it went public, twenty-four of the first seventy-nine schools were "charter" rather than "contract" schools. In the fifteen years since then, charter schools have become a generic symbolic of efforts to improve public schools outside of the constraints of the existing bureaucracy. As in many intense political battles, the operational track records of fellow travelers are not always examined closely. So Edison alumni have come to be embraced by school reform advocates as charter school pioneers, despite the dramatic public implosion of their business enterprise.

More astonishing are those who have continued to invest with Whittle after having been previously disappointed, sometimes more than once. Even if one were lucky enough to make money with Whittle by getting out early, surely the logical reaction when the inevitable collapse came would be: there but for the grace of God go I. Yet a significant number of investors have come back for more. Liberty only represents the most extreme case. There are many others.

Michael Moe, the one-time Merrill Lynch research analyst who ran their Global Growth team, was the most public and vocal supporter of the Edison IPO in its early days. When he left Merrill in 2001, Moe founded ThinkEquity Partners, the investment bank that continued to publish research on the company even after the stock collapsed and the established banks had stopped. ThinkEquity complained loudly about Edison's lack of disclosure in connection with the go-private transaction, accusing management of bad faith and irresponsibility in its treatment of shareholders.

One might think the embarrassing experience of losing clients' money by vouching for Whittle at two successive institutions would have soured Moe on backing Whittle again. But today Moe is the chief investment officer and portfolio manager for GSV Capital, a public vehicle he founded that buys private stakes in venture-backed companies. Avenues has been one of GSV's top ten holdings, along with the likes of Twitter and Palantir Technologies, and remains a significant part of the portfolio.[93] In addition to the $10 million put into Avenues in May 2012, GSV bought a $1.5 million stake in an Avenues affiliate called Whittle Schools in September 2012. Finally, Moe sought to invest more in the new Avenues deal that Pearson ultimately withdrew from. Since its IPO at $15/share in 2011, GSV shares have traded down significantly, settling between $5–6/share by the beginning of 2016.

The resilience of Whittle after a quarter century suggests that his remarkable marketing and promotional skills are even more effective in the educational domain. Psychological research strongly suggests that we are more likely to believe claims that confirm our previously held views.[94] This tendency may be even more powerful where these views take on an intense, personal aspect borne of formative developmental experiences.

If our preconceived views on education cast a powerful spell, making us particularly susceptible to misguided investment decisions in this arena, is there any protection? In *The Lost Princess of Oz*, L. Frank Baum reveals how the benevolent sorceress, Glinda the Good, protects herself from evil spells. "Of all the magical things which surrounded Glinda in her castle, there was none more marvelous than her Great Book of Records." The Book contained a contemporaneous account of everything that transpired in the kingdom, and this wisdom provided Glinda with a singular defense against any dark arts that she might encounter. "No thief, however skillful, can rob one of knowledge," wrote Baum, "and that is why knowledge is the best and safest treasure to acquire."

The educational realm is broad and complex, and knowledge can only be acquired through a detailed examination of the unique attributes of each of its distinct constituent parts. There are, unfortunately, no easy shortcuts to attaining such knowledge. The stories of how others have lost their financial way in their search for riches in different corners of the Land of Ed are probably the best way to start.

CHAPTER TWO

Rupert and the Chancellor

A Tragic Love Story

THE ALLURE OF the digital dream in education has been persistent and pervasive in the face of serial disappointment. For frustrated politicians and administrators, the absence of actual evidence of effectiveness has proven no match for the burning desire to deliver a dramatic new solution to the seemingly intractable problems in education.[1] For managers and shareholders, the bodies of those who came before have not dissuaded them from seeking the next magic elixir offered to cure the sector of its slow growth and propensity for missed earnings.[2]

In K–12, policy makers who still dare to dream must confront not only the lack of demonstrated results to date but also the substantial opportunity costs of diverting resources to pursue digital solutions. For instance, a recent influential analysis concluded that once the network, content, training, management, and needed devices are accounted for, the cost of using an iPad textbook is more than five times that of using a traditional print textbook.[3] The prospect of being able to ultimately deliver a "personalized" electronic solution to every child's problems is so compelling, however, that few pause to consider fully what this really means or whether it is either practical or desirable.

Investors are also hungry for dramatic change in primary and secondary education and seem all too ready to believe in the latest catalyst for upending the historic financial trajectory of the industry. A long line of small digital businesses—with names like Plato Learning (IPO in 1992), Riverdeep (IPO in 2000), K12 Inc. (IPO in 2007), and Archipelago Learning (IPO in 2009)[4]—has convinced the public markets that they really represent a very big idea. Some have crashed and burned more spectacularly than others. What they all have in common is the vast gulf between their originally articulated aspirations and their ultimate results.

Even outside of education, the conceptual appeal of the disruptive paradigm has not been matched with results. Historian Jill Lepore has shown that the handpicked examples used in the bible of disruption—that is, Clayton M. Christensen's *The Innovator's Dilemma*[5]—were actually more often than not the result of "incremental improvements" rather than transformative technologies.[6] The more fundamental problem, from a financial perspective, is that the ability to digitally disrupt an established marketplace is unlikely to lead to a particularly good business. Whatever kink in the armor of the established order that allowed the introduction of a new competitor is very likely to attract many more and make the new order much less profitable than the old one was.

Two leaders who have nonetheless managed to demonstrate an ability to successfully disrupt an entrenched incumbent regime are Rupert Murdoch and Joel Klein. Murdoch has created multiple profitable and resilient franchises in established domains, often by fundamentally changing the rules of the game. Many others had tried and failed to become credible competitors to the BBC, the three U.S. broadcast networks, and CNN, but only Murdoch found ways to do so. In an entirely different realm, Joel Klein used his perch as chancellor of the New York City public schools to discard a wide range of stultifying institutional orthodoxies that previous heads had found immovable. Although controversial, it is hard to argue that Klein did not succeed in changing the landscape of the possible in public education—not just in New York but nationally as well.[7]

These kindred spirits found in each other the perfect partner through which to apply their unique abilities and track records to fundamentally disrupt the K–12 educational marketplace. They did this by simultaneously taking on the global multibillion-dollar leaders in educational hardware, software, and curriculum. But after five years and more than $1 billion spent, with no serious prospect of ever turning a profit, their venture, called Amplify, would be sold for scrap value. In the interim, Amplify played a role in the break-up of Murdoch's overall media empire. It is worth taking a closer look at how this promising partnership came to be and how it then unraveled, having made no significant ripple in an increasingly crowded field of more focused early-stage educational ventures bent on leading their own education revolution.

Breaking Up Is Not So Hard to Do

With unprecedented frequency in recent years, public corporations have been splitting themselves up. Alternatively spurred by activist investors, a desire to shed underperforming assets, or simple frustration with a perceived "conglomerate discount" in the company's stock price, tax-free spinoffs have been embraced by the public markets. On the mere announcement of a company's intention to spin off a division, shares frequently rebound sharply. Indeed, shareholders are so appreciative of the separation that the remaining company frequently is valued higher without the offending holding than with it—even before taking into account the value that shareholders receive for their ownership of the spinoff company.

The market euphoria over the advantages of spinoffs has led to significantly less focus on the behind-the-scenes "sausage making" that goes into the corporate preparations preceding the separation. By the time the newly independent company actually starts trading, a series of critical questions must have been answered: Which assets should be included? Who from management and the board should go with the spin? How much of our debt should we burden the spun company with? What kind of business arrangements should continue between the two companies, and what are the "fair" terms of those arrangements?

These questions are all highly politically charged. Those who will go with the spinoff vehicle want to ensure that it is poised for success on its own. Their interest will be in getting as many attractive businesses as possible, starting out with a pristine balance sheet, and having access to any critical resources retained by the remaining company on an acceptable basis. The team staying behind, by contrast, often will be focused on something altogether different: how do I use the spinoff to get rid of all the problems that have historically constrained my operating flexibility and tempered my unconditional embrace by investors?

The tension between these diametrically opposed perspectives invariably results in lively internal, but decidedly lopsided, negotiations. The ultimate decision makers are almost always the senior management team and board members who will stay behind. As a result, spun-off companies are often larded with debt, other unwanted balance sheet obligations, and various random troubled businesses that don't fit anywhere. That is not to say there aren't exceptions to this rule. IAC/InterActiveCorp's core business model, for instance, is to nurture new digital businesses and "perpetually spin them out to the benefit of shareholders."[8] Yet, the fundamental incentives make these exceedingly rare nonetheless.

The complexities around all the details of a separation frequently require a year or more to execute. Financial, legal, and accounting advisors are hired, corporate project teams established, and code names given for "SpinCo" and "RemainCo." Given the predictable political dynamics described, however, one informal name for the to-be-spun entity often emerges as an internal company favorite: "ShitCo."

Viacom's 2006 spin-off of CBS was typical in this regard. Viacom kept the sexy businesses, like the movie studio, and its faster-growing segments, like the cable channels. CBS, by contrast, got the slow-growth businesses like book publishing; a disproportionate amount of the company's debt; and, for good measure, legacy liabilities, such as asbestos exposure litigation dating back to predecessor companies. Tensions between the companies from the treatment of CBS as "ShitCo" linger to this day. But CBS had the last laugh by outperforming Viacom in the ensuing decade and recently even executing a spinoff of its own of the company's billboard assets. More often than not, however, "ShitCo" remains "ShitCo," floundering as an orphan stock, sold, or broken up.

The decision by Murdoch to split up his media empire into two separate companies had particular resonance with public investors. Historically, Murdoch had made daring unconventional bets that, over the decades, had accrued to the benefit of all shareholders, even as, at times, they risked the company's very survival: the launch of the Fox Broadcasting Network in 1986, the creation of BSkyB in 1990, and the establishment of the FX Network in 1994 and Fox News in 1996. By most key operating metrics, News Corp. appeared to be the best run major media company through most of this era. The net result was that, with the exception of the first five years of Michael Eisner's tenure at Disney, News Corp. had consistently been the best performing media conglomerate for decades.

Murdoch had always made his share of mistakes and always pursued personal interests that had questionable strategic and financial benefits to the company. But one of Murdoch's great strengths as a CEO was his ability to reverse course quickly—some might say ruthlessly—when found to be in error. And his well-documented affinity for the newspaper business seemed harmless enough while newspapers continued to be a relatively profitable enterprise. Even his insistence on retaining a perpetually money-losing property like the *New York Post*—reported to cost the company upward of $50 million annually to maintain—were on such a relatively modest scale, that it was largely deemed well worth the value of keeping the visionary Murdoch engaged on all fronts.

Over the first years of the new century, however, the mix of visionary and value-destructive decisions shifted sharply to the negative. The speed with which mistakes were corrected slowed. The scale of the seemingly personal pursuits expanded as the results deteriorated. It wasn't just misguided digital acquisitions and investments anymore, but projects as unlikely as a chicken farm in Australia.[9] Many of the most respected senior operating and corporate executives departed, sometimes in direct reaction to the company's new ethos.

Write-offs had been piling up since 2001, totaling almost $25 billion,[10] and the share price lagged both the market and its peers. Indeed, where once there had been a Murdoch "premium" in the stock, the growing perception of unreliability among investors had created a Murdoch "discount." So when rumors first surfaced in 2012 that News Corp. would establish a "ShitCo" of its own to house Murdoch's various "enthusiasms," it surprised no one that the shares of the company jumped almost 10 percent.[11]

The Birth of ClownCo

The devil, as with all such plans, was in the details. As first reported, News Corp.'s "ShitCo" was characterized as encompassing Murdoch's various publishing interests. These included not just the *New York Post* and a coupon-distribution business in the United States, newspapers in the UK and Australia, and HarperCollins, the global English-language book publisher, but also the entirety of Dow Jones (owner of the *Wall Street Journal*), which Murdoch had purchased for $5.6 billion in 2007. The fact that the company had been forced to write down fully half the value of the Dow Jones acquisition only a year after closing the transaction may have represented a turning point in investor attitudes toward Murdoch.[12]

Together, this pure publishing company would generate around $1 billion in profit in 2012 on more than $8 billion in revenues.[13]

Surely that would represent adequate scale to establish a credible independent company and even provide room to put billions of debt on the business. But several significant countervailing factors made this an unlikely scenario.

First, unlike most spinoffs, Murdoch would remain executive chair of *both* companies. This was also true of Sumner Redstone's relationship to Viacom and CBS, though at the time, he had been clearly more focused on the long-term value creation from a high-growth Viacom. By contrast, Murdoch actually had a stronger personal emotional attachment to "ShitCo" than to "RemainCo." Although he was nominally CEO only of "RemainCo," the day-to-day management reality reflected his primary preoccupation with "ShitCo." Executives back at what would soon be called 21st Century Fox had never had any interest in the publishing assets and viewed the Dow Jones acquisition as a costly distraction. That said, they knew that any attempt to pull cash out before the spin and encumber "ShitCo" (which would retain the News Corp. name) with debt would be angrily dismissed by Murdoch. So rather than the typical situation, there was a genuine commitment to ensuring that the company had all the resources it needed to survive independently, indefinitely. Given Murdoch's perspective, management at Fox was thrilled to see these businesses jettisoned at all.

Second, absolute size notwithstanding, the operating trajectory of the publishing assets was troubling. In 2012, the profit of the news and information business fell almost 20 percent and was anticipated to continue to experience double-digit percentage declines for years to come. Although the low-margin Harper Collins book business had managed to keep profits relatively stable, in 2012 it represented less than 10 percent of the profits of the other publishing businesses.

Third, and maybe most important, in 2010 Murdoch had decided to go into the education sector through the acquisition of a small business called Wireless Generation. Since then, the company had broadened its educational sector ambitions into areas far beyond those in which Wireless had originally operated. By 2012, Murdoch's collective educational endeavors were losing close to $200 million annually, with no near-term prospect of profitability. In the context of a company the size of the combined News Corp., losses like this or that of the *New York Post* could be managed without bringing undue attention to them. In the context of a far smaller News Corp., however, with fast-shrinking profits in its core businesses, these numbers mattered.

The net result was that to be rid of these publishing assets and cash-devouring educational ventures, 21st Century Fox would need to do more than simply forgo the cash dividend that "RemainCos" traditionally exact from their departing siblings on the way out the door. In this case, just to ensure that there would be no risk to the long-term solvency of News Corp., Fox would need to actually contribute more than $2.5 billion in cash, along with valuable Australian cable and digital assets worth maybe even more.

It was an unusually hefty divorce settlement but, based on the market reaction, a very fair price for independence. The value came not just from eliminating the distraction from managing this mix of mostly declining or money-losing activities of no apparent strategic value. It also came equally from the implicit understanding that News Corp. would be the vehicle from any future shareholder-unfriendly Murdoch initiatives.

For the remaining management at Fox, almost any price was viewed as a bargain. They had long been pressing for a separation, which Murdoch had resisted even as the pace of his shareholder-unfriendly actions quickened. It was only when the *News of the World* hacking scandal erupted in London that Murdoch allowed the spin-off to move forward. To be fair, the code name used at the company during preparations for jettisoning Murdoch's beloved assets was not "ShitCo." In fact, the name of this book is partially an homage to the only slightly less pejorative name used internally: ClownCo.

If the Dow Jones write-down represented a turning point in investor attitudes toward Murdoch, the decision to take on the business and political education establishment on the shareholders' dime was something else altogether. This decision reflected a willingness to take on challenges completely unrelated to the core business that had no obvious limitation on their required investment. If not subject to some constraint, this venture had the potential to take the "Murdoch discount" to an entirely new level. It was this, more than any other single financial consideration, that made the separation of ClownCo so essential to the shareholders.

Newspapers had always been Murdoch's acknowledged first love—his long-time desire for ownership of the *Wall Street Journal* was well known. The price and the value destruction of the Dow Jones deal were infuriating but not ultimately surprising. The good news was that there really wasn't much else he could buy in this vein, as the other national papers were unavailable and likely to spark regulatory review. Most local papers would have triggered cross-ownership restrictions that applied to the Fox TV stations in those markets. In addition, although Murdoch could be criticized on any number of grounds, no one knew the newspaper business better than he. Finally, given the huge success of Fox News—and affiliated news organizations such as Sky in the United Kingdom and local U.S. station news operations— an argument could be made that there were some positive spillover effects from owning the *Wall Street Journal* brand.

The entry of Murdoch into the education business, however, had none of these mitigating considerations. Part of operating management's frustration was that the initiative began just as they were trying to focus the company by divesting or closing a long line of earlier distracting, Murdoch-sponsored projects. MySpace was sold in 2011, *The Daily* was shuttered in 2012, and IGN Networks was sold in 2013, all for a combined loss of over $1 billion. The company had little expertise in the educational sector and no significant assets to which it was strategically connected. Although Murdoch had previously owned educational publishing assets, they were ultimately divested after he, along with a number of his media conglomerate peers who had made the same strategic mistake realized their tenuous connection to the rest of his media empire.

That had been almost twenty years earlier.[14] Since then, Murdoch had gotten a taste of just how much money could be quickly lost trying to "transform" education when his friend Michael Milken asked him to invest in his Knowledge Universe venture. It was never completely clear to Murdoch precisely how the money had disappeared so fast, but he certainly knew that education had not been transformed and that he had gotten a small fraction of his investment back. Although buried in the footnotes, Murdoch wrote off $92 million of his $100 million investment in a subsidiary of Milken's Knowledge Universe.[15] The losses envisioned for this new educational initiative dwarfed anything he had given Milken and even a decade of losses at the *New York Post*. Education, it could be said, is what gave "ShitCo" its stink.

Murdoch's announcement at the time of the Wireless Generation acquisition did nothing to temper concerns about the scale of future investment being contemplated. "We see a $500 billion sector in the U.S. alone that is waiting desperately to be transformed," Murdoch gushed. In his view, the business he was buying was "at the forefront" of technology that was "poised to revolutionize public education."[16]

The announcement of the acquisition of Wireless Generation came only weeks after the announcement that Joel Klein would be joining News Corp. in the ambiguous role of "executive vice president, office of the chairman." At the time that News Corp. bought the company at a $400 million valuation, Wireless Generation had around $60 million of revenues and was cash flow negative. It is true that many digital or software companies that lost money as they invested to achieve high growth had sold at multiples of revenue as high as or higher than this transaction. But Wireless Generation revenues had actually declined in the most recent year, making the price completely irrational from an economic perspective.

News Corp. went to great pains to provide public assurances that Klein, who would remain at the Department of Education through year-end, had no involvement in the purchase.[17] What was clear, nonetheless, was the extent to which Klein had influenced Murdoch's thinking on the subject of education in the months leading up to the transaction and his hiring. Although a long-time charter school advocate and supporter of Teach for America, Murdoch had begun speaking out on education reform and making high-profile donations.[18] Also evident was the regard with which Murdoch now held Klein. In response to a *New York Magazine* survey, Murdoch identified Klein as "the most important living New Yorker."[19]

Regardless of whether Klein played a direct role in Murdoch's acquisition of Wireless Generation, it is incontrovertible that Klein's tenure as chancellor fundamentally shaped that company's development. That history is central to understanding both the otherwise inexplicable acquisition and the apparent belief that this modest educational business could serve as a platform from which to fundamentally transform K–12 education as we know it.

Welcome to the Wireless Generation

For all of Murdoch's breathless talk of revolution, at the time of the 2010 acquisition, Wireless Generation had been around for a decade and operated mostly within a tiny slice of the half-trillion-dollar sector apparently being targeted. When friends Larry Berger and Greg Gunn launched the business in 2000, they imagined piping all students' educational needs to handheld devices. As Berger described their early ambitions, he viewed mobile applications as uniquely able to transform how teachers worked in the classroom, "creating tools that would make teachers feel empowered."[20]

The large educational publishers he approached, however, expressed little interest in partnering with him to help achieve this vision. As it turned out, the main practical application of the wireless technology was for DIBELS (Dynamic Indicators of Basic Early Literacy Skills), a formative reading assessment product serving the K–3 market. Particularly in the early grades, allowing a teacher to observe individual student performance and enter it into a handheld device was an extremely efficient way to administer assessments and collect data. The DIBELS assessment was owned by the original developers, not Wireless, and its validity was a subject of heated controversy among academics and school administrators.[21] But, wisely or not, it had been adopted broadly, and Wireless Generation's application—called mCLASS—became very popular, driving the company's growth.

The entire K–3 formative assessment market, however, was not very large. Although DIBELS-related activities still represented a majority of Wireless Generation's revenue, by the time of the Murdoch acquisition, that market had already been saturated, and overall revenue in 2010 was actually down from the prior year.

An opportunity for Wireless to expand beyond its niche came in the form of Chancellor Klein's belief in the potential for technology to accelerate his efforts to transform New York City's public schools. Although much of the focus of his tenure after being appointed in 2002 had been on organizational and school design issues, Klein had early on signaled that technology would play a central role in his overall Children First reform strategies.[22] Technology, Klein asserted, "is one of the most underused assets in terms of the future of educating our children."[23]

By 2006, Klein was ready to put his money where his mouth was. The first order of business was to develop a request for proposal (RFP), typically used in major government procurement decisions, with specifications for the largest outside contract of any kind the department had ever undertaken. Klein had in mind building an $80 million instructional improvement system (IIS) that would not only track student performance in real time online but also perform certain administrative and reporting functions associated with what are known as student information systems (SIS). As conceived, the product would facilitate both the design of individualized instructional plans for students and the management of resources and personnel systemwide.

Although the initiative reflected laudable aspirations, there were no successful systems currently in place that did everything sought by New York. In addition, a number of similar but less ambitious efforts had ended badly—and expensively—with angry recriminations all around.[24] In North Carolina, the first year rollout of an accountability system had taken ten years. Chicago had fired its first vendor, only to have to shut down the system installed by a second vendor due to massive data errors and lost student information. Large districts in Florida and Texas both faced system meltdowns, resulting in lost data, millions in cost overruns, ad ultimately more rather than less work for existing staff. Thus, any procurement process of this magnitude would need to be carefully managed. In this case, given the lack of favorable precedents, additional care would be required to establish sensible and achievable technological and operational requirements.

Klein hired a chief accountability officer to spearhead technology initiatives. This new chief accountability officer would report directly to the chancellor and be responsible for developing standards, selecting contractors, and managing implementation. Selected for this role, however, was not an expert in technology, education, or procurement, but James Liebman, a professor at Columbia Law School with an impressive record as a public interest lawyer and a leading expert on the death penalty.[25] The incumbent chief information officer (CIO) of the department, Irwin Kroot, who had been a senior consultant at IBM and Price Waterhouse Coopers, would quickly depart within months. The next CIO, Ted Brodheim, would not be appointed until the following year, after the contract had already been awarded.[26]

Not very much was publicly disclosed about the procurement process Liebman led. And the thirteen-member oversight board that had been put in place when the mayor took control of the public schools did not review the process.[27] A number of the nineteen competitors for the massive contract thought its scope was overly broad and that the proposed timelines for project implementation were simply impractical. Some suspected that onerous technical specifications had been included at the behest of IBM, which was ultimately awarded the contract.[28]

Whatever the truth about the selection process, even IBM ultimately needed to align with a half-dozen subcontractors to credibly claim it could fulfill the contract requirements. Serving as an IBM sub-contractor created the opportunity for Wireless Generation to develop revenues and establish credentials beyond early-grade formative assessment work. Although a highly respected company, IBM's previous large-scale public education projects—notably, in North Carolina and Chicago—were characterized by delays, cost overruns, and, ultimately, termination. Wireless Generation would initially represent a small percentage of the overall contract,[29] but it would provide an important platform from which to expand its role when IBM faltered again later.

Another competitor for the New York City Department of Education contract was a consortium that included a business called SchoolNet. Although a relatively small business, SchoolNet had focused exclusively on developing scalable, data-driven IIS since it was founded in 1998. By 2006, it was on the fifth version of its core software. The company was by far the market leader in large school districts and had been operating successfully in neighboring Philadelphia since 2002. Indeed, it had also been operating its IIS successfully in Chicago, even as IBM was in the process of losing its SIS contract there.

SchoolNet did not have the capabilities to perform all the functions required by the RFP and had partnered with Deloitte. Jonathan Harber, the CEO of SchoolNet, had met with Liebman to argue that the proposed timelines—three months to have a pilot up and running and an initial full release four months later—were not achievable. Only SchoolNet, he argued, had an existing IIS product that could be up and running that quickly, allowing the additional functionality to be built on top later. Liebman was not convinced and remained committed to launching a system that would represent the first of its kind.

The IBM system, ARIS, would not be fully implemented for years. By late 2008, after almost $50 million had been spent, principals, teachers, and parents still did not have access to ARIS.[30] Liebman would resign in July 2009.[31] Fortunately for Wireless Generation, the company would be given more and more of the contract to execute for IBM as ARIS's deficiencies became more apparent. Ultimately, Wireless was assigned the entire project (without a new RFP). Liebman still considers ARIS a success and believes that it performed more effectively than any other comparable system even today, almost a decade after IBM's initial selection. The only aspect of the decision making that Liebman questions in retrospect was their "instinct" that the school system needed to use a "big established and well-known firm" in the first place to minimize the risks associated with taking on a project of such scope and novelty.[32]

The other potential piece of good news for Wireless Generation was the establishment in 2009 of the $4.35 billion Race to the Top Fund for which states would compete.[33] Race to the Top (RTT) was a boon to IIS providers because each winner was required to set aside part of the funds for a statewide IIS. Although Wireless Generation's experience with ARIS could make it a contender for these funds, the reality was that being asked to "fix" a troubled project that was already "well under way"[34] was a far cry from having a commercializable product to market—but it definitely represented a new opportunity.

The other key asset that Wireless Generation had was its CEO, Larry Berger. At a time when education funds were frequently directed or influenced by philanthropies and think tanks, having a leader who played well to that constituency was crucial. Despite the relatively narrow domain in which his company operated, Berger had become a popular evangelist for both the potential of technology to transform education in general and—reflecting his own bitter experience trying to get them to adopt Wireless Generation's technology—the "challenges to breaking the monopolies held by the educational publishing companies."[35] In fact, it was through a widely delivered PowerPoint presentation on these and other "barriers to innovation in the education sector" that Berger established himself in the community. He served on boards of influential educational philanthropies and thought leaders like the Carnegie Foundation for the Advancement of Teaching, the Annenberg Institute for School Reform at Brown University, and even the nonprofit corporation that owned the leading industry trade publication, *Education Week.*

This work proved particularly valuable in securing a contract to create the algorithm for something called the School of One. This program was the brainchild of New York City Department of Education employee Joel Rose, who conceived of developing a daily individual learning plan for students based on their specific needs—identified after collecting data and applying predictive algorithms. So compelling was this concept that it ultimately attracted funding from thirty different private entities—notably, the Bill and Melinda Gates Foundation and the Carnegie Corporation, a sister organization to the one on whose board Berger at. Again, there was no RFP for the project.

An initial design *charrette* was organized in 2009 and a pilot program established in a school in 2010. Wireless Generation secured the contract to develop the software for that program in June 2010. Like the ARIS contract, however, School of One had far broader ambitions. If ARIS provided hopes of Race to the Top largesse, School of One promised even greater riches if its dream of individualizing instruction for every public school kid in America was ultimately achieved. And there was no shortage of believers in the School of One. Philanthropies aside, *Time* magazine cited the program as one of the "100 Best Innovations of 2009" and the former head of Columbia University's Teachers College called it the "future of education."[36]

So, after a decade of struggle, as Wireless Generation started 2010, it had a great deal to feel good about. Although its core business had slowed, Berger had cultivated a couple of promising new avenues through which to reaccelerate its growth. The company faced one existential problem, however, that it urgently needed to address. It was running out of money.

Wireless and Cashless

Wireless Generation had raised just under $20 million over five funding rounds between 2001 and 2005. The last of these, at more than $6 million, had been the largest; it valued the business at $58 million, or just over three times revenues at the time. By the beginning of 2010, the company still had close to $8 million in the bank, but it had eaten through more than $6 million just in the previous year. These amounts understate the peak cash needs of the business. In K–12 education, cash flows fluctuate dramatically over the year. Even the largest and most profitable businesses have quarters—when product is being developed and customers are being solicited in anticipation of the fall enrollment—that are a significant drain on cash.

What's more, Wireless Generation would need to spend more than $10 million in the coming year on software development and other capital expenses to support its hoped-for growth. This amount would ramp up in future years as the new initiatives developed. To deal with these cash needs, the company arranged to borrow $5 million during the year from the Kellogg Foundation. It was clear, however, that a more permanent liquidity solution needed to be found.

The only practical options were two—find a new, deep-pocketed equity investor or sell the company. Given recent trends, neither was certain, and time was not on their side. Wireless Generation and its investors realized that even if the company were offered the same revenue multiple obtained in 2005, when the company was actually growing, they would barely get $200 million. Although a straight sale would provide immediate cash and more certainty, the only likely buyer that might offer a "strategic" value at or through this level would have been one of the large K–12 publishers. These businesses could reap significant cost and potential revenue benefits from combining operations, but they were precisely the "monopolists" that Berger had railed against in his well-publicized PowerPoint presentation. K–12 publishers not only had national sales forces with relationships with all the key districts, but they also had invested hundreds of millions on their own software development efforts.

At just that moment in early 2010, as Wireless was pondering its options, Berger was approached by Pearson about acquiring the company. Based in London, Pearson is the largest global education publisher. At that time, neither of the two other major K–12 publishers were in a position to pay an outsized price for the company. Houghton Mifflin Harcourt had just undergone one of its now regular restructurings and was in no position to make an acquisition. McGraw-Hill's educational unit had been a drag on its overall performance, such that shareholders would likely be horrified by the announcement of a significant acquisition of a money-losing, slow-growing business. (Indeed, the following year, an activist investor would push McGraw to spin off its educational business altogether.)

In contrast to the questionable appetite of the other two publishers, Doug Kubach, the senior executive who had contacted Berger, emphasized that Pearson would be divesting much of its noneducational portfolio in order to aggressively pursue digital education properties. When Pearson announced the multibillion-dollar sale of its financial information business in May, Kubach's assertion was confirmed. Rather than return any of the proceeds to shareholders, Pearson stated that it would instead "look for bolt on acquisitions with a particular focus on technology and services."37

As distasteful as the idea of becoming a division of a publishing "monopolist" may have been to Berger, Pearson expressed a willingness to potentially pay a staggering $300 million for the business.

Given the company's precarious situation, conversations began in earnest. Then, out of the blue, News Corp. reached out to express an interest in buying Wireless Generation.

The call from News Corp. was unexpected and came from an unlikely source. Rupert Murdoch, they learned, had apparently hired Kristen Kane, the former COO of the New York Department of Education under Joel Klein, to "educate" him about the sector. The call was actually about another company—a digital education company called Time To Know, funded entirely by successful Israeli entrepreneur Shmuel Meitar.[38] But when Berger told Kane that Wireless was having sale discussions, she immediately expressed interest. Given the obvious lack of strategic fit, Wireless was skeptical about News Corp.'s commitment to transact at a value that would be of interest to them, but Kane assured them that Murdoch's interest in the sector was genuine. The good news was that this was true. The bad news was that absolutely no one else of importance at News Corp. had any interest in the sector and, indeed, they would all try to kill the deal at every opportunity.

True to her word, Kane called back quickly, and within days Berger found himself in a four-hour meeting with Murdoch himself. Murdoch did not blanch at the valuations that Wireless had been discussing with Pearson. To ensure that it wouldn't leave any money on the table, Wireless had reached out to investment bankers to manage the process of selling the company or, if that failed, raising a sixth round of funding. Goldman Sachs had been hired in the summer of 2010 and was as surprised as anyone that News Corp. had expressed interest. The bankers were thrilled that they had been handed a horse race that was starting at the incredible price of at least $300 million.

Goldman knew both Pearson and News Corp. as well as anyone. The financial company had just managed the $3.4 billion sale of Pearson's financial information business, and a former Goldman partner sat on the News Corp. board. Pearson, which owned the *Financial Times*, and News Corp., had a long history of animosity, arising not only from their competition in the newspaper market and ancient disputes stemming from their once-shared ownership of BSkyB but also from deep cultural differences.

Pearson's interest in Wireless Generation was completely different from that of News Corp. Murdoch saw ARIS and the School of One as the key to transforming education and had modest interest in the legacy K–3 assessment business. Pearson, by contrast, saw significant cost savings and upside from eliminating duplicative K–3 assessment products and planned to use Wireless Generation development resources to build new products in the later grades. Indeed, the internal pro forma model built by Pearson showed that $300 million was very affordable once the cost and revenue synergies were taken into account. Pearson was highly skeptical of both ARIS, which was not obviously marketable beyond New York City, and School of One, which was a nascent venture. Pearson did, however, see value in Berger's relationships with the foundation community that had become an increasing source of funding in education and that had been historically as hostile to the publishing "monopolists" as Berger had been.

Goldman adroitly used the deep-seated competitiveness between Pearson and News Corp. to ensure that the ultimate price would reflect most, if not all, of the synergy value from the most strategic buyer. Goldman shared a term sheet reflecting Wireless's wish list of financial and commercial terms in a deal and asked both parties to put their best foot forward in marking up the document. The lack of any internal constituency for the acquisition at News Corp. beyond Murdoch led the company to cool somewhat on the transaction. In the early fall, however, bankers were still able to use the *perception* of genuine competition to force Pearson to move its price to an astounding $360 million.

Having now agreed on the price and key contract terms, Pearson knew that no other party was still involved in the process. This led to a lack of urgency and increasing intransigence on remaining open issues on its part and a building frustration on Wireless Generation's part. By November, the contract was still not quite signed.

Then, on November 9, Joel Klein announced he was leaving the schools job for the Murdoch empire at year-end. Shortly thereafter, News Corp., which had previously terminated conversations with Wireless Generation, suddenly reached back out to Goldman to see whether the contract with Pearson had actually been executed. In fact, at this point, all of the key outstanding issues had been resolved with Pearson, and an agreement on a final signing the following Monday had been reached. That said, Berger not only was annoyed with the pace of final negotiations but also was ambivalent about being owned by one of the educational publishers he had long railed against. He let it be known that if News Corp. topped Pearson and agreed more or less to the original "wish list" term sheet, Wireless Generation would be theirs.

So to own it, News Corp., which had no synergies, had no choice but to pay more than the price extracted from Pearson reflecting their full synergies. Just as he had done in buying MySpace out from under Viacom, within a matter of days and with very little incremental due diligence, Rupert Murdoch bought Wireless Generation. He paid the same $360 million in cash offered by Pearson, but for only 90 percent of the business. The 10 percent equity "kiss" above the cash paid would be retained by Berger, the COO and chief product officer.

Berger and his team spent the weekend finalizing in days with News Corp. what had taken months with Pearson. So worried were they that Pearson would find out what was afoot that Wireless didn't even tell their own banker, who they feared could not resist engaging with the educational publisher. When frantic Pearson executives were unable to contact Wireless, the Goldman bankers admitted to having no idea where their client was or what they were doing. As announced publicly, the total value placed on Wireless Generation was $400 million. In fact, the actual price ultimately paid was substantially more.

When the least strategic buyer agrees to more than the most strategic buyer, it is a sure sign that the new owner will not make a return on its investment. As another CEO of a venture-backed digital education venture wrote in *Fortune* at the time, "[The] News Corp. deal for Wireless Generation is great, but it doesn't make sense."[39]

As little sense as the initial acquisition made, it was genius compared to the strategy undertaken once the asset was owned by News Corp. The subsequent losses incurred would dwarf the price paid.

Enter the Chancellor

Joel Klein is a very impressive person. After clerking for the Supreme Court and a few years at a well-regarded litigation boutique, he founded a firm with two colleagues that was widely viewed as developing the premier Supreme Court and federal appellate advocacy practice in Washington, D.C.[40] What followed was a distinguished career in the Clinton White House and Justice Department, culminating in a stint as antitrust chief, where he successfully prosecuted Microsoft.

To appoint Klein as New York City schools chancellor, Mayor Michael Bloomberg was obliged to seek a waiver from the state education commissioner because of Klein's limited background in the education sector.[41] Notwithstanding his lack of experience, even the usually skeptical journalist Steven Brill, while not ignoring his failures, concluded that Klein made substantial progress in that role.[42] Where Brill did err, however, was in suggesting that Klein had a track record in running any kind of business.

Brill described Klein's eighteen-month tenure at the German media conglomerate Bertelsmann after leaving the Justice Department as "a daring jump out of law and government" into a corporate operating job.[43] According to Brill, Klein "was responsible for business ranging from Random House books to Sony BMG Music to Gruner + Jahr Magazines." This statement is not accurate. Each of the businesses mentioned by Brill (only one of which was wholly owned by Bertelsmann) had its own management teams, none of whom thought that Klein had much of anything to do with them.

Although Klein had the title of chairman and CEO of Bertelsmann Inc., this was merely a holding company for the U.S. assets of a number of the company's divisions. Indeed, "Bertelsmann's most prominent feature is its decentralization," with generations of leaders leaving all key strategic and operating decisions to the divisions.[44] Bertelsmann CEO Thomas Middelhoff brought in Klein for a staff role to "advise on legal and strategic governmental issues, working closely with the heads of Bertelsmann's U.S.-based operations."[45] Klein had limited staff of his own and never had any authority over any of the company's business units. The *Wall Street Journal* referred to Klein as "a roving executive-without-portfolio."[46]

Klein's weakness in operational management was also viewed as an Achilles heel during his eight years at the New York City Department of Education. The *New York Times* speculated that Klein had been pushed out due, in part, to his resistance to accepting a new chief operating officer imposed by the mayor's office.[47] None of this dissuaded Murdoch from agreeing to employ Klein when he called over a weekend to say that his tenure as chancellor would be ending imminently.[48] The sudden decision to hire Klein was not as surprising to News Corp. executives as was the agreement to put him on the News Corp. board of directors. A hastily arranged board call effectively ratifying this promise could solve the short-term awkwardness caused by Murdoch's decision. And yet, the longer-term awkwardness created by having the architect of what would become a costly mistake serve as part of the supposed oversight body could not be as easily resolved.

Murdoch had always had a favorable impression of Klein. Their earliest interaction may have been when Klein, as Bill Clinton's antitrust chief, reversed his staff's decision to sue to block News America Marketing's acquisition of ActMedia in 1997.[49] As an advocate of charter schools and a detester of unions of all kinds, Murdoch had been a fan of Klein's chancellorship from early on, and the two had crossed paths on multiple occasions. It was only in the last year of Klein's tenure as chancellor, as tensions with Mayor Bloomberg grew, that Klein and Murdoch had begun to compare notes more regularly.

To be fair, in addition to being the leading advocate for the school reform initiatives in which Murdoch deeply believed, Klein had other important skills that could prove useful to Murdoch. Klein had not only shown himself to be a singularly effective advocate both in and outside a courtroom, but he was also a highly respected Democrat at a time when Murdoch had recently lost his most important conduits to the other side of the aisle. Both Peter Chernin, the highly respected president and COO of News Corp. for over a dozen years, and Gary Ginsberg, an executive vice president "who often served as a liaison between the conservative Mr. Murdoch and the Democratic Party," had left the previous year.[50] More broadly, Klein had a remarkable ability to not just network but also connect individuals of diverse interests and backgrounds with unexpected and sometimes truly spectacular results. For instance, Klein's introduction of real estate and media mogul Mort Zuckerman to neuroscientist Eric Kandel resulted in the establishment of the $200 million Zuckerman Mind Brain Behavior Institute at Columbia University.

But that still left the question of what precisely Klein would do at News Corp. It was initially suggested that he would "advise . . . on opportunities to invest in digital initiatives in the educational market."[51] Although the company said Klein would advise Murdoch on a "wide range of initiatives," sources emphasized the focus would be specifically on "seed investments" in "entrepreneurial ventures."[52] When the Wireless Generation deal was announced soon thereafter, Klein's role became even more unclear. Wireless Generation was not a seed investment and had a complete management team under Larry Berger, all of whom would be joining News Corp. Indeed, the Wireless senior management had been explicitly assured that they would be operating independently and not reporting to Klein.

As Klein and Wireless Generation joined the News Corp. fold at the beginning of 2011, many questions remained about the assets that had just been purchased and the company's broader ambitions in education. It would be a few years before the company formally unveiled its vision for the educational division. By that time, it would be clear that Klein was firmly in charge, Wireless Generation was far smaller than anticipated, and the scope of educational activities being undertaken by News Corp. was far more expansive.

The Education of Rupert Murdoch

The education division at News Corp. when Klein took over was simply Wireless Generation. Given that Klein's salary in the first year was guaranteed to be at least $4.5 million, the division would need to exceed its already explosive promised growth in 2011 if it were still to achieve overall profitability. As Klein began quickly staffing up the division's corporate center that would sit atop Wireless Generation, it became clear that additional investment, rather than early returns, would be the focus.[53] During the course of that first year, significant impediments to the promised growth in the Wireless Generation business emerged.

The first round winners of the RTT competition among states had been announced in 2010, and late in 2011, statewide IIS contracts were being awarded with those funds. The results were foreshadowed, as some of the states that had been unsuccessful RTT finalists, such as Kentucky, had already begun to contract for these systems with their own money. The winner of the Kentucky contract, and ultimately of a majority of the competitive RTT contracts, was SchoolNet, the company New York City had earlier rejected in favor of IBM and Wireless Generation for the implementation of ARIS. By 2011, SchoolNet's system had already been adopted by a third of the large urban school districts. Pearson purchased SchoolNet in April 2011 for about half of what News Corp. paid for Wireless Generation.[54]

News Corp. did get good news when New York State, an RTT winner, sought to award Wireless Generation its IIS contract. State education officials sought approval from the state comptroller to grant the $27 million deal on a no-bid basis to News Corp.[55] Although the comptroller initially granted this request, it was later rescinded in reaction to the controversy surrounding News Corp.'s phone-hacking scandal involving its UK tabloid newspapers.[56] The result was that the state would put the contract out for competitive bid, just as all of the other RTT winners that sought an IIS vendor already had done.

Although Wireless Generation did take over the original ARIS contract from IBM in its entirety in 2012, New York City announced soon thereafter that the ARIS system would be phased out entirely. The problem, it seemed, was that very few people—principals, teachers, or parents—actually bothered to use the system, which had been subject to continual complaints once it was finally fully installed.[57]

In the aftermath of the collapse of News Corp.'s educational foray, some would point to the hacking scandal—and the loss of the New York contract, in particular—as an unforeseeable external event that doomed what would have been an otherwise successful venture. But such claims do not hold up to scrutiny. First, New York didn't bar the company from doing business with the state or city. Indeed, it would continue to work with Wireless Generation as part of a $44 million foundation grant the company had received in 2011 to build the Shared Learning Collaborative, as well as in connection with the city's School of One contract. Second, Wireless Generation ultimately did not win any of the competitive bids for state IIS contracts, some of which were awarded before the scandal broke. Finally, the legacy Wireless Generation business represented a tiny fraction of the overwhelming losses that would eventually force the termination of the venture.

A related argument is that Murdoch's decision to tap Klein's legal and regulatory expertise to help deal with the hacking scandal for the company was what doomed the educational initiative. But the truth is that although he provided Murdoch with counsel on the topic, Klein never had primary responsibility for managing it and always spent the majority of his time on the education division. Furthermore, Klein had never actually run the business on a day-to-day basis. In addition to the operating teams, Klein had filled the corporate staff with senior executives, including Kristen Kane, who joined as COO of the division, along with a raft of "some of the biggest names in education."[58] Klein was responsible for the overall strategy, and there is little evidence that his temporary corporate distractions either changed these or slowed their implementation.

The Shared Learning Collaborative mentioned above was initially an unexpected boon to Wireless Generation. The idea was to create a national student data warehouse that would facilitate personalized learning in public schools. The project was primarily funded by the Carnegie Corporation and the Bill and Melinda Gates Foundation, under the direction of former Wireless Generation board member Stacey Childress. Within three years, however, the entire effort—after briefly changing its name to the friendlier-sounding InBloom—would be shut down in the face of student data privacy concerns.[59]

Wireless Generation's association with the School of One initiative that some saw as a potentially revolutionary initiative proved similarly disappointing. Although School of One continues, it has failed to gain much traction in the half-dozen years since it launched. In 2011, Joel Rose established a nonprofit called New Classrooms Innovation Partners to further scale his personalized instructional initiative, now branded as Teach to One. By 2015, the model had attracted only fifteen schools in the entire country. Although some studies showed improvements in student performance from the program, others yielded more mixed results. Potentially more troubling was that even those who believed in the positive impact of Teach to One were not convinced it was worth the cost and disruption of implementation.[60] From a financial perspective, the challenges were heightened by the fact that the program's biggest customer—New York City public schools, representing six of the fifteen active sites—did not have to pay a license for the software because it had been developed when Rose was an employee of the system.

The net result was that after the first full year of ownership, Wireless Generation was far behind the projections that management had provided during the sale process. In addition, the effective purchase price had risen dramatically. Not included in the original $400 million were a variety of additional payments (on top of the $360 million and the 10 percent retained equity stake) related to certain specific performance targets. With Klein brought in as the leader of the overall effort, he wanted Wireless management focused on his various other new initiatives. Although Berger and the team agreed to redirect their energies, the quid pro quo was for News Corp. to simply pay out these substantial bonuses, regardless of the achievement of the targets. Whereas at the time of the purchase, Wireless Generation looked like it might be on the brink of breaking even, in 2011 the business had hemorrhaged cash. Results for 2012 looked even more dire.

In June 2012, the formal announcement of the spinoff of ClownCo was made. Although News Corp. stock reacted well, little of detail had been shared publicly about how the educational division was doing—and certainly nothing about the magnitude of the losses. Although it would be a full year before the spin was complete, it would be necessary before then to familiarize investors with the collection of assets that would be included—in particular, the education division, about which little had been said.

A month after that announcement came the first hint regarding the extent of the expanding ambitions of the division. The company unveiled a new brand—Amplify—which would be broadly "dedicated to reimagining K–12 [e]ducation."[61] Although the Wireless Generation brand appeared late in the press release, its legacy activities were consigned to one of three divisions—now called Amplify Insight. The two other divisions were Amplify Learning, aiming to "reinvent teaching and learning" through new digital reading, math, and science curricula, and Amplify Access, which promised to introduce a new tablet-based platform with AT&T that bundled content and analytics for schools. No financial details were provided, and it did not appear that the two newer divisions had any sales or even products. It was clear, however, that Amplify had not been idle. Links in the release provided "early glimpses" of the "game-changing" products being developed. Amplify's "next phase," according to Klein, would be "ushering in a new age of teaching and learning."[62]

Any specifics had to wait until the education division and Klein's strategic vision had their coming-out party, of sorts, at the UBS Global Media and Communications Conference in December 2012. This long-established annual event attracted investors from around the world and featured presentations from almost 100 companies in the sector.[63] There Klein and chief product officer Laurence Holt took the group through almost sixty slides outlining their full ambitions for Amplify. It was only then that investors learned how much money was being lost and where it was going.

Amplify Conquers the World

More than half of Klein's presentation to analysts was strangely reminiscent of the Chris Whittle/Benno Schmidt road show from over a dozen years earlier, leading with dramatic slides (updated of course) contrasting the growth in student spending with the intransigence of student performance and ending with the promise of doing more for less. The nuance here was the extent to which Klein connected the potential opportunity to the establishment of Common Core standards among the states and the emergence of disruptive digital technologies.

When he turned to the details, Klein was brief but breathtaking. Both the scope of the long-term vision and the extent of the immediate-term losses were unexpectedly massive. Although the legacy Amplify Insight business had grown to $100 million in revenues, far behind the original plan, losses were now projected to approach $25 million—even before the new $10 million in annual costs accumulated at Amplify corporate. But the presentation made clear that, though they still contributed no revenues, the real focus of Amplify would be the start-up Access and Learning segments.

In the two substantive slides on the Access division, Klein essentially informed the assembled guests that News Corp. would be taking on Apple and all the other computer hardware manufacturers by introducing a dedicated device for sale to schools. And the Amplify Tablet was entering a segment of the market that had recently become increasingly crowded. The previous year, Samsung and Acer had begun shipping Google Chromebooks. By the time of Klein's presentation, schools had already become the largest category of customer for such devices. Klein nonetheless argued that existing consumer market devices were not "optimized" as "learning tools." Product chief Holt provided a "sneak peek" of their "complete reskinning and reworking of an Android tablet . . . so that it works in K–12 classrooms."[64] Klein characterized the market positioning of their late entrant to the category incongruously as an "affordable, high-end" tablet.

According to Klein and Holt, the Amplify Tablet would be sold as a subscription product bundled with content. Holt demonstrated a variety of uses of the tablet, such as creating lesson plans and taking attendance. However, it remained unclear why these functions required entirely new hardware rather than just software. Of course, if there was compelling proprietary content included with the tablet, schools might be willing to spring for the device. Yet Holt emphasized instead open-source content that Amplify had simply curated. When it came to proprietary content, the offerings were the antithesis of cutting edge—deals with Encyclopædia Britannica and associated News Corp. trade publisher HarperCollins were highlighted. It quickly became obvious that Klein was having no more luck than Berger had

had years before in negotiating distribution agreements with the major educational publishers that held long-term curriculum contracts with the major school districts. Undeterred, Klein's answer for that hole in the bundle lay in what would end up being the biggest loss leader of the group—Amplify Learning.

Amplify Learning also rated two dedicated substantive slides. From the voice-over, it was clear that they intended to build "brand new curriculum from the ground up" in English language, math, science, and even arts. Thus, in addition to competing with the leading hardware vendors, Amplify wanted to take on Pearson, Houghton Mifflin Harcourt, and McGraw-Hill Education, along with all of the focused start-ups targeting various aspects of the K–12 curriculum. The major publishers might spend $50 million or more on the competitive adoption process for a single subject in a major state and had invested hundreds of millions in digital curriculum. Klein, however, suggested that the Common Core standards would massively simplify this adoption process and allow for the development of a single national curriculum that was "digitized," "gamified," and "personalized," with "very sophisticated analytics."

The problem with this view is that all of the existing curriculum publishers would also align their materials to Common Core standards. More important, states adopting these standards could still decide which provider to adopt and impose additional state-specific requirements as part of their selection process. It is not surprising that the track record of educational companies that try to break into the national curriculum market is poor, given the structural advantages of the scale incumbents. The record of those that conceived of curriculum as a way to enhance the attractiveness of their entrance into the distribution business is particularly abysmal.

A good example of the challenges associated with developing digital curriculum is K12 Inc., the leading provider of online public schools. In 1999, K12 wisely targeted a growing population of families who wanted to homeschool their children. Increasingly, state and public funds were being made available for these students to be served, usually through distance-learning charter schools. K12 provided the technology solution for these charters.

A former investment banker who had gone to work for Michael Milken's Knowledge Universe education venture, Ron Packard had founded K12 with Milken's backing.[65] K12 was the first to identify this market, and as such, it grew quickly, executing a successful IPO in 2007. But Packard, along with Milken, wanted to do more than run a profitable business; he wanted to "transform" education. Inspired by the writings of former U.S. Secretary of Education Bill Bennett, part of the core K12 proposition was delivering an entirely new, all-digital curriculum.

The trouble was that the cost of delivering the curriculum was so overwhelming that the business failed to deliver any cash flow. A competing business, Connections Academy, started years later but decided to focus exclusively on perfecting its technology solution and simply adapting the best of existing curricular solutions to its digital environment. Even at a fraction of the size of K12, Connections was far more profitable—which should not have been the case in a scale business. It also attracted fewer operational problems and less regulatory scrutiny.[66] In addition, there was no evidence that the new digital curriculum performed any better. Pearson ultimately purchased Connections Academy, and almost ten years later, K12 still trades below its original IPO price.

As disturbing as the ballooning of Amplify Insight's losses were, these were far smaller than those being generated by each of the two newer divisions. Amplify Access was slated to lose more than $61 million in the first year, and Amplify Learning would lose $85 million. The total projected operating losses of $180 million for the year were included on a slide headed "Amplify Disciplined Investment."

If the general assurance that the investments were to be disciplined was not comforting to investors, the slide dedicated to the overarching investment thesis would provide little additional solace. In addition to not providing much of a thesis, it suggested that whatever software they had developed to improve English-language writing skills still had kinks to work out. "Amplify," the slide declared in large enough font to fill the page, "is a balanced investment opportunity in the disruptive innovation in education."

Most of the slides contained only a handful of words, and even the voice-overs contained more hyperbole than detail. The financial section, such as it was, while revealing the scale of the losses for the year, did not provide any specific milestones for when breakeven would be achieved, what rate of return was being targeted, what steady-state profit margin for the businesses investors could eventually expect, or how quickly businesses would grow individually or collectively.

Two aspirational targets were provided, though without any time frames. These dealt not with how big the business would become or how profitable it would be. Instead they narrowly discussed the composition of the revenue that would ultimately be generated. Both of these slides were head-scratchers.

Typical of traditional software businesses, the current $100 million in revenues came overwhelmingly from enterprise software development and "professional services" (mostly in the form of consulting to customers). One of Amplify's revenue mix targets was that it expected fully 75 percent of its expanded business to be generated by subscriptions. It is true that the emergence of so-called software-as-a-service (SaaS) business models has transformed how many software businesses get paid. Whereas enterprise software businesses obtain huge upfront implementation fees followed by relatively modest annual maintenance fees under a fixed-term contract (supplemented by hefty ongoing consulting services), SaaS businesses have relatively modest implementation fees followed by consistent open-ended subscriptions (which require more modest ongoing consulting). The result has been that software businesses that once required new sales every year to make their numbers could now rely much more on their ongoing subscription backlog. In the educational realm, however, this improved earnings visibility confronts a largely immovable object: local politics.

Companies serving local public schools are overwhelmingly paid pursuant to specific grants from state or local political authorities. These entities are not only subject to dramatic and unexpected turnover of personnel, but they also often have statutory limits on the duration of the financial commitments they can make. Many times, appropriations for a particular purpose are subject to a "use it or lose it" restriction. Nothing about the economics of SaaS business models changed the reality of the public appropriations process. Even if, in the abstract, a subscription business model is more attractive, those operating in the public school environment are often wiser to take whatever funds are made available as soon as possible.

That said, some providers of relatively low-cost supplemental educational services have, over time, been able to migrate their businesses to a predominately SaaS subscription model. Renaissance Learning, a formative early-grade-focused assessment business analogous to Amplify's Insight segment, had succeeded in doing precisely that. The problem for Amplify, however, was that its objective was to move a majority of its business to hardware and core curriculum—areas in which there is little evidence of local willingness to contract on a subscription basis. The largest K–12 basal publishers receive scant revenues as subscriptions. Amplify's assertion that its business would achieve a 75 percent subscription revenue base suggested a fundamental lack of understanding regarding its core customer base.

Amplify's other performance target—again, provided with no time line—related to the intended mix of revenues among divisions. At the time of the presentation, 100 percent of the revenues were coming from the Insight division. Eventually, as Klein told the assembled investors, this would decline to 40 percent, with the Access division contributing a similar percentage and the Learning division responsible for the remaining 20 percent. The trouble was, to justify the level of investment currently being consumed by Amplify, these targets either assumed a rate of growth that was inconceivable, a level of profitability that was unprecedented, or both.

At the end of the presentation, only a few minutes were available for questions. The first of the four questions asked was obvious from even quick math that a research analyst could do in her head: if the Learning business was only going to be 20 percent of revenues, why was Amplify investing almost as much in it as in the other two divisions combined? "Your slides were whizzing through so fast, I may have misunderstood," a research analyst offered apologetically. "What's the reason for that kind of mismatch?"

Klein responded by explaining that curriculum required significant upfront costs and that he would "expect [that] the revenue piece will accelerate in the further years out." This response was not satisfactory for two reasons. First, as every curriculum developer knows, the need for significant ongoing investment is constant, reflecting the need for updates, changing state and local requirements, and any new funding opportunity—"upfront" costs aside. Second, the revenue mix target Klein provided for some point in the indefinite future presumably already should have reflected his hoped-for accelerated growth.

As the actual spinoff date approached in the middle of 2013, Klein's presentation would be refined, and the revenue mix target slides would quietly disappear.[67] As more historical financial results were released in advance of the separation, it also became clear that, in addition to the $180 million that Amplify was projected to lose in its current fiscal year ending June 2013, it had previously already lost as much again since News Corp. had purchased the business eighteen months earlier.

Given the magnitude of the cash flow drain, the new News Corp. would do everything it could to direct attention away from Amplify and leave the division's precise ongoing losses ambiguous. In reporting its financials, News Corp. hoped to emphasize its four other operating segments—News and Information, Cable Network Programming, Digital Real Estate, and Book Publishing—along with its valuable 50 percent stake in the Australian pay-TV company, Foxtel. Amplify would be subsumed under "Other," which included various general corporate expenses, along with the results of some small, noncore Australian businesses.

The strategy of diverting the focus away from Amplify initially appeared successful. The first Wall Street research reports on the independent company, issued in late 2013, often barely mentioned the educational division. In valuing the business based on the sum of its parts, some analysts gave News Corp. full credit for the $360 million in cash it had paid for Wireless Generation and added this to the values ascribed to the other operating divisions.[68] Even those who simply valued the education division at zero were implicitly giving the company the benefit of the doubt by making no adjustment for what were anticipated to be hundreds of millions of dollars in losses over an unspecified number of years.[69]

Within a few months, however, some were publicly becoming more skeptical about Amplify. By September, Morgan Stanley had published research under the headline, What if Amplify Was Closed? "Amplify operates in a very competitive industry with entrenched interests on all sides that may be averse to change," the analyst argued with significant understatement. Faced with the prospect of at least three more years of losses at similar levels, he drew the inescapable conclusion that "[a] path to an attractive return on investment for this business is unclear."[70]

In fact, for the fiscal year ending June 2014, revenues for Amplify actually declined and losses increased, as did both operating and central sales, general, and administrative (SG&A) expenses. This finding had implications for News Corp.'s regulators and auditors. Regulators wanted to ensure that investors had all they needed to make informed decisions and pushed the company to disclose Amplify's results separately, rather than subsuming them within the "Other" segment. Auditors would need to be convinced that the value of News Corp.'s Amplify investment did not need to be written down. In the last quarter of the fiscal year, the company agreed to report Amplify as a separate segment. News Corp. somehow succeeded, however, in convincing its accountants, Ernst & Young, that no impairment charge needed to be taken—yet.

By early 2015, it was clear that changes were afoot. During the most recent quarters, Amplify was still not growing, which suggested that any modest incremental sales in the company's two new divisions receiving the bulk of investment were exactly offset by declines in the Insight business. Although professing a continued commitment to Amplify, in February, News Corp. CEO Robert Thomson ominously noted that he would "review the situation" once the next school selling season was completed.[71] Around the same time, Klein issued an internal memo stating that the time had come "to begin the process of fully integrating Amplify" through a major reorganization code named "One Amplify."[72]

The potential value of the One Amplify initiative was not just in reducing the duplicative overhead and functions associated with each of the completely independent operations under Amplify—an organization that had ballooned to 1,200 employees. Those separate organizations often used different development tools and project architectures, making collaboration difficult. There were also complaints by former employees that "it was sometimes difficult to know who was in charge."[73] A scathing profile in *BloombergBusiness* described the uncoordinated sales processes pursued by the various divisions, with one client complaining, "The left hand doesn't necessarily talk to the right hand."[74]

In the end, the structural flaw in Amplify was not whether it had an integrated management structure or a decentralized one. It was that the organization was trying to do far too many things at once in the name of transformation. The K–12 educational market is characterized by large integrated players, on the one hand, and focused, product-oriented start-ups, on the other. In between are a variety of established niche players who focus on either a single product or service or a collection of tightly related ones. Amplify sought to be a combination of the two incongruous ends of the spectrum: a large integrated collection of mostly start-up initiatives. Given the inherent difficulty in simultaneously starting up and integrating, Amplify's ambitions, on their face, presented a highly dubious proposition.

Most large integrated market leaders, whether in education or otherwise, started by dominating a segment and building or buying adjacent businesses along the value chain that leveraged the strength of the core. Amplify started by buying a small business that had a solid but modest position and product in part of what it did (early formative assessment). It followed up by quickly entering many new businesses that were largely unrelated and highly competitive. This approach has the double disadvantage of combining multiple uncertain initiatives with a likely loss of focus on the existing ones.

The decision to enter the hardware business—something even the largest integrated K–12 leaders from both a technology and publishing heritage have absolutely avoided—was only the most extreme manifestation of this inevitably unsatisfying growth strategy. Within the Insight and Learning divisions were multiple independent initiatives, each with its own leadership team tackling areas, such as gaming and professional development, which were themselves the primary focus of numerous early-stage and established companies. These were all significant undertakings—for instance, it was reported that the games team managed contracts with thirteen independent studios and had produced thirty educational games.[75]

The simplified industry map in Figure 2.1 provides a flavor of the insurmountable fundamental challenges that Klein's strategy presented. News Corp. would have been far better off if "One Amplify" had signaled a decision to focus on the single business line in which

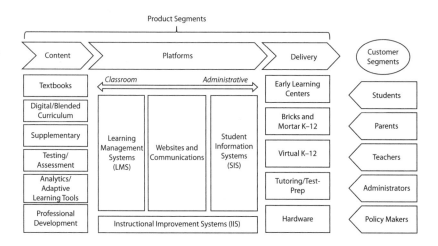

Figure 2.1 K–12 industry map

it had gained the most traction rather than a strategy of integrating a series of diverse subscale initiatives.

The great irony is that the only major segment of the K–12 market eschewed by Amplify was the one that was growing the fastest and in which scale seemed to matter the most—that is, learning management systems (LMS). This is not surprising given Klein's demonstrably false view that "technology in itself has no inherent value in education."[76] According to Klein, "a cool tech platform without the content" would be "useless."

One Amplify felt less like a new organizational strategy than a triage effort to address the building pressure from investors. CEO Thomson publicly promised in June 2015 that investments in the division would be "significantly lower" going forward.[77] Soon thereafter, the company stopped actively marketing tablets. The CEO of Amplify Access had left the company in February and was not replaced. As the fiscal year came to an end, it was also clear that there would be no way to avoid writing down almost the entire value of the Wireless Generation acquisition. The company hastily began discussions with billionaire Laurene Powell Jobs, the widow of Steve Jobs, who had a long-term interest in the segment and serves as President of Emerson Collective.[78] News Corp. hoped that when the financial results (and corresponding write-off) were announced in August, a clean exit could be simultaneously announced.

The history of Amplify highlights the huge gulf between admirable aspiration and effective execution in education. This has been replayed over and over again in the sector, with no end in sight. In an internal memo on the decision to sell Amplify, Klein acknowledged the failure of many of the far-flung products to gain market traction. In that memo, Klein diagnosed the problem with respect to all of their businesses, tablets included, was that they were *too* good: "In my view, Amplify's work has been so innovative and transformative that we've been ahead of the market."[79]

Klein has since become more forthcoming regarding Amplify's failures in strategy and execution. For instance, with respect to the Amplify Learning products, he concedes it was a mistake to "serve people a full meal when what they wanted was a few appetizers." That said, he continues to believe strongly in the product and in the animating proposition that "high quality curriculum coupled with an effective delivery system" is the key to driving improved student outcomes. And while Klein insists he wanted to succeed financially, that was not the primary driving force: "We were trying to change K–12."[80]

Although initial reports noted that Klein would be an investor in the newly private Amplify, no one was surprised that he departed, once it became clear that its new owners had decided to go in a different, scaled-back, refocused direction. Powell Jobs insisted that News Corp. eliminate 500 jobs before agreeing to take on the business. She also decided to revert to Larry Berger as CEO of the much smaller operation. Berger was not only the original head of Wireless Generation but also a long-time denizen of the education foundation sector in which Powell Jobs had previously been operating.[81] Klein remained on the board of the now-private entity, Berger said Klein would continue to provide "critical strategic advice" but have no operational role.[82]

Jobs and Berger moved quickly after the sale to reorganize and refocus the enterprise. Four business lines, including gaming and professional development, are being spun off. The remaining core activities are now organized in two divisions: the Centre of Early Literacy, which integrates the early English language curriculum with the legacy Amplify insight business, and a significantly narrowed middle-schooled focused version of what was Amplify learning. The business now has around 400 employees. Although the Amplify middle school English curriculum was adopted in California around the time of job purchases, total revenues remain only slightly above what they were when Murdoch bought wireless generation. Losses are expected to continue for three more years.

Ironically, it is the effective exit of the two transformational leaders of Amplify—Murdoch and Klein—that creates the opportunity for its future. Well-intentioned revolutionaries can become so singularly focused on where they hope to arrive that they neglect the messy details of how to get there. The inherent complexities and structural aversion to radical change of the educational ecosystem condemn such an approach to certain failure. Jobs's and Berger's potential path to success going forward involves a fundamental reorientation of the organization toward the specific incremental needs of the multiple constituencies that drive buying decisions, rather than the general transformational goals of the founders.

The objective of Amplify was to disrupt a wide range of entrenched incumbents operating across the educational value chain. Their failure was a function of a lack of focus and a lack of understanding of the source of the incumbent's competitive advantage. In the next chapter, a series of investors instead aimed to find hidden value within an entrenched incumbent from a more aggressive operating and acquisitions strategy. The results, unfortunately, were no better.

CHAPTER THREE

Curious George Schools John Paulson

TEXTBOOK PUBLISHING IS possibly the the oldest and largest segment of the for-profit education industry. Unlike other parts of the educational sector, there has never been significant public pressure to limit curriculum development to public or nonprofit entities. This does not mean, however, that the publishers have not been the subject of controversy or attack. Policy makers, parents, and students have often complained about product, content and price, and the historic profitability attracted plenty of competitors. Indeed, the cash-generating ability of textbook publishing despite the perceived inadequacies of the product is precisely what attracted Rupert Murdoch and many others who have sought to disrupt what was long viewed as a smug oligopoly.

Some investors have sought to join rather than beat the incumbent market leaders in textbook publishing. Achieving superior returns from this alternative strategy requires no less of an understanding of the sources of competitive advantage that allowed many of these businesses to perform so well for so long. The failure of some of the newer owners to appreciate the nuance of business and market structure has resulted in a surprising number of bankruptcies in the sector. To understand how this happened, it is worth looking at what has changed and what has stayed the same about textbook publishing. The best way to do that is to look at the full arc of the life, multiple deaths, and rebirth of one the most prestigious names in the industry.

The Rebirth of Houghton Mifflin

In November 2013, the venerable publishing house previously known as Houghton, Mifflin and Company sold just over $200 million of stock to the public. At the turn of the twentieth century, Houghton had built a school publishing and testing business on the back of a great literary house that boasted the likes of Ralph Waldo Emerson and Henry David Thoreau as authors. With a former Microsoft executive newly installed as CEO, the focus of the offering was on the future, not the past. Under the headline "Curious George Gets a Tablet," Morgan Stanley recommended investors buy the stock of what was now, in its view, "a leader in the digital evolution of K–12 content."[1] Surely these changes epitomized the triumph of technology in driving a successful corporate transformation and offered vistas of new possibilities for educating our young. But in fact, there was not much new here.

After a relatively calm first hundred years of existence, Houghton's ownership has changed a half-dozen times since the turn of the twenty-first century. Houghton had actually gone public once before, almost fifty years earlier. At that time, the owners, including descendants of the original partners who had steered the business since its founding in 1880, were looking for new capital to further grow the business. This time, however, all the proceeds would go straight into the pockets of its new hedge-fund owners, who were looking to salvage what they could from their disastrous foray into the arcane world of K–12 publishing.

The great irony of Houghton's fate at the mercy of a series of financially reckless owners and managers is that the business had origi-nally been the most conservative of its peers. Established as a printer, Henry Houghton became a reluctant publisher when he took posses-sion of the stereotype plates produced for publishing customers who fell behind on their bills during the "Panic of 1857."[2] These metal molds developed in the eighteenth century significantly reduced the cost of printing and contained the underlying intellectual property of the publishers. A second irony is that although its acquisition of these plates marked the birth of Houghton as publisher, the failure of its subsequent owners, more than a century later, to appreciate the cash flow implications of plate development for educational works ulti-mately and repeatedly drove the business into insolvency.

Some of the publishing partners who came together in 1880 to create Houghton had already been operating independently for almost fifty years. Even as an integrated printer/publisher, Houghton generally eschewed large author advances and was constantly looking for ways to repurpose classic texts in anthologies and new editions. At the time, non-American works did not benefit from copyright protection, which created multiple opportunities to pursue such a low-risk publishing strategy. Houghton also used the marketing heft of its stable of magazines, which then included *The Atlantic,* to attract authors on better terms than would otherwise be available to the publisher.

This cautious approach to publishing, combined with some key assets of Houghton's, lent itself to educational publishing. Although the educational market at the time was crowded, with well over a hundred competitors,[3] a separate education division was established at Houghton in 1882. There were three reasons for this development. First, many of the classic texts published by Houghton could easily be repurposed for use in schools. Second, Houghton had a strong children's "list"—its established stable of titles and authors—that sold through both traditional trade and educational distribution channels. As early as 1868, the predecessor company, Houghton & Hurd, had convinced Hans Christian Andersen to both write for their children's magazine and become a staple of their list. Finally, Houghton was able to have an outsized impact on the market because of its unique credibility in the sector. Houghton's *Atlantic* magazine had established an education department in 1874 (not long after the federal government established the Office of Education in 1867), which had become a national thought leader in educational policy and pedagogy. It had particular resonance among the local Superintendents of Public Instruction, who were responsible for many school buying decisions.[4]

The launch of the educational publishing business was met with skepticism by George Mifflin, who took over upon Henry Houghton's death in 1895. By the time Mifflin died in 1921, however, that division had eclipsed the company's other segments in both revenues and, in particular, profit. This turn of events was driven both by demographics and Houghton's continuing thought leadership, even after it sold *The Atlantic* in 1908 at the time of the company's incorporation.[5]

On the demographic front, the number of schoolchildren had doubled since the establishment of the education division. On the intellectual front, in addition to staying ahead of the nearly constant reassessments of the ideal curriculum as new schools of education emerged around the country, Houghton had also published the modern form of the IQ test. Most notably, the U.S. Army adopted this test after the declaration of war in 1917 to assist in screening and assigning the waves of new enlisted men. By 1921, Houghton was the fourth-largest U.S. educational publisher. That said, it was still a modest business, with less than $4 million in total revenues from its educational, book, magazine, and printing operations (around $50 million in today's dollars).

Houghton continued its smaller literary business alongside the educational division and built what would become one of the most respected children's lists in the book industry. In 1941, Houghton published a book by a German Jewish couple who had escaped Paris on bicycles with their manuscript the previous year, just as the Nazis had moved in. *Curious George* and its successor titles would ultimately sell more than twenty-five million copies. George, the inquisitive monkey who managed to capture hearts even as he got into one close call after another, would become the single brand most closely associated with Houghton. But he also became an unexpectedly appropriate symbol of the company's own more recent adventures.

Curious George Goes Public

In 1967, the Houghton Mifflin Company went public on the New York Stock Exchange. At the time, Houghton could boast that for the full quarter-century since Curious George had swung into the family, the business had enjoyed continuous organic growth—with the single exception of 1954. Educational publishing had generally enjoyed a renaissance during this period, as it benefited from the postwar baby boom and the flood of federal money from the GI Bill. The company topped $50 million of annual revenues (around $350 million in today's dollars). Size aside, however, what was most striking is how little had changed at the company. Although Houghton had gotten out of the magazine business, its other business lines were intact: education, book publishing, and printing. Henry O. Houghton—a direct descendant of the original—was a corporate officer. The finance chief, Franklin K. Hoyt, had been at the company since 1930, and his father,

Franklin S. Hoyt, had served as editor-in-chief of the education division from 1907 until 1938.

The offering itself was a modest affair. The company raised just over $8 million "to help finance its expanding activity."[6] The cash mostly sat on the company's conservative balance sheet in marketable securities, where it exceeded the totality of its outstanding debt. Going public increased the number of shareholders from 368 to 3,700.

By the mid-1970s, when Houghton began reporting divisional revenues, it was clear not only that the company had continued its growth trajectory but also that the educational division now dwarfed all else. Printing had been closed in 1971, and all trade book publishing, including the children's list, constituted barely 10 percent of overall revenues. The balance of the business was educational—overwhelmingly K–12, though with small but growing college and testing operations as well.

The overall growth in the still-fragmented United States educational publishing sector attracted frenetic activity not only from the general industrial conglomerates of the era but also from media conglomerates. For instance, in 1962, Time Inc. bought school publisher Silver Burdett and, a few years later, contributed this to a partnership with General Electric called the General Learning Company. The General Learning Company was sold at a loss to educational publisher Scott Foresman in 1974, but Time Inc. then purchased Foresman in 1985, only to turn around and sell it to Rupert Murdoch's News Corp. three years later.

In 1967, Litton Industries purchased the American Book Company, the publisher that had held the top market share at George Mifflin's death in 1921. The number two player at that time, Ginn & Company, ended up as part of Paramount after Gulf and Western's 1975 purchase of Simon & Schuster. Simon & Schuster then spent much of the 1980s rolling up the educational publishing industry.

Houghton resisted active participation in the game of musical chairs being played in the sector. The company's deep conservatism led it to pursue only modest acquisitions while fiercely guarding its independence.[7] In 1978, when Western Pacific Industries announced that it had accumulated a stake in the company, Houghton marshaled the resources of its impressive list of authors and powerful friends to beat back the takeover attempt.[8] Arthur Schlesinger Jr., John Kenneth Galbraith, and Senator Ted Kennedy, who was chair of the U.S. Judiciary Committee's Antitrust Subcommittee, all got involved in the dispute, which ended quietly with Houghton buying back Western Pacific's shares.[9]

Houghton's fierce leader at the time of the Western Pacific assault was Harold T. Miller. As his retirement approached in 1990, after forty years at the company (with seventeen as chair and chief executive), Miller continued to insist that the company would remain independent and defended Houghton's cautious approach to acquisitions, leverage, and paying big advances. "I can't think of anywhere where we wouldn't have gotten worse results," Miller insisted.[10] The company's performance under his leadership, significantly outperforming the industry and the market as a whole, seemed to justify Miller's confidence.

But the market was not so sure. A number of factors led many to conclude that an imminent takeover was all but unavoidable if Houghton did not do something to change its strategic approach. Houghton was, after all, "the closest thing to a pure play in an industry with 20 percent pretax margins."[11] The slowing in the overall textbook market was expected to put pressure on Houghton's high trading multiple. The continuing mergers and acquisitions (M&A) activity in the sector, combined with the lack of any debt on Houghton's highly leverageable balance sheet, would make the business attractive to strategic buyers, conglomerates, and the emerging leveraged buyout kings. Finally, literary culture had shifted so that it now seemed acceptable to be published by an industrial behemoth or even a corporate raider. Houghton author John Kenneth Galbraith, whose uncompromising stand had been so important to the company's takeover defense a decade earlier, was now quoted as saying, "In case of a takeover, I probably wouldn't resist the inevitable."[12] In February 1989, when the Texas billionaire Robert Bass disclosed that he had a 5.6 percent stake in the company, many expected a bidding war to quickly ensue.

But it was not to be. Some of the speculation on the company's future had stemmed from its failure to name a successor to Miller, who turned sixty-six a few weeks before the Bass stake became public. When Miller announced his replacement later in the year, however, it signaled no radical change in course. Miller selected a twenty-five-year company veteran who, like himself, had started as a junior sales representative. But if Miller hoped that those similarities in résumé would translate into a similarity in approach and outlook, he would be sorely disappointed.

Curious George Goes to Iran

Nader Darehshori, who was named Miller's replacement, liked to tell the story of walking from his family apple orchard in southern Iran to a one-room schoolhouse with outdated textbooks.[13] He would later become a schoolteacher before emigrating to the United States and securing his job at Houghton in 1966. Darehshori was one of a number of new U.S. publishing CEOs born overseas who emerged in the early 1990s.[14] But of this group, none used this background to press the strategic importance of internationalization as enthusiastically as Darehshori did.[15]

This internationalization was neither the only nor the most significant break with the conservative traditions of the past. Although soft spoken and deferential, Darehshori had a taste for the limelight. He often appeared in the society pages. As the *Boston Globe* described Nader and his wife, Cynthia, in an article titled "Partying with Pavarotti": "They are one of the hardest working social couples in the city and they do not miss many key parties. Indeed, they are often behind many of the best ones."[16]

Darehshori was also prone to grand public pronouncements, particularly around what he viewed as the limitless opportunities that would come from emerging technology and intensified competition. "We are in the very early stages of what promises to be a rebirth of publishing," he told a crowd at the Bookbuilders of Boston dinner. This brave new world on which he was embarking "will parallel that of the Renaissance, when Gutenberg pulled Europe out of the Dark Ages."[17] Darehshori had a new age aspect to his futuristic vision, as he took up meditation and sent has senior management to meditative training sessions.[18]

Atmospherics aside, however, business results were weak. In the first few years of Darehshori's stewardship, school publishing revenues actually fell in both 1992 and 1993. Staff reductions and corporate reorganizations were not able to drive significant bottom-line growth. An effort to outsource distribution operations proved disastrous and had to be reversed. Even as core operations struggled, however, Darehshori increasingly focused on diversifying and acquisitions. The buying binge started slowly, with three relatively small acquisitions in 1992. Then, in 1994, Houghton undertook its largest acquisition ever, spending $138 million on McDougal Littell, a Chicago-based school publisher.

In April 1995, in conjunction with the reporting of the company's anemic financial results for 1994, Darehshori made his grandest pronouncement yet. Houghton, he assured investors, would be a billion-dollar company by 2000. This more than doubling of revenues from the most recent year, he said, would be achieved, in part, by diversifying into entirely new areas, such as network software for colleges and consumer electronic publications.[19] A cursory review of the company's organic growth trajectory made it clear, however, that this goal could not be attained without lots of acquisitions—big acquisitions.

This fact was confirmed a few months later when Houghton announced that it had beat out a half-dozen other bidders to acquire D. C. Heath from Raytheon for $455 million. Houghton's ability to outbid much larger competitors in a cash deal of this size was not simply a function of its willingness to overpay. Houghton had established a small software division in 1982 that developed spell-checking and reference software. The fast-growing division had $14 million of revenue in 1993, and Houghton had sold a majority stake to the public in 1994 as InfoSoft International. Although InfoSoft would crash and burn within a decade,[20] Darehshori was able to realize almost $200 million of cash from its stake long before then, and this money was critical to financing the D. C. Heath acquisition.

The price paid for D. C. Heath was almost double what Raytheon had originally expected to achieve.[21] Even with the benefit of the InfoSoft offering proceeds, the purchase left Houghton with a level of debt unprecedented for the once-conservative company. The normally sympathetic hometown paper expressed skepticism that the transaction was "historic," as Darehshori had claimed, given that the "company has had a hard time growing either sales or earnings."[22] The *Wall Street Journal* was even more critical, pointing to the "whirlwind of activity" that, to date, had only yielded consistently "missed earnings estimates."[23]

This increasing lack of predictability of earnings was partly a function of Houghton's own operating and strategic missteps, but it also reflected some structural changes in the K–12 publishing market. What was once a relatively steady, franchise-driven business had begun to display significant similarities to the hit-driven movie business. Although so-called open territory states still allowed local districts to select their own materials, K–12 schools were increasingly making critical buying decisions on a statewide basis through a textbook-adoption process that followed a five- to six-year cycle by subject. What had started as an effort by poor Southern states to buy efficiently had turned into a broader high-stakes arms race among publishers to secure big contracts in key jurisdictions.

With reading and math representing upward of two-thirds of so-called basal spending, it was now not unusual for a publisher to spend well over $50 million to try to secure a major adoption in one of the three largest adoption states: Texas, California, or Florida.[24] As the industry consolidated around a handful of deep-pocketed diversified players, the ante to win was continually upped. In this context, Houghton was increasingly marginalized, given its capital constraints. In addition, competitors that were part of larger industrial or entertainment conglomerates could mitigate the impact of a missed adoption on overall earnings. Even a more diversified educational publisher with a larger college presence could better manage the inherent gyrations in basal publishing. In higher education, individual professors typically "adopt" a textbook and are averse to switching, which makes for much less volatile results.

The fundamentally capricious nature of the K–12 end market—subject as it is to local political whims, influence peddling, and budget crises—makes for tough sledding as a pure-play public company. A review of those that serve this industry sector and that have tapped the public market in recent decades—whether in publishing, services, or technology businesses—reveals that they are highly prone to missing expectations and that their half-life as independent public companies is brief indeed. That these are usually small-cap stocks (less than $2 billion in equity value) adds to the burden, as small-cap investors are particularly unforgiving. It is hard to think of a single K–12-focused stock that lasted long enough in the public markets to become a large-cap stock (more than $10 billion in equity value).

Houghton exacerbated its structural challenges by spending the latter part of the 1990s buying a dozen other, mostly technology-oriented companies that further diluted earnings. Notwithstanding Darehshori's unprecedented acquisition spree, as his first decade as CEO came to a close in 2000, Houghton was still the number four K–12 publisher—the same relative position it had held in 1921.

Its stock also had significantly underperformed the market over this period. In October 2000, Houghton's closest public comparable company, Harcourt General, would be sold and split up between two much larger diversified publishing companies—Reed Elsevier, which kept the K–12 business, and Thomson, which added the higher education publishing to its Thomson Learning division.[25] A few weeks earlier, Houghton had repeated what one analyst called its "unfortunate history of missing earnings expectations and disappointing investors" by announcing that its "full-year 2000 results would fall dramatically short of expectations."[26]

Houghton had been the subject of takeover speculation on and off since Darehshori had taken over, but this speculation now began to take on a life of its own. After collapsing in the face of the bad news about company performance, the stock crept up to the low 40s in early 2001.[27] By the time Dahreshori announced his retirement in April 2001, the stock was in the mid-40s. The stock ran another 20 percent in the next month, until the first reports of talks with France's Vivendi Universal appeared.[28] In June 2001, Houghton formally announced that it had reached an agreement to be sold to Vivendi for $60 per share for a total value of $2.2 billion.

Curious George Goes to France

For all the increasing speculation about Houghton being an "obvious" takeover candidate as the last independent major educational publisher, no one seemed to have much of an idea who would actually buy it. Once word of the concrete talks with Vivendi surfaced, the *New York Times* reported that "analysts were hard pressed to think of other possible bidders."[29]

It was widely assumed that antitrust considerations would preclude any of the three larger K–12 publishers from taking on Houghton. As recently as the late 1980s, there had been a dozen "major" K–12 publishers. But over time, the four top players had swallowed up almost all the smaller competitors, so that together they now represented almost 90 percent of the basal market. Acquisitions aside, overall market shares were remarkably stable. Pearson and McGraw-Hill each had close to 25 percent of the market, and Harcourt and Houghton were closer to 20 percent.

Even if such a transaction might ultimately be approved, however, the authorities would certainly require the purchaser to divest a significant number of titles in disciplines where the combined business would otherwise dominate. Paying a lofty price for the company only to be required to undertake significant forced sales at low prices was not a particularly attractive proposition. Although there would be real cost synergies in such a pairing—not only overhead savings but also other major benefits from rationalizing duplicative marketing and distribution infrastructure—there would likely be revenue dis-synergies as well. Even in the absence of government intervention, wherever the two publishers had directly overlapping programs, the optimal strategy would be to close or migrate customers of the weaker one.

Such considerations only left corporate conglomerates or an opportunistic financial investor as possible suitors for Houghton. But this was 2001. The era of conglomerate buildups in the 1960s and 1970s had already been largely repudiated and had unwound in the 1980s and 1990s.[30] Although the media industry did not get the memo about conglomerates for a few years, and Time Warner had recently announced what would become the most value-destructive conglomerate merger of all time, even this industrially retarded sector had concluded that educational media added nothing of value to a consumer media conglomerate. Time Warner, News Corp., and, most recently, Viacom[31] had all exited educational publishing by this point, having realized how awkwardly the locally focused institutional sales channel fit within its mass consumer franchises.

Luckily for Darehshori, one media mogul was content to ignore the historic lessons of his peers. Former investment banker Jean-Marie Messier was brashly committed to turning Vivendi, the once-sleepy French water utility he ran, into "the world's preferred creator and provider of personalized information, entertainment, and services to consumers anywhere, at any time, across all distribution platforms and devices."[32] If there was any question about the scope of Messier's ambition and self-regard, one only had to look at the title of his memoir cum manifesto: *J6m.Com*. The appellation stood for "Jean-Marie Messier Moi-Meme Maitre du Monde," which translates to "Jean-Marie Messier, Myself, Master of the World."[33]

Messier would become a broader symbol for the excesses of an era in general and of the media industry specifically.[34] In the context of the more than a hundred transactions totaling more than $100 billion perpetrated by Messier during his mercifully brief tenure as Vivendi's CEO, the Houghton deal "does not really stand out in either absolute size or strangeness."[35] That said, many of the allegedly strategic justifications for the purchase provided by Messier dovetail nicely with the strategic imperatives championed by Darehshori, albeit on a much smaller scale.

Messier marketed the transaction to the public largely based on rights to Curious George that either Houghton did not own or had already been licensed to Messier's Universal Studios before the transaction.[36] With respect to the educational core of the business, however, Messier echoed Darehshori's earlier pronouncements on the importance of globalization and technology. Messier emphasized that, although nothing about the deal would move Houghton from its stubbornly held fourth-place position in the U.S. market, when combined with its own largely francophone publishing business, Vivendi would now be the number two educational publisher globally. The problem was that, given the intensely local nature of educational publishing, a strong position in one national market does not translate into a meaningful benefit in another.

Messier had earlier spent $1 billion on a U.S. educational software company, and the suggestion was that this digital element would create synergies by spreading development costs across the global platform. But the essentially local nature of the business limited the possibility of combining these efforts within print or electronic media. The lack of any meaningful savings was underscored by the fact that Vivendi provided assurances that there would be absolutely no job losses at Houghton.[37]

Messier stressed the boundless unexploited global opportunity in the realm of what he termed "edutainment," even touting the potential educational software applications of the film *The Mummy Returns*. Peter Jovanovich, the CEO of Pearson Education, the market leader both globally and in the United States, described this proclamation as "utter nonsense," stating, "We have had twenty years of these movie execs exclaiming that 'edutainment' is the future."[38] Research analysts were no more credulous. On the record, the most that could be mustered was that the deal was "not totally illogical."[39] Off the record, they complained, "There are no synergies with Universal Pictures, Universal Music or Canal Plus, which Messier has said would be his emphasis."[40]

Former Houghton Mifflin chief Harold Miller could only look on in horror. The sale to a foreign conglomerate was only the icing on the cake. Unable to do anything about the dismantling of his legacy, Miller had long before begun a series of more than a hundred interviews with former colleagues and peers to create a testament to the disappearing publishing culture he had tried to preserve as CEO. In 1970, Houghton itself published a book chronicling the company's formative years through 1921. Miller's angry effort, which focused on the more recent decades through his retirement, would need to find a different outlet. The final chapter of Miller's book is titled "Independence: How We Protected It and Why." He ends the chapter by listing dozens of once-independent U.S. publishing houses that had been subsumed by foreign conglomerates. After detailing the various synergistic defenses of these transactions, he rejected these as "boiler plate explanations [that] soon submerge discussion into the deep swamp of confusion and self-justification."[41] Although many of Miller's criticisms of conglomerate publishing acquisitions are well founded, his complaints at times take on an almost nativist tone. "We were Boston and independent publishing," he wrote. "That's what the entire project and this book seek to make known."[42]

Barely a year later, Vivendi would sell Houghton at a loss to a Boston-based consortium of private equity buyers. This next chapter in Houghton's history does not provide much support for Miller's belief in independent, hometown ownership as a panacea for what ails educational publishing.

Curious George Plays with Junk

Vivendi's acquisition of Houghton closed on August 1, 2001. Within six weeks, the 9/11 tragedy would bring the global economy to its knees and heightened investor scrutiny to the expansive strategy pursued by Messier. Although it is hard to imagine a scenario in which Messier's Vivendi would not ultimately be dismembered, the terrifying events of late 2001 undoubtedly accelerated that process.

Within months of the closing, Messier's CFO sent him a private handwritten note describing "the unpleasant feeling of being in a car whose driver is accelerating in the turns and that I am in the death seat."[43] The company would report a staggering $12 billion loss for 2001, and Messier would be fired in July 2002.[44] Messier's successor rushed to hire lawyers to radically pare back the $18 billion of debt left in his wake. Houghton was high on the list of noncore assets to monetize.

Vivendi's bankers scoured the landscape for potential buyers of Houghton Mifflin, but no "strategic" buyers emerged. As the final bid date approached, a who's who list of well-known names in private equity were rumored to be interested. When the smoke cleared, the winner was a group led by two of the largest Boston-based firms. Together, Bain Capital and Thomas H. Lee Partners represented 80 percent of the equity required to fund the deal, which, at just under $1.7 billion, reflected a discount of 25 percent to what Vivendi had paid the previous year.[45] But just because the private equity buyers were paying less than Messier had didn't mean they were getting a bargain. In a broad auction like the one run by Vivendi's investment bankers, competition ensures that the clearing price is relatively full.

When a number of private equity firms compete against each other for the same asset—and when none of them contributes any strategic synergies through an existing portfolio company—what determines which one will pay the highest price? Contrary to what is often assumed, the answer is not differences in which firm has better access to leveraged financing. Major private equity firms usually are offered very similar debt terms, and any differences are rarely significant enough to change the outcome. Instead, two related factors overwhelmingly determine which fund wins an auction conducted exclusively among private equity participants—who takes the rosiest view of the company's prospects and who is willing to accept the lowest financial returns for their investors. Each of these factors, in turn, has its own drivers.

A relatively optimistic view of an acquisition target's future can be based on a perspective on broader trends affecting the sector, as well as specific opportunities to enhance revenue and improve margins in an undermanaged asset. This conviction can be justified based on industry knowledge gleaned from previous companies owned or by working with an experienced executive. The level of confidence a particular fund has regarding its base case projections also affects what level of returns is required for the investment. The riskier the investment, the higher the returns required to justify it. Deep sector knowledge can sometimes lower perceived risk and provide a rationale for accepting lower returns. More parochial considerations, however, can have an even greater impact on the required level of returns.

The economics of the private equity business are concisely summed up by the phrase "two and twenty." This means that the fund's General Partner—those who actually run the fund—are paid 2 percent on total assets under management plus 20 percent of the returns generated on the investments (often only after a specified threshold return has been delivered to the Limited Partners, whose capital is being invested). Although there are variations to this basic structure, it means that a firm will be paid $200 million annually for every $10 billion it has under management before generating any returns at all to investors.

The most successful funds raise a series of increasingly large funds. The General Partner, however, can only begin raising the next fund once about 70 percent of the capital from the existing fund has been deployed. As a result, the private equity fund-raising cycle often plays an outsized role in the psychology of private equity investors on individual deals. Experienced sellers often target private equity firms that have just raised a new fund or that need one more major investment in order to reach the threshold required to launch fund-raising.

Other factors of course also come in to play. Who knows if Bain and Thomas H. Lee shared, at least to some extent, Harold Miller's romanticism around hometown ownership of this Boston publishing icon. What is clear, however, is that they could not have been relying too much on existing management. Just before putting the business up for sale, Vivendi had hired an executive without educational publishing experience.[46] This CEO was initially kept on and was positioned as the organization's leader going forward on the highly successful road show to raise $1 billion in junk bonds to finance the deal. He left the company, however, in June 2003. After a brief period with an internal interim CEO, Houghton hired Tony Lucki, the internal candidate at Harcourt who Reed Elsevier had passed over for their global education CEO role.[47]

Private equity firms typically hold their investments for between three and seven years. So, from the very start, they are focused on one burning question—how will I exit the investment? There are three primary means to monetize private equity investments: going public in an IPO, selling to another private equity investor, or selling to a strategic buyer. Many of the most successful private equity investments have been achieved from the last of these. Strategic buyers are willing to pay over to the seller at least a portion of the synergies they believe are achievable in a combination. This explains the sometimes significant "control premium" present in such deals. In an IPO, however, there is no control premium, because only a minority of the shares is being sold to the public. In a sale to another private equity firm, control is being sold, but there are no operational synergies to share with the seller.

When private equity firms buy a company in a broad auction that attracts no strategic buyers, they cannot count on an ultimate strategic exit. If strategic buyers did not show up at one auction, what are the chances they will suddenly become interested later? In the case of Houghton, the conventional wisdom was that antitrust considerations made it unlikely that an acquisition by a direct competitor would be possible. By 2002, conglomerate buildups had been replaced by split-ups as the favored path to value creation, even among media companies. Given Vivendi's experience, any potential international buyer would be particularly wary.

All of this suggested that the Bain/Lee group would need to make its money the old-fashioned way—that is, by significantly increasing the cash flow generated by Houghton Mifflin. To be fair, increasing profitability—whether through internal investments in growth, operational improvements, well-executed acquisitions, or some combination thereof—is the primary source of value creation by private equity firms. Cheap and plentiful debt certainly juices returns, but business performance is the primary driver.

Another much-coveted potential source of appreciation is called "multiple expansion," in which returns are achieved not by how much more profit is produced but by the increase in the multiple obtained on exit for every dollar of profit. Even when a business doesn't grow, a private equity firm can find success if it buys at a low multiple and sells at a high one. Multiple expansion, however, is typically reserved for strategic deals or cases in which a truly dramatic business transformation has occurred. Although Houghton may have been under-managed, no one expected that it would ever be anything other than primarily an educational publisher.

Once Bain/Lee had put into place a new team, they quickly turned to assuring employees, customers, and the Boston community that they were committed to "reinvigorating" Houghton for the long term. Lucki, a local boy who had started his career at Houghton almost thirty years previously before moving to Harcourt, exulted that their "goal is to be leaders in everything we publish."[48] As proof of the private equity firms' commitment, they pointed to the fact that the new owners had "poured about $155 million into expanding the company's product line" in the first eighteen months of ownership.[49]

On closer examination, however, remarkably little had really changed under new management. The money that was "poured" into the business was not done so at any greater rate than had been done previously, even under Vivendi's ownership. And that money was essential to the operations of the business.

"Plate capital expenditures" (plate) are the lifeblood of any educational publisher. This is the modern version of the physical "plates" that turned Henry Houghton into a publisher in the 1850s. The mammoth investments required to compete in state adoption processes are the contemporary form of plate development. Ongoing spending on the publisher's core intellectual property, though required every year, is treated as a capital expense because its useful life spans several years. Darehshori had conceded that the continuing escalation of the scale of investment required to be competitive in key state adoptions was a major reason he had sold the business when he did: "Frankly, I was finding it difficult to compete with the big boys."[50]

As a result, a clear picture of the business's cash flow generation can be achieved only by looking at operating profit *minus* plate. At Houghton, plate capital expense was about $100 million. Although the precise annual amount varied based on timing of state adoption cycles and a general upward secular creep, something on that order of magnitude needed to be spent every year. As Darehshori lamented, "If you don't invest, you don't have products in three or four years."[51] And that fact would be perfectly obvious to any potential buyer. Accordingly, simply stopping the plate spend to milk the business was not an option.

This characteristic of educational publishing makes it very different from almost all other publishing and information businesses. The industry's financial attributes are more reminiscent of the movie business—if the film library is not continuously refreshed, the business will slowly atrophy. The other analogy to the movie business noted earlier is its hit-driven nature. These qualities make movie studios, like K–12 education businesses, extremely difficult stand-alone public companies. This combination of high investment requirements and volatility is why all the major studios are embedded within much larger companies with cash flows dominated by the much more predictable cable channel business.

In general, both equity and debt markets focus on a term called EBITDA—earnings before interest, tax, depreciation, and amortization—as the key indicator of operating cash flow. EBITDA is not an official generally accepted accounting principle (GAAP) expression; therefore, it has been subjected to many creative definitions by aggressive financiers. But broadly it means operating profit (also known as EBIT, which *is* a GAAP term) with noncash items, such as depreciation and amortization, added back. In most publishing businesses, where there are limited capital expenditures, EBITDA is an adequate representation of the cash-generating capabilities of a business.

When Bain/Lee looked to the junk markets to finance their acquisition, they accordingly pointed to EBITDA as the relevant metric, and their "bankers pitched the Houghton Mifflin bonds on a similar business profile to two large Yellow Page bond deals that were successfully sold last year."[52] But those two high-margin Yellow Page businesses had no plate expense and almost no capital expenditures to speak of. With 2002 EBITDA of just over $250 million, the extraordinary success of the junk deal was due, in part, to successfully positioning it as being leveraged at a relatively conservative four times EBITDA. But if the correct number to look at was EBITDA minus plate, Houghton was actually leveraged at almost seven times—nosebleed levels that would leave very little margin for error.[53]

So enthusiastic were Bain/Lee about the apparent willingness of the junk markets to ignore the plate spending inherent in their business that they quickly returned to put even more debt on the company. Within a few months—even before their new CEO was in place—Houghton had raised an additional $150 million. This money was not to be "poured" into the company; it was simply to serve as a dividend straight back to the private equity firms in order to reduce their exposure to the business. Although the credit ratings agencies quickly downgraded or revised to negative their outlook on the acquisition debt that had been issued earlier that year, the offering remained a complete success.[54]

Houghton continued to aggressively express the view that its significant investments would soon yield dramatic results. But, of course, all of their competitors were also making investments. The best indicator of strong barriers to entry in an industry is the stability of market shares. Ironically, if Houghton's claims of the ability to quickly shift market shares through investment were true, it would have shown that the industry was less attractive overall.

The good news and the bad news was that Houghton's claims were not true. By the end of 2004, Moody's had downgraded the junk bonds to reflect "heightened concerns regarding Houghton Mifflin's financial results, which continue to fall short of Moody's expectations and the risks associated with the company's strategy to expand its product offering."[55] Faced with challenging results, a lack of strategic buyers in the K–12 publishing sector, and inadequate cash flow to pay down debt, the private equity owners looked to whether there was a way to bulk up their small higher-education publishing business. Two other companies, John Wiley and Macmillan (the latter owned by the private German company Holtzbrinck), had similar-sized higher-education businesses. The private equity owners engaged in strategic conversations with both about some kind of combination but to no avail. Although there were clear benefits from combining the college textbook businesses, neither was as interested in the more volatile K–12 business, and they certainly were not willing to give Houghton credit for its continued optimistic view of future results.[56]

With no strategic buyers for the business, stagnant results, and increasingly high leverage, a sale to another private equity buyer seemed unlikely. This left very few liquidity options for the investors, beyond trying to continue to pull out dividends as long as the junk market allowed and potentially taking the company public. The Bain/ Lee group pursued both of these avenues aggressively in 2006.

Goldman Sachs was directed to prepare a prospectus to take the business public. Not wanting to leave anything to chance, however, the private equity owners also sought to pull even more cash out of the business in advance—twice as much as had already been taken out in 2003. This move was all the more remarkable because the company had not managed to pay down any of its debt since the 2002 buyout. Indeed, as Moody's pointed out, leverage had already increased to almost eight times 2005 EBITDA minus plate. The leverage, after the Bain/Lee group took out another $300 million, would approach an eye-popping ten times.

The dividend was successfully financed in May 2006, and Goldman was preparing to file IPO documents in June. At that point, what was truly remarkable about the transformation in Houghton Mifflin during the almost four years of much-touted hometown ownership was that it hadn't transformed at all. EBITDA minus plate in 2002 had been $158 million, and by mid-2006 EBITDA minus plate was $159 million. What *had* changed was the amount of debt on the company. At the time of the original LBO, the private equity buyers put $1.097 billion on the company. Now Houghton boasted $1.6 billion in debt. This difference was due, in part, to the $450 million in dividends that the private equity owners had taken. In addition, not only hadn't the company been able to pay down any of the principal, but also the net cash flows from the business had not even covered the interest and other expenses.

All of this did not bode well for the coming IPO. The good news for the private equity owners was that they had already pulled out almost three-quarters of their original equity investment. That said, a deal is usually not considered a success unless a firm doubles its money, and even if a public offering were successful, at any conceivable valuation Houghton would fall far short of this benchmark.

Then the equivalent of lightning struck. Private equity owners and sellers of all stripes often dream of crazy foreign buyers turning up to offer far more than any conventional purchaser, but those buyers rarely materialize. But in this case, one did, and it made the Houghton Mifflin acquisition one of the most successful ever for the private equity owners.

Curious George Goes to Ireland

Barry O'Callaghan was a self-described "professional middle-class boy, likely to do well in his Leaving Cert" from the Jesuit-run boarding school he had attended in his native Ireland.[57] After graduating with a law degree from Trinity in Dublin in 1991, he spent the 1990s as a M&A banker, bouncing from Morgan Stanley to Salomon Smith Barney (now part of Citigroup) to Credit Suisse in 1997. Then in 1999, an Irish schoolteacher turned serial entrepreneur, Pat McDonagh, decided to make O'Callaghan—then thirty years old and with no operating experience—CEO of one of his companies.[58] The company was called Riverdeep. McDonagh had already made his first fortune taking CBT Systems public in the early 1990s.[59] Although billed as an educational software company, Riverdeep had barely twenty employees, significant losses, and scant revenues.[60] Thus, at the height of the first Internet boom, McDonagh may have concluded that what he needed was not an operator but a banker to exploit the window of opportunity.

Just as NASDAQ topped 5,000 for the first time in 2000 Riverdeep went public.[61] By then, Riverdeep had achieved losses of over $20 million on barely $2 million of revenues. So, O'Callaghan went about using the public sale proceeds of almost $125 million and the highly valued stock currency—at one point, Riverdeep's stock was worth more than $2 billion—to acquire seven companies for more than $300 in quick succession over two and a half years.[62]

Notwithstanding O'Callaghan's deal-making frenzy, when the music stopped, Riverdeep's stock collapsed and was delisted from NASDAQ in late 2002. At the time, the board considered replacing O'Callaghan as CEO because of his "fractured relationship" with investors.[63] O'Callaghan then hired the same bank that had orchestrated the sale to the public only a few years earlier to find a way for him to buy back the company at a fraction of that price.[64] It would also come to light that those same bankers had purchased shares at a steep discount in the months leading up to the IPO and had sold many of them before the share collapse, even as their research analyst touted the stock's upside.[65]

Before the 2003 go-private transaction, O'Callaghan owned 6.3 percent of Riverdeep. McDonagh was so appreciative of O'Callaghan's efforts, however, that he agreed to pool his shares and split their combined stake of 42.4 percent equally with O'Callaghan. Soon thereafter, McDonagh and O'Callaghan bought out two private equity investors who had backed the delisting in the company rather than take the original buyout.[66] Then, in 2006, O'Callaghan purchased McDonagh's remaining stake for $120 million—still less than the original IPO back in 2000 and a fraction of the value O'Callaghan would shortly tell new investors it was worth.

O'Callaghan had also already bought out many smaller shareholders who remained in the company rather than take the original buyout. Where he got the money to make these various purchases, as well as subsequent ones, is the subject of much speculation and debate.[67] After subsequent deals led to the company's insolvency, a political uproar ensued over the prospect that the Irish taxpayers would foot the bill for bad personal loans made to O'Callaghan by the then-nationalized

Allied Irish Bank. The controversy led O'Callaghan to make public assurances that he would honor his commitments without specifying what precisely those commitments were.[68]

What is beyond question is that by 2006, O'Callaghan had secured majority control of Riverdeep. That summer, O'Callaghan met with Houghton CEO Tony Lucki for dinner in Boston to discuss a strategic alliance. Lucki had briefly served on the public Riverdeep board of directors after Reed Elsevier had invested $25 million as part of a strategic alliance with the Harcourt division Lucki had then still headed. O'Callaghan learned over dinner about the planned Houghton IPO and began in earnest to come up with a way to offer the private equity owners a more attractive alternative that would leave him in control of both companies.[69]

But how to engineer such a transaction was not obvious. Riverdeep was a fraction of the size of Houghton. In 2005, the company experienced the third consecutive year of revenue declines and had operating profit of just $10 million. Houghton's 2005 revenues, at $1.29 billion, were almost ten times greater than Riverdeep's, though its operating profit margin was similarly anemic. In the end, O'Callaghan agreed to pay $3.33 billion in cash to the private equity owners of Houghton Mifflin. This represented an unprecedented multiple—more than twenty times trailing EBITDA minus plate—for a business that essentially had been flat for years. It is not surprising that the private equity buyers took this offer, which ended up delivering them almost four times their original investment. What is surprising, even shocking, is that O'Callaghan was able to secure funds to consummate the deal.

Where did the money come from? The answer is a mix of gullible and sophisticated equity and debt investors around the world. In 2005, Riverdeep and Houghton together produced operating profit of less than $100 million. With the help of some of the world's most respected financial institutions, O'Callaghan was able to raise $4 billion of new equity and debt based on a valuation of $5 billion for the combined enterprise. This, in turn, was justified by looking not at the modest operating profit but rather at the almost $500 million in something described in deal marketing materials as "pro forma adjusted EBITDA with full synergies."

The $500 million included $100 million in cost ($70 million) and revenue ($30 million) synergies from the combination in 2007. But fully a quarter of Riverdeep's modest revenues had nothing to do with the school business; rather, they came from selling productivity and other software through retail, direct-to-consumer, and computer equipment manufacturer channels. Another 16 percent of revenues were sold internationally, mostly through joint ventures and resellers, with little opportunity for cost savings. In addition, the $70 million in promised total cost synergies represented more than Riverdeep's entire expense base. The rest of the inflated number came from neglecting to subtract "plate" or other capital expense and making adjustments for various supposedly one-time expenses, including more than $20 million in "special" bonuses received by Houghton management.

Despite his already checkered track record, O'Callaghan was viewed as something of a folk hero in Ireland. He described the ultimate failure of Riverdeep's foray into the public markets as exclusively the fault of short-selling U.S. hedge funds, and he positioned his actions in almost nationalistic terms. By valuing the contribution of Riverdeep at $1.2 billion in the transaction, the continuing investors looked like they had quadrupled their money on paper since the go-private transaction. Never mind that their stake sat behind $3.6 billion in other securities that far exceeded the value of the underlying assets. O'Callaghan could position himself as a hero to the few investors who stayed with him in the face of the short-selling onslaught.

To raise more than half a billion dollars in new equity, O'Callaghan enlisted the Davy Group, Ireland's leading stockbroker and wealth manager. At a series of exclusive presentations at locations like Dublin's Four Seasons and the Royal College of Physicians, they made their pitch. At these highly secretive events, Davy required their wealthiest clients to sign confidentiality agreements as the price of admission.

Of course, if someone believed that $500 million was the relevant financial metric, then at around ten times, $5 billion might seem like a reasonable number. Based on press reports, the presentations did not stop at rosy positionings of various pro forma adjustments and accounting definitions. Davy apparently also was not shy about suggesting that synergies could really be $200 million and that investors could double their money in two years.[70]

The presentations to debt investors were similarly aggressive. The capitalization summary showed the debt-to-EBITDA ratio of a full but apparently manageable level of six times, giving credit for everything Davy had marketed except the $30 million of revenue synergies. Buried on page 37 of the lender presentation, however, was a summary of the business's actual cash flow. EBITDA (with all the previously discussed add-backs included but no credit for "synergies") for the past twelve months was $391 million, but this did not account for $149 million of capital expenditures ("capex")—mostly in the form of ongoing plate needs. In addition, a footnote stated that this amount excluded $49 million in costs associated with online development and a major enterprise software implementation. If the full $198 million actually spent were subtracted from the $391 million in EBITDA, then the cash flow generated in the past year was actually $193 million, at best.

Recast in this fashion, it became clear that the correct debt-to-EBITDA ratio actually approached a mind-boggling fifteen times. The need for so much debt was a combination of the unprecedented all-cash purchase price being insisted on by Houghton's private equity owners and the fact that consummating this complex transaction would entail $325 million in fees alone. Roughly half of the expenses went for prepayment penalties for the existing debt, and the rest went for fees associated with the new debt and various advisors. Even more horrifying for the new equity, O'Callaghan was raising an additional $750 million of preferred equity on top of the debt. This meant that before any of Davy's well-heeled customers would see a penny of their original investment returned, O'Callaghan would have to find a way to satisfy more than $3.5 billion in claims ahead of them.

The required infusion of $660 million of new equity was nonetheless accomplished, attracting not only rich Irish interests but also rich Middle Eastern interests, including the Saudi Obeikan Investment Group.[71] One tool O'Callaghan used to overcome potential skepticism was the assurance that he would be personally contributing millions in the deal. As noted, where precisely this money came from is a subject of continuing speculation. More relevant, however, is that although he and some co-investors contributed about 10 percent of the new money, O'Callaghan and his team would control more than 50 percent of the equity. Part of the difference in equity came from rolling his stake from Riverdeep into the new entity at the outsized valuation described. But the biggest single source of his equity—roughly half—was simply given to him as a "promoter and management incentive," supposedly "designed to incentivize and lock-in Mr. O'Callaghan."[72] Although some preferred equity is often reserved for management in a buyout, the 25 percent provided here is more than twice as much as would be typical.

It is less difficult to comprehend why the major investment banks agreed to sponsor this questionable capital structure in the marketplace—there were hundreds of millions of dollars in fees and significant bragging rights on the line. In particular, Credit Suisse as an institution benefited, as did the individual bankers involved,[73] due to their long-standing association with O'Callaghan. Banks make money from transactions, and a deal-junkie client like Barry O'Callaghan was the gift that keeps on giving. Thus, there seemed to be every reason for the bank to continue to milk the relationship for all it was worth.

That said, the deal was not without risk for the investment banks. In debt offerings, the lead banks usually agree to hold a certain amount of the offering, and if it trades badly, the bank can lose millions. Furthermore, in this deal, $1 billion of the debt was in the form of so-called bridge financing. Because sellers want to close transactions quickly, they are often unwilling to wait for bonds to be marketed to investors. In such instances, the lead banks may offer to "bridge" the deal themselves, with the expectation that their temporary loan will be replaced with permanent financing shortly thereafter.

When the private equity buyers originally bought Houghton, they had used a bridge. That deal closed on December 31, 2002, and was followed by a very successful refinancing in the junk bond market a few weeks later. When it works out, as in that deal, a bridge is a very useful tool—it provides speed and certainty to the seller, while giving the buyer time to determine and secure the best long-term capital structure.

But bridges don't always work out, and they can quickly become the proverbial bridge to nowhere. These instruments are structured to have the interest rate increase every month that they are outstanding in order to incentivize a quick refinancing. But if there is no market to refinance the instrument, this increasing interest rate is almost certainly not enough to compensate the investment banks for holding it on their books. The result is that the investment bank is losing millions, while the company's cash is being increasingly devoured by the ballooning interest payments. This phenomenon is called a "hung bridge." Eventually the hung bridge automatically turns into a bond at the highest possible interest rate, often placing a crushing permanent burden on the company, and the investment bank is left to sell off the bonds at a huge loss.

Goldman Sachs had been working closely with Houghton's private equity owners to either find a buyer or take the company public.

In the early reporting on the deal that fall, Goldman was described as being on board as a leader of the financing.[74] By late November, however, when the lender presentations were made, Goldman had quietly disappeared from the underwriting group, leaving only Credit Suisse and Citigroup. Both would soon wish they had followed Goldman's lead and left Barry O'Callaghan to pursue his grand vision without their help.

Curious George Eats a Whale

When Reed Elsevier, the Anglo-Dutch professional information conglomerate, purchased Harcourt General for $5.65 billion in 2001, it knew almost nothing about the U.S. K–12 educational market. The Harcourt auction had attracted its attention because the company also owned a well-regarded scholarly publisher called Academic Press, which was highly strategic to their Elsevier Science division. When Harcourt rebuffed efforts to break up the business, Reed pursued partners for an entire company bid. After securing an agreement with Thomson to take Harcourt's higher-education assets for $2.1 billion, Reed had to decide whether it was willing to keep the K–12 assets as the price of getting its hands on Academic Press. Reed concluded that managing a leading educational business in an oligopolistic market like the United States couldn't be that hard. They were wrong.

By 2007, Reed and its shareholders had long tired of its educational foray. Multiple earnings misses tied to the lumpy and unpredictable nature of the business came as something of a shock to the owners of remarkably steady subscription businesses characterized by high renewal rates and regular price increases.[75] In February 2007, Reed announced that it planned to sell Harcourt. Once it sold the student assessment and international businesses to Pearson in May for almost $1 billion, the company turned to off-loading the core Harcourt K–12 business.

Before making adjustments or subtracting plate, Houghton and Harcourt had almost identical, basically flat EBITDA of about $350 million in both 2005 and 2006. Harcourt generated this EBITDA on about $250 million less of revenue, resulting in higher profit margins. But Harcourt had also been investing significantly more in plate than Houghton, suggesting that, contrary to the claims of O'Callaghan and the private equity investors before him, Houghton had actually been relatively starved of curricular development investment for some time. From Reed's perspective, this meant that potential buyers would be looking at EBITDA *minus* plate of around $150 million. If buyers paid Reed the same multiple of EBITDA minus plate that the private equity investors had given Vivendi in that auction, Harcourt would end up attracting about a $1.6 billion purchase price. Reed knew it would be very lucky to get $2 billion.

When Reed's bankers got under way, they did not seriously think that any of the three other major K–12 publishers would participate in the auction. Neither Pearson nor McGraw-Hill had looked at Houghton during any of the times it had changed hands in recent years, and they had similarly ignored the original Harcourt sale. Houghton was now so over-leveraged—as O'Callaghan had still been unable to refinance the previous year's acquisition bridge—that the idea of their involvement seemed financially inconceivable.

Furthermore, almost as soon as the Houghton acquisition closed, O'Callaghan's auditors quit, "[a]s a result of incorrect representations made to us by the company's parent."[76] The departing Ernst & Young had been replaced by KPMG in 2003 but had returned as the company's auditors in 2004. Houghton would now try out a third set of auditors, PwC—hardly a good omen for investors, lenders, or business dealings of any kind. In any case, the conventional wisdom was that the antitrust authorities would require so many divestitures before it would permit such consolidation, that any deal would be uneconomic. Reed and its shareholders wanted Harcourt gone quickly and cleanly. Any proposed deal that had regulatory risk—or even significant regulatory delay—would be dead on arrival as far as Reed was concerned.

And yet, none of these impediments struck O'Callaghan as overwhelming. In the past, he had found that enough money could overcome any objections. But how could he get enough money to interest Reed in a deal with him over any simpler alternative? The answer was that he had to convince the investors and lenders in the Houghton deal that if they didn't double down on the Harcourt deal, they would risk losing it all.

Reed was highly skeptical. Reed Elsevier is a highly conservative Financial Times Stock Exchange (FTSE) 100 company created through the merger in 1993 of two century-old publishing houses—Reed in the UK and Elsevier in the Netherlands. But O'Callaghan was correct in that enough money could overcome that skepticism. However, the price required was not a generous $2 billion but a staggering $4 billion.[77] Only O'Callaghan's own purchase of Houghton the previous year had even approached the multiple reflected in this transaction. In addition, in order to secure Reed's assent, O'Callaghan still had to agree to pay Reed a $550 million reverse breakup fee if it did not receive regulatory clearance within a year.

The Harcourt financing made the Houghton transaction that preceded it seem almost conservative. To take out the hung bridge, the banks agreed to replace it and the term loan with new permanent facilities more than twice as large. Of course, they would benefit from the more than $250 million in financing fees and transaction expenses generated. (In combination with the Houghton deal before it, this added up to well over half a billion in less than a year.) The existing equity investors had to come up with an additional $235 million. Reed also ultimately agreed to take $300 million of the $4 billion purchase price in equity—but internally, they assumed this would be worth nothing, knowing that even at $3.7 billion, they were being paid an astounding twenty-five times EBITDA minus plate.

Closing the transaction required more than $7 billion in new financing raised through a new Cayman Islands holding company called Education Media & Publishing Group. The marketing materials the banks used pointed to the potential for $377 million in cost savings. These were claimed to cost an unbelievably low $100 million to achieve.[78] Typically, one-time costs of achieving permanent savings are one to two times the projected level of annual benefits. Furthermore, O'Callaghan asserted that the company had already exceeded the $75 million in cost savings promised in the Riverdeep/Houghton combination. According to the documents, $90 million in cost savings had already been realized or "actioned" with the realization to come later. Yet, suspiciously, for the first nine months of 2007, actual EBITDA remained stubbornly flat, and plate expense actually increased, which suggested that any synergies supposedly generated had been offset either by dis-synergies or by business declines.

Although the banks launched the deal in late October 2007, within a few weeks, the debt markets had turned against them, as the beginnings of what would become the 2008 subprime financial crisis began to manifest themselves. By the time the deal closed in mid-December, Houghton had announced the sale of its higher-education business for

$750 million to support the troubled financing. Despite these efforts, the offering was downsized to a fraction of its original size, and on much less favorable terms. The banks were left holding the balance of the debt, and a five-year downward spiral of the newly rechristened Houghton Mifflin Harcourt (HMH) had begun.

Curious George Keeps Running Out of Money

The banks spent much of 2008 unloading their positions in the debt used to purchase Harcourt at significant discounts. Credit Suisse in particular had profited handsomely from its long association with the O'Callaghan deal machine, but now both the institution and its employees would experience even larger losses. Part of the remaining debt was placed in an illiquid vehicle used to pay bonuses to Credit Suisse employees in 2008.

Despite the difficulty in finding buyers for its debt or its products, O'Callaghan and his bankers continued to hype the story. In the summer of 2008, O'Callaghan sent shareholders a letter assuring them of their ability to repay the debt, meet covenants, and "comfortably" remain within their credit lines. Synergies in year three could total $340 million, and an incremental $100 million of product development savings, he assured investors, would yield "total cash synergy of $420 [million] to $430 [million]."[79] Analysts from Davy, his Irish brokers, were even more expansive, suggesting that the latest investors to put new equity behind O'Callaghan could "double their investment over the next two years."[80] This outcome was assured because there was "likely to be a deal with a large international publishing company such as Newscorp or Viacom"[81]—despite the fact that both alleged suitors had divested their educational publishing businesses long ago and had made clear their intention never to return to the sector.

Within months of these words of encouragement, the company underwent a series of ratings downgrades to the most speculative levels possible based on liquidity concerns and the high likelihood of default.[82] S&P named HMH one of the European companies at the highest risk of default, while the company publically challenged the latest Moody's downgrade.[83] Even as the company touted its "ample liquidity to meet its needs" and predicted market share gains and double-digit growth, Houghton's trade imprint, the storied publisher of Curious George, stopped buying new books altogether and put itself up for sale.[84] The business was taken off the market when it became clear that the multiple of cash flow offered by potential buyers was lower than the debt multiple that burdened the overall business.[85]

In March 2009, just months after the letter from O'Callaghan expressing confidence in the ability "to meet all covenant requirements," the company reached an agreement with lenders to pay a fee and higher interest in return for the loosening of covenant restrictions.[86] Because Credit Suisse served as agent and itself still owned a significant portion of the debt, securing the majority approval of the holders was not challenging. But this did not come close to bridging the fundamental disconnect between the company's cash needs and what it could generate. That accord was followed by further negotiations to convince some debt holders to exchange their debt for equity in the company and find some new investors. This tactic was also successful, with the Dubai royal family entering the fray, but the equity was at half the price of earlier rounds.[87] In the end, $800 million of the debt became equity, and another $1.7 billion deferred interest payments for a higher payout later. The result was that the company's $500 million annual interest bill was reduced to $400 million.

It became almost immediately apparent that there was no way the company could service even this reduced debt load and that the dramatically lower equity price was still far too high. The shareholder base and the list of debt holders had quite significantly transformed. The balance sheet restructuring, though inadequate to solve the fundamental issues the company faced, had diluted the existing shareholders by 45 percent. O'Callaghan himself had gone from an effectively controlling position of nearly 40 percent to just 22 percent. In addition to the new shareholders from the Middle East, the debt holders who converted into equity now had a significant say in the company's affairs. These were overwhelmingly not the original lenders; instead, they were highly opportunistic, distressed-debt hedge funds that had seen a chance to exploit the banks' desperation to get out of the credit at almost any price.

One surprising aspect of the restructuring was that these highly sophisticated and aggressive investors did not insist, as a condition of accepting the proposed deal, on securing management with experience in operating and integrating these kinds of businesses. Tony Lucki was a generally respected publisher, but he had no experience with anything of this scale or with operating with these kinds of liquidity constraints. O'Callaghan, a former banker, did hire a president at the holding company level in 2007, between the Houghton and Harcourt deals, to complement the team.[88] But this executive, Jeremy Dickens, was a former corporate lawyer from Weil Gotshal & Manges. Whatever his faults, Lucki remained the only credible senior publishing executive associated with the now massive enterprise. But then he announced his retirement in April 2009, and his replacement was the now thirty-nine-year old Barry O'Callaghan.[89] Then, even Dickens would announce his departure shortly after the restructuring, leaving no meaningful bench of talent at either the operating or the holding company level.

The largest single outside buyer of the distressed debt, at what seemed to him to be a bargain-basement price, was one of the largest beneficiaries of the financial collapse: John Paulson. Paulson's hedge funds had earned more than $15 billion in 2007, when he bet against subprime mortgages, 20 percent of which he and employees of Paulson & Co. pocketed themselves.[90] As 2009 drew to a close, Paulson and the other distressed-debt owners—notably, Guggenheim Partners—negotiated a transaction in which more than $4 billion of the remaining debt was converted to equity. The transaction left about $2.5 billion of debt, even as $650 million of new equity—secured from the largest debt holders themselves—were scheduled to come in for working capital. Annual interest payments would now fall to $200 million.

This time, the almost $1 billion of equity previously invested along the way would be largely wiped out. The restructuring caused political repercussions in Ireland, as many of the local investors wooed by Davy had been financed by the Anglo-Irish bank, which was now owned by the Irish taxpayers after being privatized during the financial crisis. O'Callaghan, as usual, was unapologetic, complaining that "I can't be blamed for things I can't control" like state budgets and insisting that "operationally and strategically it has all worked out."[91] Despite the obvious evidence to the contrary, O'Callaghan asserted: "I don't think you can say that the investment thesis was flawed."[92] As evidence for his blamelessness, he repeatedly pointed out that "no one has lost more than me."

O'Callaghan's claim that no one had lost more than he was not strictly accurate. On the one hand, he had paid far less than others for his stake by virtue of the enormous financial "promote" that he had secured in the transaction financings. On the other hand, unlike other equity holders who were being offered a small share in any eventual value accretion above $10 billion, O'Callaghan would negotiate a huge incremental financial incentive to stay on with the company.

The decision to keep O'Callaghan was highly controversial among the debt holders. Many advised Paulson to cut O'Callaghan loose. O'Callaghan held out for a massive financial package—potentially worth over $100 million—that many of the investors viewed as unconscionable. Indeed, part of the package was to make good on $30 million of the outstanding loans from the Anglo-Irish bank for which O'Callaghan was personally liable.

Paulson's thinking remained something of a mystery to the other bondholders.[93] He was usually represented by an inscrutable young partner, Sheru Chowdhry, in discussions over the company's fate. It soon became clear, however, that O'Callaghan had managed to convince one other important bondholder that he was a visionary with the key to unlocking long-term value at HMH. In public statements, the face of Guggenheim Partners was managing partner Todd Boehly. During one critical bondholder debate to decide O'Callaghan's fate, however, the principal whose interests were being represented by Guggenheim emerged from behind the curtain to make the case for keeping the current CEO: Michael Milken.[94] Milken was apparently the largest investor in the Guggenheim fund that had made the investment in Houghton.

Although Milken's track record in education, which is the subject of chapter 4, is undistinguished, at the time investors knew of his interest in the sector but nothing about his returns. And high-yield investors viewed him with awe due to his foundational role in the sector. Milken's relationship with Guggenheim in general and Boehly specifically would later become the subject of a Securities and Exchange Commission investigation. During the bondholder negotiations, the other stakeholders simply assumed that Boehly spoke for Milken.[95]

Others at the meeting pressed that even if O'Callaghan's vision were credible, his reputation in the marketplace would undermine the long-term value of their stake. After all, given how unlikely a strategic sale was, the most likely exit was clearly through the public markets. In light of how many public debt and equity investors had been disappointed by O'Callaghan in the decade since the original Riverdeep IPO, he was hardly an ideal public company CEO.

Paulson did not know Milken but had agreed to meet with him privately before the fateful bondholder session. By virtue of the size of their collective holdings, Guggenheim and Paulson together would control the outcome of any bondholder vote. Milken argued forcefully to Paulson that, as the mastermind of the Houghton-Harcourt combination, it would be a mistake to fire O'Callaghan when so much of the bad news was due to market forces outside of his control.

In what would be a very expensive decision, Paulson decided to go along with Milken's recommendation to keep O'Callaghan. Despite Milken's assurances, Paulson had done enough diligence on O'Callaghan to have some serious reservations. For instance, he learned that O'Callaghan insisted that he not be in the country for more than 180 days a year for personal tax reasons—despite the operations being overwhelmingly U.S.-based—and often had staff in Boston fly to Ireland for meetings. Paulson reasoned, however, that given the company's strong market share, the company would rebound forcefully when the spending cycle returned. And he viewed the bigger risk as coming from losing market share if the company was forced to file for bankruptcy in lieu of a negotiated settlement among bondholders. The fear was that states and localities would be unwilling to do business with a "bankrupt" textbook publisher.

Both of Paulson's assumptions were mistaken. When the cycle returned, it was not nearly as robust as hoped. And as the company learned when it was nonetheless forced to file for bankruptcy two years later, this could be managed effectively without any meaningful risk to the company's relative market position. To the disappointment of a number of the smaller debt holders, the restructuring moved forward with O'Callaghan at the helm and his generous package intact.

Another aspect of this second restructuring still rankles investors. When the company was trying to syndicate the unsold debt from the Harcourt acquisition in 2008, it touted the huge upside from international expansion. After talking with O'Callaghan, the *Irish Independent* reported that despite the tough operating environment, "the real kicker could be EMPG's fledgling international arm, EMPGI." Davy's research analyst exulted, "You're basically talking about transferring existing intellectual property into other markets—the upside is enormous." But somehow, in the restructuring, the existing shareholders, with O'Callaghan being the largest among them, were able to exclude the debt holders from ownership in this division.

Paulson indicated no second thoughts. He publically expressed "great admiration" for O'Callaghan. Speaking to employees, Paulson assured them that, in his view, with the team in place and the restructured balance sheet, "Houghton Mifflin Harcourt is well positioned."[96]

Curious George Goes Bankrupt

Paulson's professed optimism was short lived. Throughout 2010, the bad news just kept coming. Although O'Callaghan kept up a busy schedule announcing feel-good initiatives, such as free books for public libraries and a $100 million global education innovation fund, revenues continued to head downward. O'Callaghan had attracted new capital from the distressed-debt investors in the restructuring on the promise that the business had bottomed out and was poised to benefit from the promised massive synergies. But even with a reduction of 60 percent in the outstanding indebtedness, it became clear that the company could not service even these much-diminished obligations.

In early 2011, this became even more apparent, as the auditors finalized their accounts. Just a few days after O'Callaghan mused on the future of education at an expo that HMH underwrote, along with Goldman Sachs, News Corp., and AT&T for the glamorous Aspen Institute,[97] PwC signed papers highlighting "material uncertainty" regarding the company's standing as a going concern.[98] In March, after feverish negotiations, O'Callaghan quietly stepped down—but not before negotiating the effective forgiveness of an $11 million loan and a one-year consulting deal that would pay $2 million up front, with potential for $3 million more.[99] The CFO responsible for developing the unreliable projections, a long-time Milken associate, was promoted to CEO on an interim basis.[100] The company insisted that the sudden departure was "not a commentary on our financial situation" and pointed to unspecified increases in market share and profit, despite the continuing overall revenue declines.

A company spokesperson assured investors that the year 2011 had "started strongly," despite the unexplained removal of the chief executive. But, in fact, revenue for 2011 would soon fall another 14 percent. In addition, during the treacherous first half of the year, when working capital needs peak in the seasonal business, the company had to scramble to pay its bills.

To provide a more permanent solution to its cash needs and to refinance its shorter-term borrowings, the company launched a bond deal for $1.35 billion, even in the absence of a permanent CEO. The offering attracted scant investor demand and closed in May 2011 after being downsized by more than a billion dollars to a mere $300 million.[101] Even this modest result was achieved only after the existing lenders agreed to buy $115 million of the $300 million deal.[102] Adding insult to injury, as the company struggled to make ends meet while it searched for a new CEO, Paulson had to read that O'Callaghan was poised for a $150 million payday as he prepared to take a Chinese English-language-learning subsidiary of EMPGI public, leveraging the exclusive license for HMH's e-learning software in China.[103]

Six months after O'Callaghan's departure, the company announced his replacement. In the interim, the company had reported disastrous results, with EBITDA in the second quarter down 67 percent.[104] Linda Zecher was a respected Microsoft executive who had no education experience. She had been in charge of Microsoft's $8 billion global public-sector business, but she did not cite this experience with selling to governmental entities as a key driver for being attracted to the job. "I love reading," she later said. "So I couldn't pass up the chance to work there."[105]

Within months, Zecher announced that she would be cutting 10 percent of the staff and would replace both the head of the education group and the CFO.[106] She was soon thrust into negotiations with the owners and continuing lenders over the terms of a prepackaged bankruptcy. The key questions were not only how to divvy up the ownership among the various interests but also, critically, how much debt the company could support. The company once supported close to $8 billion of obligations. This amount was reduced by around $1 billion in the first restructuring and another $3 billion in the second. After much debate, an optimal level of debt was determined—none whatsoever. The company would have ample credit lines to manage the significant working capital swings inherent in the business, but no permanent debt.

When the company made its official bankruptcy filing on May 21, 2012, it looked remarkably like the stand-alone Houghton Mifflin before it had been combined, first with Riverdeep and later with Harcourt.[107] Revenue was almost identical, and profit had shrunk somewhat. Revenue in 2011 and 2005 was $1.295 and $1.289 billion, respectively.

The corresponding EBITDA figures before plate were $238 and $297 million, respectively. It was almost as if the deals had never happened at all. After plate spend, EBITDA remained not much more than $100 million.

It is hard to believe that only five years earlier, O'Callaghan had painted the picture of a combined entity with $2.5 billion in revenues and well over $1 billion in "pro forma adjusted EBITDA with full synergies." To be sure, the industry had undergone significant retrenchment as states reduced their educational spending during the financial crisis. But HMH's most direct competitors, Pearson and McGraw-Hill, had not experienced anything like the deterioration reflected in these shocking results.[108]

Curious George Goes Public Again

When the company emerged from bankruptcy a month later, Paulson was by far the largest owner, with 26 percent, and the group of a half-dozen of the largest hedge fund holders together controlled two-thirds of the equity. And yet, one of the previous major hedge fund owners—the third largest, in fact—was conspicuously absent from this group as Houghton emerged from bankruptcy. Guggenheim and Milken had been the chief proponents of the misguided strategy of keeping and paying Barry O'Callaghan after the previous restructuring. Representing almost 10 percent of the equity at the time, they had almost immediately started liquidating their position in the company as soon as the radically downsized bond offering in May 2011 had closed.

Now the question was how Paulson would make a return on the investment. It is impossible to calculate how much Paulson actually paid for his stake without knowing precisely when his fund purchased the debt and at how great a discount. Based on the size of Paulson's position and the overall debt trading levels, along with his contributions to new equity in the second restructuring and his purchase of new senior notes shortly before the final bankruptcy, it seems very unlikely that the ultimate investment was less than $1 billion.

Hedge funds like Paulson's look for annual returns in excess of 30 percent to justify the risk they are taking in distressed securities. Paulson had built up his position over many years at this point.

Given that the latest restructuring had eliminated all the remaining $3.1 billion of debt, it was clear that the company was worth less than that. The restructuring advisor presented a value range of $1.6–$1.9 billion.[109] Thus, under any plausible scenario, Paulson had not only failed to meet his return threshold, but he had also lost hundreds of millions on an absolute basis.

The options for liquidity had only gotten worse since the previous private equity owners had faced the same issue a decade earlier. The absence of any potential truly strategic buyer had led them to prepare for an IPO, while hoping for someone to make them a better offer than what would be available from the public. Lightning struck for the Bain/Lee group in the form of Barry O'Callaghan. Given the tragic and very public history of all that ensued, however, the chances of that happening again were slim. At a minimum, any private deal for Houghton would need to involve much lower leverage than had made any of the previous mergers and acquisitions transactions possible.

Unfortunately for any potential public offering, Houghton revenue fell again in 2012. In the first half of 2013, however, Houghton showed a modest top-line gain for the first time in years and quickly filed to go public. Public offerings are usually to raise capital to fund a young company's growth plan. This "primary" capital goes directly into a company. Even when private equity investors own a company, the owners rarely sell their own stake in the IPO—so-called "secondary" shares—because of the negative signal it sends to new investors. Such a signal almost always results in investors paying a lower price than they otherwise would.

In the case of HMH, however, the distressed investors were so exhausted from their experience to date that the entire offering consisted of "secondary" shares, with the existing investors trying to sell as much of their position as they possibly could. As sophisticated market participants, they were well aware of the potential adverse impact on the offering, but they were willing to risk it. The result was that although underwriters proposed a pricing range of $14–$16 per share, the market for the IPO shares cleared at just $12 per share. Instead of the nearly $300 million anticipated, the offering in November 2013 raised just over $200 million. The entire value of Houghton Mifflin in the public market initially was almost exactly the price of $1.7 billion paid by the Bain/Lee consortium more than a decade earlier, before the assets of Riverdeep and Harcourt had been added to the mix.

Paulson, as a result of the anemic offering, was only able to pull out about $65 million. He continued to own 22 percent of the company for almost two years. After the IPO, the HMH stock steadily climbed, and by the end of 2014, it had settled at around $20 per share. Paulson was able to exit the balance of the investment in May 2015 after a brief uptick in the stock to $23 before it returned to below $20 within a few months. Even with the fortunate timing of this sale, total proceeds of Paulson's liquidation of his position were less than $350 million. Although it is impossible to calculate precisely, it is clear that he left the investment many hundreds of millions in the red.[110]

Meanwhile O'Callaghan has managed to continue to thrive personally, even as the list of unhappy partners lengthens. The planned IPO of EMPGI's Chinese operations never happened. The Dubai state investment company that had invested $50 million to acquire one-third of HMH's international business in 2008 completely walked away from its investment in 2013.[111] This was all part of a mysterious liquidation of the Cayman Islands holding company that resulted in a new Cayman-based entity with O'Callaghan squarely in control. O'Callaghan has attracted a board that includes not only former HMH stalwarts like Tony Lucki but also celebrities, such as *Chariots of Fire* producer Lord David Puttnam. Also included for added credibility is former U.S. Education Secretary Bill Bennett, who ironically made a name for himself by lecturing the public on managing excess in their personal behavior.

The restructured EMPGI now goes to market with its network of owned and franchised English language learning centers across Asia and the Middle East under the RISE brand. The RISE website describes Chairman O'Callaghan as "a high profile entrepreneur with a strong educational pedigree." The site touts the fact that "foundational content is provided by Houghton Mifflin Harcourt," and it prominently displays the logo of the company O'Callaghan had led into bankruptcy. Given this outcome of their previous efforts, it is remarkable that RISE further brags that "its leadership [has] overseen an investment in excess of US$1 billion in [e]ducational content and IP."[112]

Although the HMH stock performed well in the first year after the reintroduction to the public market, the underlying realities of the industry dynamics had not changed. After an initial burst of enthusiastic utterances about growth in adjacent markets[113] and the digital future,[114] new CEO Zecher seemed to settle into the hard slog of selling educational materials to states and localities, which continues to be HMH's core business. The good news was that 2014 was a banner adoption year, with Houghton reporting market share gains. Although reported revenue was essentially flat again, both billings and cash flow were significantly up. The bad news was that this set the stage for an inevitably much more challenging 2015.

Zecher has always described generating organic revenue growth as her number one priority. Early on in her tenure, she said that, to complement this, she would "perhaps make some small acquisitions."[115] But Houghton's first high-profile smaller acquisition as a public company should give pause. On May 13, 2014, Houghton purchased the carcass of what was once Chris Whittle's Channel One. Channel One was strategic, Zecher explained, because it "shares our commitment to high quality digital content."[116]

As 2015 approached, however, she was mentioning the possibility of "larger strategic" transactions.[117] Given the history of Houghton, despite an activist investor's pressure to releverage the balance sheet, Zecher was sensitive to the issues of which large deals are truly "strategic" and how much leverage the company could actually support. That said, the large deal came quickly, with the purchase of Scholastic's educational technology unit for $575 million in April 2015.[118]

Zecher had approached Scholastic's long-time CEO and controlling shareholder, Richard Robinson, about buying all of Scholastic. Robinson had no interest in selling the business, which had traded for years at a single-digit EBITDA multiple, notwithstanding its storied children's publishing and education brand. Robinson was frustrated. On the one hand, he couldn't afford to buy the "ed tech" assets that came on the market and went for what he thought of as crazy prices. On the other hand, his anemic stock price failed to give credit for the significant number of digital educational assets Scholastic had developed over time. At the price Zecher offered just for Scholastic's mostly homegrown technology businesses, which reflected her belief that she could find $20 million of cost savings, Robinson netted his desired "crazy" price even after paying taxes.

HMH stock ran to over $25 per share the summer after the deal—this is the period during which time Paulson took the opportunity to sell his remaining holdings. Hugely disappointing earnings announcements, however, quickly followed, and full-year expectations were revised downward.[119] Having already releveraged the balance sheet with the Scholastic acquisition and doubled the buyback program from $100 to $200 million, the company finally acceded to activist demands and announced a massive $1 billion buyback program. This "aggressive usage of debt to fund share buy-backs" led Moody's to downgrade the rating on the company's credit facility in early 2016.[120] The full year 2015 ended with "one final miss to end a difficult year," and the share price remained stubbornly in the teens.[121] Billings for 2015 were down, even with the addition of the Scholastic technology assets, and overall market share had fallen from the impressive levels achieved in 2014.

Zecher now faces a choice. She can focus on the effective management of her core educational assets in a sector that is relatively low growth with significant volatility but in which market shares shift slowly and scale is a distinct advantage. Or she can double down on her embrace of the digital future through additional expensive higher-growth technology acquisitions and aggressive transformative investments to fundamentally change HMH's business mix and model. The financial devastation that Houghton left in its wake was due to the wrong capital structure, exacerbated by a lack of operational focus—it was not due to slow growth. Thus, before following the latter path, she would do well to examine both this history and Rupert Murdoch's experience.

CHAPTER FOUR

Michael Milken

Master of the Knowledge Universe

ON JULY 9, 2015, Michael Milken's twenty-year quest to upend education from "cradle to cane"[1] by unleashing the power of free markets came to a practical end when he announced the sale of the last and largest company his ambitious educational venture had backed. Innumerable other deals had preceded this one over the years, but the sale of all U.S. operations of a for-profit early childhood education business left Knowledge Universe—the audacious holding company name of Milken's educational foray—as little more than a corporate shell with some real estate holdings and intellectual property assets.[2] According to Lowell Milken, Michael's brother and one of the original backers of the educational initiative in 1996, Michael was unlikely to redeploy additional capital into the sector.[3]

Michael Milken, the one-time leader of the now-defunct Drexel Burnham Lambert's high-yield bond department, has long been a polarizing figure. His legacy as a financier and his ultimate felony conviction have attracted fierce debate. Although his widely praised philanthropic activities since his release from prison in 1993 have been less controversial, they are arguably as revolutionary as his financial innovations.[4] Milken's continuing business activities, however, have been mostly under the radar and are the subject of both conspiracy theories and regulatory scrutiny,[5] due to his well-documented obsession with secrecy and his lifetime ban from the securities industry.

Like much else associated with Milken's finances, the details of the Knowledge Universe sale were shrouded in mystery, with no terms disclosed. There can be little doubt, however, that the educational ventures collectively had fallen far short of their original broader objective of establishing "the pre-eminent for-profit education and training company in the world."[6] The asset being sold was overwhelmingly comprised of the KinderCare day-care centers that Milken had purchased for more than $1 billion in 2005.[7] This final transaction, selling a modest, narrowly focused business that had not distinguished itself in either innovation or operating performance, seemed strangely disconnected from the wide-ranging, futuristic vision of education painted in the heady early days of Knowledge Universe.

Even from a financial viewpoint, enough information can be pieced together to confidently conclude that Michael Milken's unique financial acumen did not translate into financial success for his overall educational investments. In just the day-care center arena, before the KinderCare acquisition, Milken's Knowledge Universe had begun, in 1998, by spending $100 million for Children's Discovery Centers; this was followed with the purchase of Aramark's Children's World Learning Centers for $265 million in 2003, as well as a number of other smaller acquisitions. Between the KinderCare acquisition and a February 2014 refinancing of the KinderCare deal junk bonds, revenues had remained stagnant at around $1.4 billion, while profitability and cash flow had plummeted. From 2011 to 2013, EBITDA margins were below 5 percent, as compared with almost 15 percent in 2003. With annual capital expenditures typically between $50 and $60 million, in some years (notably 2012), this spending actually exceeded EBITDA—meaning that cash flow was negative even before paying any interest. After the company's performance necessitated amendments to its loan covenants, the credit ratings agencies downgraded the organization's outstanding bonds to subterranean levels in 2012.

As S&P noted at the time, the fact that Knowledge Universe was the largest U.S. child-care operator did not detract from the fact that the entire segment is "mature, cyclical and highly competitive."[8] In addition, being "largest" still left Knowledge Universe with less than 5 percent of the overall child-care market. This persistent fragmentation in the face of continuing efforts to consolidate the industry strongly suggested low structural barriers to entry. More generally, there is little reward for being big in an industry in which scale has few economic benefits. Scale matters in sectors in which fixed costs predominate. When costs are overwhelmingly variable, however, any wily local proprietor can give the largest national competitor a run for its money. As we will see in the next chapter, even in industries with such structural infirmities, innovative entrepreneurs can sometimes redraw the traditional dimensions of competition to create sustainable franchises. But a blind desire to be the biggest, without a nuanced understanding of when and how bigness can actually deliver superior performance, is always a recipe for financial disaster.

Given the financial results and the fact that the ultimate buyer of Knowledge Universe was a disciplined private equity investor, it is not surprising that Milken received less than the sum of the original purchase prices paid for the stream of assets swallowed up since the purchase of Children's Discovery Centers in 1998. A few years before the sale, in 2012, Milken had hired a turnaround expert—former Old Navy CEO Tom Wyatt—who managed to stanch the persistent revenue losses and move EBITDA margins up to high single-digit percentages, but that was too little, too late. Although Milken refused to disclose the purchase price, the private equity buyer was obliged to share all the details to the junk bond investors who were being asked to take on $845 million in debt (almost $300 million more than what was already in place) in the highly leveraged deal. A Milken spokesperson at the time noted that outside investors had placed a $2.25 billion valuation on the business in 2007 and insisted that since then it had "realized substantial gains."[9] The numbers told a very different story. The actual purchase price revealed to the new debt holders was $1.465 billion, making it difficult to see how the 2007 investors could have been made whole.[10] Even for Milken, who had been extracting millions in "management fees"—fees that the private equity acquirer's financing documents insisted were not associated with any actual services—this amount could not have represented an acceptable return for the leveraged risk he undertook over such an extended period.

In the Beginning, Milken Created the Universe

The child-care properties of Knowledge Universe may have been all that remained in its final years, but these give little hint of the initial scope and ambition of the venture. In its early years, the initiative encompassed investments and acquisitions in dozens of different enterprises touching almost every segment of the educational sector. Indeed, what distinguished Milken's vision was its very vastness.

His goal was to create an education brand that stretched "from birth to post-retirement"—"I don't think anyone has tried to do it," said Milken in a rare *Los Angeles Times* interview.[11]

The breadth of Milken's aspirations dwarfed even those of Joel Klein at News Corp., who had at least limited his focus to the K–12 realm. At the height of its activity, Knowledge Universe's investments were organized into six distinct areas, from child care and interactive learning to corporate training and consulting, and most contained multiple distinct investments. The company consistently expressed a genuine belief that these far-flung enterprises were somehow synergistic. Knowledge Universe's first CEO, Thomas Kalinske, a former toy executive, described the vision of a brand that would encompass child care, educational toys in the early grades, math software in the later grades, SAT prep, and college selection. Kalinske postulated, "Then when they graduate, whatever business they are in, if they need additional training, they think of us."[12] Under this view, who would be better positioned to provide retirees with "training for a new part-time career"?[13]

As far-fetched as this notion may seem, it attracted a fair amount of breathless praise. Stan Lepeak, then at the META Group consulting firm but later the head of Global Research and Thought Leadership at KPMG, claimed that Knowledge Universe could "easily become a Fortune 100 company."[14] Kalinske encouraged the impression of inevitable world domination: "Could it be a $5 billion company? Yes. Could it be more than that? Maybe."[15] One Wall Street analyst described the assets and team as "a potential category killer" poised to "change the face of for-profit education."[16] Barely two years into its existence, after the investment of only a few hundred million dollars, another analyst pegged the hypothetical market value of Knowledge Universe as $4–$6 billion.[17]

All of this big talk distracted from the fact that Knowledge Universe was only modestly capitalized. Milken and his brother had each put in only $125 million. During the course of his career, Milken has often figured out how to control significant endeavors using primarily other people's money. Here the bigger silent partner was billionaire and Oracle CEO Larry Ellison, who contributed $250 million. Although $500 million is a lot of money, even with leverage it is a tiny fraction of what would be required to break into the Fortune 100 from a standing start. By 2000, more than 100 private equity funds were already at least this size in operation.[18] Indeed, strategic logic aside, there had always been a fundamental financial disconnect between the grandiosity of the ambition and the venture's actual scale.

Milken seemed to revel in the rumors of Knowledge Universe taking over any number of large multibillion-dollar enterprises, such as one of the largest chains of for-profit colleges. He even participated in a bid for Simon & Schuster, the leading educational publisher that ultimately sold to Viacom for $4.6 billion in 1998.[19] The reality was, however, that the venture never had anything like the capital required to lead an acquisition of this scale. The idea may have been that the publicity thereby generated would create enough momentum to attract new capital that would allow Knowledge Universe to fulfill its dreams of world domination. Indeed, much later, in 2007, Milken hired Goldman Sachs and Credit Suisse to raise $1 billion of new equity for Knowledge Universe, though it does not appear that he ever succeeded in attracting anything like that amount.

In the end, the only transaction Knowledge Universe would ever consummate that was even close to $1 billion in size was the 2005 acquisition of KinderCare Learning Centers, which would remain the troubled core of the business. KinderCare was an asset and company that Milken had known well since the 1970s[20] and for which he had financed an ill-conceived acquisition spree, including retail clothing and shoe chains, in the mid-1980s.[21] Before going bankrupt in 1992, its founder pled guilty to secretly pocketing placement fees for pledging company money to Drexel Burnham Lambert junk bond deals.[22]

Assessing Knowledge Universe's smaller investments outside of the child-care arena, whether on Milken's terms or on a purely financial basis, is complicated by the fact that the organization is so secretive and there were just so many investments. During the course of its history, Knowledge Universe changed names, ownership, and corporate structure repeatedly. For instance, in the years leading up to the KinderCare acquisition, the original partnership appears to have been unwound, with former ambassador to Singapore Steven J. Green stepping in to take Ellison's place in at least some future investments.[23]

The parts of the Milken education portfolio with greatest transparency are those companies in which he invested that went public or were already public. Chapter 2 discussed the fate of K12 Inc., the Milken-backed online charter school operator that went public in 2007. A closer examination of the four earliest public situations in which Milken was involved—the CRT Group, LeapFrog, Nobel

Learning, and Nextera—provides a sense of the breadth of his interests and an opportunity to objectively assess his success or failure, at least in these instances (see Figures 4.1–4.4).

In August 1996, Knowledge Universe's first significant purchase was a relatively large one, consuming fully a third of its cash hoard. CRT Group was a British temporary staffing and training company that specialized in information technology. Spending $169 million for 50.1 percent of a public company that was the UK's largest private technology-recruitment agency might not seem like an obvious acquisition for Knowledge Universe. However, it apparently fell within their expansive conception of their remit: "We define education as anything that helps people improve, helps train them, or have a new career."[24] The investment reflected a broader effort to capitalize on what Milken saw as an inevitable shortage of high-tech professionals to feed the exploding "human capital industry."[25]

In adjacent areas, Milken purchased most of the franchisees of Productivity Point, a Florida facilities-based IT training company; Symmetrix, a Boston consulting firm; and MindQ Publishing, a Virginia computer-based provider of Java training. Some were impressed with the strategy reflected in this eclectic collection of IT training and consulting assets. As tech guru Lepeak explained, "You would have to be an

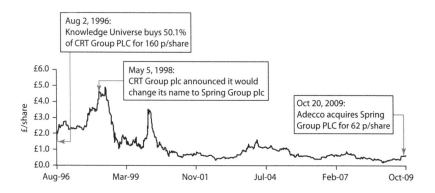

Figure 4.1 CRT Group/Spring Group share price (£/share)

Point 1: August 2, 1996: Knowledge Universe buys 50.1 percent of CRT Group PLC for 160 p/share
Point 2: May 5, 1998: CRT Group PLC announced it would change its name to Spring Group PLC
Point 3: October 20, 2009: Adecco acquires Spring Group PLC for 62 p/share

idiot to lose money in the knowledge market over the next few years."[26] Other industry insiders were not so sure. With competitors of both the broad-based entrenched variety, such as "all the major accounting giants," in addition to well-regarded "specialists occupying every niche,"[27] some questioned whether simultaneously attacking every vertical from scratch represented a coherent strategy. Such concerns were largely swept to the side, however, after the infusion of capital into CRT supercharged not only its marketing efforts but also its stock price. Knowledge Universe bought its shares of CRT at 160p; the price tripled over the first two years, reaching a high of 491p by June 1998. Indeed, this very public performance seems to have driven the early perception of Milken's Midas touch in education, along with outsized valuations of the overall Knowledge Universe portfolio. Ellison himself served as a Knowledge Universe board representative for a time, as did Stephen Bollenbach, the Hilton Hotels CEO and former Disney CFO.

In May 1998, CRT Group announced it would be changing its name to the Spring Group. In the previous year, the company had made eight acquisitions, diversifying into a number of new IT and vocational training and recruiting areas. It had also established an Educational Services division. The name change, it was said, would facilitate "a consistent and coherent message to be communicated" and permit rationalization of the marketing spend being made across what were now "more than 15 different names."[28] But the bloom on the roll-up rose faded quickly. The share price collapsed to just over 100p by December 1998. In May 2000, Milken pushed out CRT's founder and replaced him with a new CEO, Jon Chait, who quickly set about reversing the diversification strategy.[29]

Although Chait, a former Manpower executive, announced the planned divestiture of Spring Education, Spring Skills, and Spring Personnel, this move did not halt the share price slide. By December 2000, he had managed to sell two of these three divisions but had to pull one off the market.[30] The shares still continued their downward spiral, remaining stubbornly under 100. Chait was replaced as CEO in 2002 by the finance director, Richard Barfield, who lasted until 2006.[31] Although Barfield turned the business profitable again after consecutive money-losing years, operating margins were rarely above 1 percent during his tenure and the share price fell as low as 39p in June 2006 shortly before his departure. The shares hit an all-time low of 20p in November 2008.[32] On August 11, 2009, simultaneous with announcing interim results showing continued double-digit percentage revenue declines, Spring revealed that its board was recommending acceptance of a 62p-per-share offer from Adecco—the largest global staffing company or, as it describes itself, "the world's leading provider of HR solutions."[33]

This relatively modest deal merited barely a mention by the acquirer, who announced it between two much larger transactions.[34] Although the offer represented a 67 percent premium to the share price of 42p before the company revealed the proposal's existence, the total equity value was about the same as Knowledge Universe had spent for roughly half the company thirteen years earlier. A Milken-controlled entity, which still owned 36 percent of the company (and 60 million of the 72 million shares he had started with thirteen years earlier), had provided an irrevocable commitment to vote for the deal.

The educational toy company LeapFrog was started by a law firm partner who had developed a product using a Texas Instruments chip to help his child learn to read. His original Phonics Desk was first carried in stores during the 1995 Christmas season, and Knowledge Universe made its controlling investment in the product in 1997 for $50 million.

Figure 4.2 LeapFrog Enterprises share price ($/share). IPO to February 2016.

Point 1: July 25, 2002: LeapFrog IPO at $13/share

Point 2: September 2, 2004: LeapFrog founder Michael Wood resigns

Point 3: September 4, 2015: Company receives delisting notice from NYSE

Point 4: February 5, 2016: Acquired by Hong Kong's VTech Holdings for $1/share

In 1999, the company launched its flagship LeapPad product, which became a best-selling toy in the United States for the period[35] leading up to its IPO, which was the best performing in 2002.[36]

Milken's decision to target a technology-enabled business in the so-called edutainment sector was not surprising given his fascination with both entertainment and futuristic science fiction. His speeches were filled with both *Star Trek* and *Star Wars* references, and the Knowledge Universe board was filled not with educators but with media moguls whose loyalty had been earned during the junk bond era.[37] Although in 1999 LeapFrog launched an educational division, LeapFrog Schoolhouse, the company was and would remain overwhelmingly a retail toy business. The toy business is a difficult, hit-driven enterprise in which scale in manufacturing, marketing, and distribution matters immensely. The persistently anemic margins and highly seasonal nature of the business (Christmas sales make or break the year) have led even the largest players to diversify into broader entertainment ventures.[38] When an upstart introduces an unexpectedly successful product, the scale players are well positioned to quickly flood the market with their own variations on the theme. These structural industry challenges have long made it highly challenging for toy start-ups to attract funding.[39]

When LeapFrog went public in 2002, it had a hit toy, but it didn't have scale. Unfortunately, hits are sporadic, whereas the lack of scale is persistent. The public markets focused on the hit, and the offering at $13 per share was wildly successful. After experiencing a more than 20 percent pop in the share price on the first day of trading, Knowledge Universe's overall stake was valued at more than a half-billion dollars. But not everyone was enamored with the LeapFrog IPO at the time. The *Wall Street Journal* highlighted a number of unusual aspects to the offering and the governance structure as causes for concern.[40] First, companies typically sell no more than 20–25 percent of their equity in an IPO—and often much less. The simple notion is that if the owners believe in the growth potential unleashed by the new capital, they should want to retain as much as possible. Selling any more signals to investors a lack of confidence in the business. Knowledge Universe was selling an almost unheard of 75 percent of the company's equity. Second, the company was issuing low-vote shares to the public so that Knowledge Universe—with ten vote shares—would continue to control the company even after it sold a majority of the equity to the public.

For the first year after the IPO, it felt like the *Journal's* cautions were misplaced as the stock soared to almost three times the offering price. The first signs of trouble did not appear until autumn of 2003, when the company missed its numbers. When the company followed up early in 2004 by missing its first-quarter numbers—only a month after providing very different guidance on the coming year's performance—the stock collapsed back into the teens[41] and began a largely uninterrupted decade-long descent. Michael Wood, the founder, chief creative officer, and former CEO, abruptly resigned in 2004.[42] In September 2015, the New York Stock Exchange notified the company that because the shares had fallen below $1 for more than thirty consecutive trading days, it was potentially subject to delisting.[43]

Many tech entrepreneurs and investors get rich by selling enough of their stake in a temporarily hot company before it comes crashing down. The fact that Broadcast.com no longer even exists does not make Mark Cuban, who sold the company to Yahoo for $5.7 billion in stock that he hedged, any less a billionaire. Nor does it seem to have done much to harm Cuban's business or financial reputation. In the case of Milken, however, it does not appear that he was able to translate LeapFrog's brief early success into significant financial success. In the 2002 IPO, all of the selling shareholders jointly took out barely $5 million. Milken, as part of the unwinding of the original Knowledge Universe partnerships, did distribute the stake in LeapFrog to the individual investors—just before and just after the disastrous 2004 earnings announcement. But at the time, both Ellison and the Milken brothers insisted that they had "no present intention to sell any of their LeapFrog stock."[44] In 2015, as pointed out by an activist investor frustrated with the company's continued decline, Milken and his family still owned almost 4 percent of the shares and controlled almost 40 percent of the vote. That stake, however, was only worth a few million dollars. Milken had sold a few hundred thousand shares near the peak in 2003 for almost $35 per share, but he sold most of his other shares between 2009 and 2011 for an average price of not much more than $5 per share. Although this amount was well above the penny-stock levels the company found itself trading at by 2015, it was still a fraction of the original IPO price.

In February 2016, shareholders got some much-needed good news. A Hong Kong–based "supplier of corded and cordless phones and electronic learning toys" announced the acquisition of LeapFrog for

$1 per share. Although this purchase price represented a 75 percent premium to the previous closing price, Milken's small economic interest in the $72 million deal would still represent only a few million dollars. Collectively, the proceeds of these sales plus the modest value of his remaining stake amounted to less than the $50 million that Knowledge Universe originally invested. Given that the original investment was by an entity only partially owned by Milken, it is conceivable that he personally got back what he put in, but it is inconceivable that he achieved an acceptable return over his holding period, which is now approaching twenty years.

Milken's dalliance with for-profit K–12 school operator Nobel Learning is one of the odder episodes in the Knowledge Universe history. Nobel had started its life as Rocking Horse Child Care Centers of America in 1984 and was taken over in 1992 by banker Alfred "Jack" Clegg, who accelerated the company's move into preschools and elementary and middle schools mainly through acquisitions. By 1998, when Knowledge Universe took a large stake in the public company, it had changed its name to Nobel Education Dynamics and was operating more than 120 schools in fourteen states.

Figure 4.3 Nobel Learning share price ($/share)

Point 1: January 14, 1998: Knowledge Universe buys 1,000,000 shares at $5.63 each.

Point 2: July 25, 2003: George Bernstein is appointed CEO.

Point 3: July 17, 2008: Milken buys just under 1,000,000 shares at $16 each, and the company institutes a poison pill.

Point 4: September 22, 2008: Milken proposes a buyout at $17 per share.

Point 5: March 11, 2009: Milken proposes a buyout at $13.50 per share.

Point 6: August 8, 2011: Leeds completes the buyout at $11.75 per share.

The basic positioning of Nobel was as an affordable alternative to elite private schools for relatively well-heeled middle-class families. A higher student-teacher ratio and a more disciplined cost regime supported the business model. However, new schools typically took eighteen to twenty-four months to achieve profitable enrollment levels, and a burst of openings depressed 1997 profits, when shares fell from $12.50 to $4.50 during the course of the year.

Knowledge Universe seemed to view this decline as a buying opportunity. Unlike the case of CRT, however, new money was not put into the public company to accelerate its growth plan. The Milken vehicle simply purchased 1.28 million shares in the open market beginning in late 1997 and into early 1998, gaining a more than 20 percent stake in the company. One million of these shares were purchased at $5.63 each on January 14, 1998.[45] Although the corresponding public filing indicated a potential interest in eventually taking a majority stake in the company, direct communications with Nobel about their interests or intentions were vague beyond generally encouraging a more aggressive new school rollout.[46]

Nobel's stock popped on the news of the Knowledge Universe purchase, but nothing much else seemed to change. Although Clegg had moved the business from being a child-care company to a predominantly pre-K–8 private school operator, it was still very much a "microcap" (a public company with an equity value of less than $300 million).[47] What's more, Clegg ran the business essentially as a family enterprise. Four of his children were on the payroll, including one son eventually positioned as the heir apparent. At the time of the investment, Clegg expressed hope that Knowledge Universe would help with technology in the schools but claimed indifference overall and said he had never even met Milken. "At this stage, I am relatively neutral until I see if there are some benefits," Clegg asserted five months into the relationship with Knowledge Universe.[48]

Any "synergy" between Knowledge Universe and Nobel never materialized. Over the following years, growth continued, but the company lost focus on the core school business. Indeed, the pace of new general education private school openings slowed. Instead, the company entered the markets for charter schools, schools for special needs children, and summer camps; it also purchased a company that ran pre- and after-school programs.[49] These initiatives were accompanied by a significant expansion of Nobel's geographic footprint. All of this frenetic activity placed significant strains on the company's capital structure. In the years after Milken's investment, the shares remained volatile but never exceeded $10 per share and sometimes fell below $5 per share.

In August 2002, Clegg partnered with two small private equity firms to take the company private for $7.75 per share, a 32 percent premium over the $5.85 that it had been trading at.[50] Although there was speculation that this move came to avoid a Milken takeover of the company, presumably Milken could have simply offered more once Clegg had effectively put the company in play. If the deal had closed, Milken would have achieved a paltry return on his investment. The deal, however, didn't close. In November, the buyout group informed Nobel that it had been unable to secure the financing needed for the deal.[51] The stock immediately collapsed below $5 once again, and in February 2003, the buyout agreement was formally terminated.[52]

The company was in a precarious financial position, with its lender threatening to put the company into receivership. The Milken group threatened a proxy fight but settled by making a $5 million loan with warrants to the company and by getting two board seats.[53] This loan did not resolve the company's capital structure challenges, and Milken saw it as a first step to gaining further control, as the agreement also permitted him to buy an additional 10 percent of the company on the open market. Ultimately the company was only able to avoid Milken's control by accepting help from a "white knight," Camden Partners which agreed in June 2003 to invest $6 million of new preferred equity in the company—but only if Clegg stepped down.[54] In July, an entirely new management team, led by George Bernstein, was put in place, and the Clegg family departed the stage.[55]

To Bernstein's surprise, the company he took over was still facing default. In September 2003, he avoided disaster by getting the company's three largest shareholders—the Milken Group, Camden Partners, and Allied Capital—to each invest an additional $1 million in preferred equity, which gave Bernstein the breathing room needed to ultimately put a more permanent capital structure in place. By the end of the year, the Milken Group owned just under 30 percent of the common stock; Camden, just under 20 percent; and Allied, just under 10 percent—with each also owning different stakes in the multiplying classes of preferred stock.[56]

Although the stock remained stubbornly under $5 at the end of 2003, Bernstein quickly moved to refocus and stabilize the company.

The shares began to rise steadily, ending 2004 at more than $7.50 and reaching $10 early in 2006. The stock reached a high of $14 in February 2007. During this period, Milken liquidated the original Knowledge Universe vehicle used to buy the shares and distributed the holdings to investors. As a result, overall Milken-affiliated entities' ownership fell, though he and his brother built up their position again—in part by buying out Allied Capital's holdings. By March 2007, the Milkens once again owned close to 20 percent of the company. News of the Milken brothers' purchases quickly drove the shares to more than $15 per share for the first time since the 1980s.[57] The Milkens continued to buy shares on the open market in 2007 and into 2008.

Throughout the period from the 2003 recapitalization until 2008 Milken's substantive communications with the company regarding either his intentions or the potential for strategic arrangements with other Knowledge Universe companies were nonexistent. His communications consisted instead of the rare brief note or of high-level conversations. Indeed, Bernstein pressed Joseph Harch, one of Milken's two initial board appointees, to step down after Harch failed to appear at board meetings.[58] On Thursday, July 17, 2008, Bernstein got a call from Milken offering to dramatically alter the nature of their previous communications. Milken let Bernstein know that he had purchased another 10 percent of the company at $16 per share and suggested that they get together the following week for a detailed discussion. Milken had purchased the stake at a price above market directly from Ellison, who had not sold his shares since getting them distributed from the original Knowledge Universe partnership.

The threat of a "creeping takeover" by Milken concerned both the board and other major shareholders, who loudly communicated their concerns.[59] Their worry was that Milken was trying to buy control on the cheap, without allowing the company to explore other, potentially superior proposals. Over the weekend, the board adopted a so-called poison pill to thwart any such effort and to give the company time to organize itself.[60] On Monday, July 21, after the pill was announced, Bernstein called Milken as promised to schedule their meeting. The call was short, as Milken told him they had nothing left to discuss.

The stock then drifted down below $13 per share. Then, in September 2008, the Milkens made a formal proposal to buy the balance of the company for $17 per share. The proposal came in a letter from Knowledge Learning Corp. (KLC), the entity that owned the

U.S. child-care properties. The letter touted the strategic benefits as a feeder for enrollments in Nobel Schools. It also emphasized the benefits of association with Knowledge Universe Education (KUE), KLC's parent, with its ownership of other K–12 businesses such as GlobalScholar, which was a roll-up of various online businesses serving that market.[61]

The independent board members established a committee, which decided to run a process to assess what could be achieved from a sale and determine whether any transaction was advisable. Given the company's progress under Bernstein, some board members felt that selling at all in the midst of the 2008 financial crisis, while stocks were all artificially depressed, made little sense.[62] Throughout the resulting process, which corresponded with a deepening financial crisis, KLC refused to receive any confidential material about the company so that Milken would maintain flexibility in the disposal of his shares. In addition, KLC repeatedly requested extensions to the date for submitting final definitive proposals. The stock price continued to fall with the market—reaching as low as $11.37 per share—and the process dragged out. Then, in March 2009, Milken publically announced a revised proposal of $13.50 per share,[63] which the board quickly rejected.[64] None of the other strategic or financial parties engaged by Nobel submitted a proposal.

In March 2010, the Nobel board decided to quietly pursue a sale in discussion with a handful of parties that had previously expressed interest and continued to track the company. Although the company had performed relatively well operationally, the recession's lingering impact and a lack of market enthusiasm for the K–12 sector in general had left the stock floundering below $10 per share since the second half of 2009. This narrow process collapsed in August 2010, after the initially selected "winner" significantly revised its offer downward and none of the other participants were willing to match the original proposal.

Leeds Equity Partners, an education-focused private equity firm, approached the company after the failure of the process and secured an exclusivity period starting late in 2010. Leeds reached an agreement to buy Nobel in May 2011 at a price of $11.75 per share. Milken had remained enigmatic throughout the 2010 process and the subsequent discussions with Leeds. He ultimately agreed to participate and sign a limited nondisclosure agreement in connection with the 2010 process, but did not submit an indication of interest with the other parties.

Even after the auction ended and discussions with Leeds began, it was not completely clear whether Milken would support a deal. In October 2010, Milken suggested he was a seller at $11 per share and worked with Leeds to provide financing for the transaction. The terms of the Milken financing were so onerous, however, that Leeds turned to more conventional sources. Then, in March 2011, when Leeds increased its earlier offers to $11.25 per share, Milken said this amount was now not high enough. Instead, he insisted on a price of $11.75, as well as a variety of other financial benefits, before he agreed to vote his shares in favor of the deal. The negotiations with both Leeds and the board dragged on for months. When the transaction was finally announced in May, more than half of the holders—including Milken, other large holders, and management—were committed to the deal.

Neither the extra fifty cents per share nor the other concessions Milken insisted on before supporting the deal would have any significant impact on the unattractiveness of his investment in Nobel. Although Milken had been associated with Nobel for more than a decade, he had purchased half of the 3.857 million shares he owned at an average price of around $15 per share, representing a loss of close to 20 percent. Even the original million shares he purchased for $5.63 in 1998 would yield him a paltry annual return below 5 percent.[65] Adding insult to injury, during four short years of private ownership that followed Milken's association with the company, the investors made four times their money.[66] This achievement was not reached by any "synergies" with other Leeds Equity portfolio companies. Rather, Leeds's main contribution was to leave CEO Bernstein alone to execute his focused strategy of building and operating efficient, locally-based clusters of preschools and K–8 schools.

When Leeds sold in 2015—to private equity firm Investcorp and Bahraini sovereign wealth fund Mumtalakat—the price paid reflected boom M&A market multiples far above what had been achievable in 2011. But Leeds's success was not simply a function of market timing. Bernstein actually grew the EBITDA of the business by more than 70 percent by growing revenues 33 percent and increasing margins from 10 percent to 13 percent. The growth achieved during these four years came through a balance of modestly priced acquisitions and organic investments. The significant capital deployed in the business still allowed a substantial reduction in the debt level put in place in the initial LBO. The contrast to the period of public ownership is a testament to the potential costs of management distraction in a small-cap company, particularly one with warring shareholders.

Knowledge Universe's first IPO was very different from any of the other three public companies discussed above. In February 1997, Knowledge Universe created Nextera out of whole cloth as a vehicle to roll up a multiplicity of established independent consulting firms. The big idea was to take the collection public quickly and use the currency to continue that "strategy." These consultancies had little in common beyond targeting large corporations as clients. The offering prospectus sought to organize the nine acquisitions it had made into four broad buckets—Strategy and Research Services, Process Transformation Services, Human Capital Services, and Information Technology Consultancy Services. The artificial and arbitrary nature of these categories was highlighted by the way they were continually adjusted to accommodate new acquisitions made between the initial filing in September 1998 and the final offering document in May 1999.

The IPO itself had a lukewarm reception. The filing range was first lowered from $13–$15 per share to $10–$12 per share; it was then priced at the bottom end of the range. Shares promptly fell more

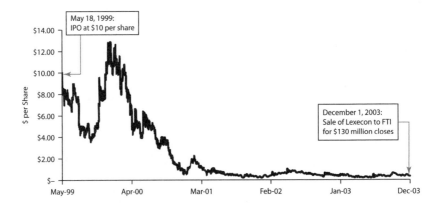

Figure 4.4 Nextera Enterprises share price ($/share)

Point 1: May 18, 1999: IPO at $1000 per share
Point 2: December 1, 2003: Sale of Lexicon to FTI for $130 million closes

than 10 percent in the first day of trading.[67] Various explanations were offered for the poor performance: the market's lack of appetite for roll-up stories, Nextera's minimal exposure to the "hot" Internet and telecommunications niches that were driving the overall IPO boom, and the unorthodox governance structure that could allow Milken to control the business indefinitely through a special class of high-vote shares. Whatever the reasons for the indifferent welcome, none would have necessarily doomed the company if it had proceeded to execute effectively on its articulated strategy.

The key to any successful outcome for Nextera would be the performance of a business called Lexecon, which was both the largest acquisition of Nextera and the least connected strategically to the rest of the roll-up. In the late 1970s, two well-known law professors at the University of Chicago and Andrew Rosenfield, a second-year law student, founded Lexecon to provide litigation support grounded in economic analysis. Over the years, a number of distinguished academics, including more than one Nobel Prize winner, would be associated with Lexecon.[68] Even as Lexecon grew in its first decade to more than 100 employees, all of its management held either part- or full-time posts at the University of Chicago. By the time of the Nextera acquisition for $60 million, Rosenfield, who once described the business as the "action arm of the Law and Economics movement," was Lexecon's chair.[69] Notably, Lexecon's principal, Daniel Fischel, was dean of the University of Chicago Law School and had written *Payback: The Conspiracy to Destroy Michael Milken and His Financial Revolution,* a controversial book defending Milken.

Based on the deal, which was just under half in stock, Rosenfield and Fischel became the largest individual shareholders of Nextera, and, on a pro forma basis, Lexecon would have represented 30 percent of Nextera's 1997 revenues.[70] In the month before the IPO, however, Lexecon experienced an unexpected windfall of $50 million when it won a jury trial against plaintiff's class-action law firm Milberg Weiss for impugning its reputation.[71] The case related to an earlier trial, in which both Milken and Lexecon had been defendants, involving the collapse of a savings and loan controlled by Charles Keating.

Shares of Nextera fell under $5 per share in its first year of trading, and the CEO was soon replaced by Milken's neighbor, Steven Fink, who was already on the board.[72] Although Fink had no particular expertise in consulting, he had undertaken a number of projects for

Milken-related businesses.[73] With the dot-com boom in full swing in 1999, Fink's primary focus as CEO was to "refocus the company and convince Wall Street Nextera is an Internet play."[74] When the boom became a bust only a year later, a new CEO was brought in[75] and all of the key operating divisions other than Lexecon were sold in 2001 and 2002 to meet the company's debt obligations.[76] In February 2003, with the stock trading in the pennies and Lexecon the only remaining operating asset, Fischel was made CEO of Nextera.

The price that Milken's vociferous public defender exacted to take the CEO job ultimately required the effective liquidation of the company.[77] By that time, Fischel had sold the 1.3 million shares he had held at the time of the IPO. The new employment agreement secured by Fischel was remarkable in a number of regards. In a typical professional services business, whether law, consulting, or banking, individual professionals typically keep between 20 and 40 percent of the revenues they generate, with the balance going to cover overhead. Under his deal, Fischel kept 100 percent. In addition, Fischel was entitled to more than a third of a bonus pool pegged at 43 percent of any operating income generated by the Chicago office. On top of all this, he received a $2 million signing bonus and another $5 million for an agreement not to compete for a year (presumably in the event that he decided to leave the sinking ship). The $5 million noncompete took Nextera only to January 1, 2004; it was then obliged to write him and another employee each another $10 million check for an additional five years of noncompetition assurance. This was the straw that broke the camel's back, as the company had less than $1 million of cash and a mountain of debt.[78] Nextera had "no viable alternatives" but to sell the last remaining operating asset "to enable us to meet these obligations."[79]

Fischel and his colleagues at Lexecon would get another bite at the apple as the division was sold for $130 million to a new owner, FTI Consulting, a $1 billion public company that focused more narrowly on corporate finance and restructuring.[80] None of the sale proceeds would be made available to Nextera shareholders, because the company had almost $100 million in debt and other liabilities to fulfill. There was little question, however, that the transaction would receive shareholder approval, as the Milken group controlled more than 70 percent through a special class of high-vote shares and still held all of the 8.8 million shares with which they had started.

In anticipation of the transaction's closing on December 1, 2003, NASDAQ sent the company a final delisting notice. The deal left Nextera an empty-shell penny stock, with little more than $30 million in residual operating losses and $17 million in cash. The value of the Milken group's collective stake was little more than a couple of million dollars. As the *New York Times* said, the sale transaction "put an end to what began as a big idea: to build a one-stop shop for companies that need advice."[81]

A Little Knowledge Is a Dangerous Thing

All four of these far-flung Milken enterprises shared several characteristics. In each case, somewhere along the line, the company's ambitions significantly outstripped what was practically achievable, due to some combination of the constraints of industry structure and operating realities, on the one hand, and the needs of domain expertise and execution capability, on the other. At some point, the public market, to a greater or lesser extent, bought into Milken's expansive vision of each company's potential role in the broadly defined educational firmament. But Milken took advantage of these moments of market euphoria to only a modest degree. The result is that his financial returns ultimately ranged from the pedestrian to the disastrous, which could reflect either bad market timing on Milken's part or the conviction of a true believer. Circumstantial evidence indicates that the latter played at least some role in these outcomes.

As public companies, these four situations represented the portion of the secretive Milken edu-world that broke through the surface to be subjected to scrutiny. Although they reflect a small fraction of the investments made by Knowledge Universe, key features are consistent with a slightly messianic and fundamentally misguided world view reflected in Milken's statements and actions. At the birth of Knowledge Universe in 1996, Milken had shared the overarching investment thesis that "entertainment, technology, telecommunications and education will continue to come together to create a new dynamic in education."[82] However, Milken was not simply predicting that educational products would incorporate innovations in these other sectors. He believed not just in product convergence but also in actual industry convergence. In addition, across the various segments of the "life-long learning" enterprises that make up the "human capital industry," he genuinely believed that "there'll be a vertical integration of all of that."[83]

More often than not, the investments made by Knowledge Universe underperformed due to lack of focus. The determination to be the biggest overall within a massive, amorphous vertically and horizontally integrated edutainment sector made it difficult to actually achieve relevant scale along the way. Establishing scale only matters within a product niche or geography. Operating K–8 schools efficiently in geographic clusters is a fine business, but combining them with day-care centers and other kinds of schools and programs—at least without a coherent integrated operating strategy—is a distraction. Lexecon has continued to operate successfully within FTI Consulting, but it never made sense for it to be combined with HR or IT consulting. The temporary staffing, IT training, and IT consulting sectors in which CRT played are all distinct businesses, and those that outperform in each business specialize. LeapFrog would never be as big as Hasbro or Mattel in toys or as big as Apple or Samsung in any kind of computer hardware for children; therefore, the only conceivable successful strategy was for it to narrowly define and defend its market segment.

The insurmountable obstacle facing Milken's ambition to become a titan of the twenty-first century's trillion-dollar human capital industry was that such an industry does not exist. "Milken is convinced that the fragmented educational-services business will allow for the creation of huge new corporations," *BusinessWeek* observed in 1999. "And he intends to be in charge of one of them."[84] Even at the time, however, those who actually did run one of the leaders in some segment of the highly regulated and idiosyncratic educational sector found this approach more perplexing than threatening. "What is the core competency, the focus?"[85] asked John Sperling, the founder and then-CEO of Apollo, which is still the largest for-profit university system.

On the ground, Milken's approach made it hugely difficult to prioritize opportunities. With a modest bankroll and a desire to dominate a market defined in the hundreds of billions, where to begin and where to end? Joseph Costello, a respected software executive and then-CEO of Cadence Design Systems, joined Milken's mission in the early days, convinced of "the potential for making a significant contribution to the educational world."[86] He lasted fewer than three months. "They were all over the map," Costello complained. "[Milken is] like an addicted shopper."[87] Part of Costello's frustration was not just the ad hoc mixture of low- and high-technology initiatives, but also Milken's tendency to fall back on traditional LBOs of traditional businesses he understood and, in some cases, had financed before. But the ultimate large-scale educational convergence that Milken foresaw required technology to fundamentally disrupt the incumbent players, and he was eager to get in on the ground floor. Many of the investments he pursued involved potentially radical digital business models far removed from providing child care; running bricks-and-mortar elementary schools; selling toys; or providing consulting, staffing, or traditional corporate training.

Knowledge Universe's digital educational efforts spanned all segments of the educational market. Chapter 2 discussed K12 Inc., but that was not the only effort on the digital side of primary and secondary education. Knowledge Universe also funded a roll-up of businesses under the GlobalScholar brand to compete with SchoolNet and Wireless Generation in the instructional improvement system market. This investment was at least financially successful for Milken, who sold it to his old friend, billionaire Ronald Perelman, for $160 million. Operationally, however, GlobalScholar's pieces were never effectively integrated, and its offering was never competitive. Perelman publically credits Milken with both his own financial success and that of the U.S. economy more generally. Yet, despite his deep admiration for Milken, Perelman sued Milken for fraud in connection with the GlobalScholar sale, describing the product as "vaporware" that was "not actually functional."[88] Perelman lost the suit—the court effectively found he should have known better—and closed the money-losing GlobalScholar.[89]

So Milken Created Education in His Own Image

Milken's most ambitious early efforts at Knowledge Universe to transform education were aimed at the higher education sector. Almost immediately, Milken focused on the idea of a "'virtual university' that would be beamed to students by satellite television or over the Internet."[90] The fate of that project, initially launched under the Knowledge University moniker, highlights a number of the structural challenges to digital business models in general. It also specifically underscores significant practical limits of many pure digital offerings in the educational context.

Knowledge University was born of the notion that the Internet could deliver broad access to the ideas produced at the world's most prestigious universities. Although the company would burn through hundreds of millions of dollars in a few short years, it would continue to soldier on for more than a decade as it repeatedly changed its name, narrowed its ambitions, and adjusted its business model. Although the carcass of what started as Knowledge University still survives as a tiny subsidiary of another Milken-affiliated company, its effective end came with U.S. attorney Preet Bharara's December 2012 announcement of a multimillion-dollar fraud settlement.[91] Given Knowledge University's obsession with affiliating with Nobel Prize winners and top-tier institutions, it is the ultimate irony that its demise came in connection with a scam directed toward career-oriented, low-income students.

Milken's basic concept for the business was to get prestigious universities to lend their names and faculty to develop courses that would make up an online MBA curriculum. The university would be paid for providing its imprimatur and access to its faculty, but students would not get credit from these institutions. Faculty participation and compensation would be the universities' responsibility. These courses would be delivered asynchronously, with faculty contributing to curriculum development—in most cases, this contribution appears to have been simply providing a course outline. The final course content and actual class management and instruction were entrusted to paid staff. The initial plan was to sell the product to the corporate market.

The first name change came quickly after it became clear that the prestigious universities whose participation was central to this vision would not lend their names to a Milken-controlled entity. Milken had backed Andrew Rosenfield, a founder of Lexecon and now a lecturer at the University of Chicago Law School, to lead Knowledge University. Although Rosenfield had no experience running an enterprise of this complexity, he had a track record of making academics rich. When Milken bought Lexecon in early 1999, Rosenfield turned around and used the proceeds to buy Knowledge University through a new entity called UNext.com (the .com would eventually be dropped). Milken would retain a 20 percent nonvoting stake in the entity and substantial ongoing informal influence. But minimizing Milken's association with UNext was a necessary but not sufficient condition to attract the caliber of institution the founders had in mind. As it turned out, the kinds of agreements required to secure their participation would place significant financial burdens on UNext, while reserving complete flexibility for the universities.

Although Rosenfield's role as a member of the University of Chicago Board of Trustees caused controversy over that institution's participation—as did the suggestion that a potential generous contribution from Rosenfield's share of the $50 million Lexecon legal settlement was being used as enticement for their involvement[92]—it was actually Columbia University Business School that first agreed to be an affiliate. That school's entrepreneurial dean, Meyer Feldberg, had a personal relationship with Milken and was unapologetic in his view that the deal was as much a "business opportunity" as an "intellectual opportunity" with "huge upside" from the value of the equity in the IPO."[93]

For all the focus on the upside, however, Feldberg clearly knew how important the association with a top business school was to Milken and negotiated for months to protect the institution's downside—both financial and reputational. The dean may have been a friend of Milken's, but all the evidence suggests Feldberg picked his pocket, which may be why the deal did not seem to engender anything like the level of controversy it had at the University of Chicago. As influential professor of finance Bruce Greenwald said, the arrangement "looked like money for nothing and a chance for some people to make salary supplements for adapting their courses."[94]

Although the contracts were not public and they varied somewhat among the graduate business schools—Columbia, Stanford, Chicago, London School of Economics, and Carnegie Mellon—each appeared to contain broadly similar provisions based on the template negotiated by Feldberg. On the one hand, the universities got meaningful upfront payments (Columbia reported receiving $2 million and assurances of at least $20 million over a five-year period),[95] based on a share of ongoing revenues that would be convertible at their option into a collective 20 percent of the company. In addition, the university maintained veto rights over how their logos would be used and even over who other partners would be. On the other hand, beyond being able to claim the association and voluntary assistance from selected faculty in course development, UNext got very little, as all of the agreements were nonexclusive.

A basic problem with many distance-learning models is the extent to which they ignore the central socialization role of most educational experiences. At different levels of instruction, the nature of this role varies but is no less critical to the overarching objective of developing high-functioning citizens. Elementary school introduces children to peers from a broader range of cultures, backgrounds, personalities, and abilities with whom they will need to interact in the real world. In college, students have a heightened level of independence that requires them to master a complex variety of interdependent tasks and human relationships, completely apart from any selected curriculum. The point is not that online learning can have no useful role to play in delivering education; rather, it is that unless the purpose of the enterprise is fully understood, the business is unlikely to be a pedagogical or financial success.

The aims of an MBA are complex and quite different from those of many other educational programs generally or graduate programs specifically. Unlike most forms of graduate study, and even many undergraduate programs, the MBA does not purport to confer domain expertise or professional training in any specific area. Rather it is analogous to a mini two-year liberal arts degree across more than a half-dozen different business-related disciplines—from accounting and finance to organizational psychology and marketing. What distinguishes the MBA is the relative importance of the social over the pedagogical in defining the aims of the overall program. Although programs and philosophies vary widely, class format is often as important as class substance, with some mix of team-building exercises, group work, "case method" teaching, and real-world projects typically defining aspects of the curriculum. In addition, the importance and experience of the social aspects of the MBA extend far beyond the classroom. MBA students have all been in the workforce and are looking to move up in their current industry or, more often, to move into something new altogether. Thus, a business school's alumni network and classmates play a critical role in this regard, both upon graduation and throughout a student's subsequent career.

These qualities of an MBA have two broad implications. The first is that if a student does not get into one of the very top programs—with access to a strong network of alumni and high-quality peers who will watch their back as they develop professionally—it is a terrible waste of money. Professor Jeffrey Pfeffer at Stanford has shown how economically unattractive it is to get an MBA from something other than a top fifteen school, particularly when compared with a graduate degree in a specific subject or with just continuing to work.[96]

The second implication is that an MBA seems like one of the least sensible programs to deliver electronically. Great software can facilitate, replicate, and even enhance human interaction in some contexts, including learning. UNext, however, was spending $1 million per class to develop curriculum in the late 1990s when the technology solutions available were limited and broadband penetration was less than 10 percent. Although UNext marketing materials emphasized interactivity and multimedia capabilities, those capabilities were designed to be "delivered adequately on dial up connections" and were usually supplemented with "textbooks and printed course packs."[97] The online courses were being touted as cutting edge for the time. However, when Rosenfield was looking for underwriters to take the company public in 1999, I had the opportunity to view a course as part of a group of bankers at Morgan Stanley. As Rosenfield breathlessly sold the notion that we were watching the "killer app" of the Internet, he clicked on an icon to reveal a short video of an elderly Nobel Prize winner mumbling the basics of the capital asset pricing model. None of us were impressed.

Another critical aspect of the value of an MBA that even Professor Pfeffer concedes can have value is the "signaling" role that a degree from a top school can play for employers. Corporations often view the selectivity of the most elite institutions as a useful form of prescreening, and many only actively recruit from the very best schools. But UNext was associated with such institutions in only the most tenuous way possible, and its students had no access to their faculty or alumni network. Supposedly, UNext students could say they took a course developed in connection with one of these respected institutions, but any credentials received would be from a new entity that UNext named Cardean University, which had no established brand value. Not only did Cardean have no resonance in the job market, but it also did not have the accreditation needed to offer MBAs in the first place. Accrediting bodies generally require several years of review before providing their imprimatur, and UNext was burning cash at a remarkable clip. Although it was able to sell individual courses for a few hundred dollars each in the meantime, this was a far cry from the $25,000–$30,000 they would charge for an MBA. UNext quietly got around this problem by buying the shell of an established correspondence school called ISIM University, which was accredited though not by the more prestigious regional accreditation bodies. UNext soon began offering Cardean MBAs.[98]

To be fair, the MBA market for students who intend to continue working while taking the courses—usually either because they can't afford not to or because their employer has sponsored them to do so as part of an internal development initiative—has some important differences from the market for traditional MBAs. UNext initially focused on the corporate part of the market and did succeed in making a few high-profile sales. This market, however, was an even more competitive space in which UNext appeared to be operating at a meaningful disadvantage. On the one hand, all of the top MBA programs—both those affiliated with Cardean and the rest—offered a variety of so-called executive MBA (EMBA) programs that bestow a real MBA from one of these institutions. Although mostly delivered live, these degrees are structured creatively, making use of weekends and short intensive periods of instruction, allowing students to matriculate while being fully employed. On the other hand, pure online MBAs had become an increasingly crowded field, with the established, fully accredited, bricks-and-mortar, for-profit universities already enrolling many thousands in their fully or partially online degree programs. Those programs, as well as a number of others established by public and private nonprofit institutions, were able to heavily leverage their existing staff and infrastructure. Although Cardean was priced far below the traditional EMBA programs, it was priced far above the competing online programs.

Although the existing for-profit higher education industry had obvious structural advantages over UNext, it is worth noting that pure online operations were not the most profitable ventures in the industry. The most successful businesses were those that leveraged their physical regional strength or their scale for delivering targeted degree programs. Although these businesses did build complementary distance and hybrid programs, in the online realm, leaders in particular geographic or subject matter niches were all suddenly able to compete more broadly, putting pressure on pricing and profitability. (The largest online degree program—Apollo's Phoenix Online—already had almost 20,000 online degree students by the end of 2000.[99]) In addition, completion rates for online programs—an issue that would be a focus of the future regulatory problems—were far below that of traditional delivery methods.[100] Notably, all of the major online degree programs (except for the very largest) outsourced the learning management system (LMS) on which they delivered their programs. UNext initially followed the sensible model of outsourcing its LMS; however, to secure IBM as its first major high-profile client, it agreed to use IBM's Lotus LearningSpace platform in a kind of barter transaction. Although this seemed like a win-win, the product was poorly designed for delivering the kind of program envisioned by UNext. Rather than select a more appropriate LMS provider, presumably one that was being successfully used by any of the other online graduate programs, the company decided to spend tens of millions of dollars to design a proprietary LMS.

The UNext approach reflected a variety of faulty assumptions not only about the size and nature of the potential market for its product in general but also about the value to students and employers of the limited association with well-regarded institutions and famous academics. The company even hired Roger Schank, a world-renowned cognitive psychologist who founded the Institute for the Learning Sciences at Northwestern University, to develop the curriculum. After Schank was publicly quoted questioning the company's actual commitment to education, he was quickly fired.

Many new ventures shift their focus and strategies as they learn more about the market they are serving or trying to redefine. UNext's most fateful decision, however, was to spend hundreds of millions quickly and commit to a particular model well before it had been able to test the validity of any of its ultimately faulty assumptions. "The whole business model depends on making huge up-front investment," the company's president and COO Richard Strubel, a former manufacturing executive, conceded as early as 2001. "I don't know that anyone will ever do it again, and they certainly won't do it the way we did it."[101] Although Don Norman, another distinguished academic and Schank's replacement at UNext, continues to defend the quality of the courses, he conceded that the business model was fundamentally flawed. Recalling a "successful" early pitch to a major global financial institution in the market for online MBA courses, Norman said their human resources executives had surveyed the landscape and declared that UNext courses "were the best." The bad news came soon thereafter. The institution could "only think of two or three people at the company worldwide to go through [the course]."

From the beginning, UNext was characterized by a remarkable combination of arrogance and naïveté. The arrogance stemmed from a conviction that the association with Nobel Prize winners, world-renowned institutions, and leading academic authorities would almost, of necessity, translate into a large, successful business that could attract endless capital.[102] The naïveté extended to almost every area in which domain expertise would be needed to actually build a large, successful business—product, market, regulation, and financing. In the 1999 meeting with Rosenfield, it was not just the pedestrian nature of the product and the narrow market they were targeting that struck the Morgan Stanley bankers. When the hyperconfident Rosenfield, who himself had no public company experience except for working at a subsidiary of the failed Nextera, introduced us to the CFO, whom he proposed would manage the IPO, we were speechless. Not only had Patrick J. Keating, the former finance executive from Carnegie Mellon, never been a public company CFO, but he had also never previously worked at a for-profit institution of any kind.[103]

The Internet boom fed this natural hubris. The NASDAQ peaked in March 2000, just around the time that UNext started to test its first handful of courses with its first handful of corporate clients.[104] By then, a third of all U.S. colleges and universities already offered their own distance-learning courses.[105] Once UNext was up and running with its full MBA, Cardean was still a tiny fraction of the size of, and had a lower level of accreditation than, its for-profit online competitors.[106] Nonetheless, UNext continued to raise new equity from sophisticated investors such as the Pritzker family at valuations that reached as high as $800 million—which would make it, on an inflation-adjusted basis, a unicorn today.[107]

In 2001, the last reported outside money came into the company. Thomson Corporation, one of the largest higher education publishers at the time, announced a $38 million investment in connection with a vague "strategic partnership."[108] Around the same time, UNext, which had ballooned to 400 employees, announced its first job cuts. By the fall of that year, UNext reported plans to cut the remaining staff in half[109] and was deep in talks to renegotiate its financial arrangements with "partner" universities.[110] But even as it faced challenges in meeting its bills and attracting customers, UNext remained, as *The Red Herring* reported at the time, "high on hyperbole."[111] Rosenfield in particular was fond of referring to the hundreds of thousands of people employed by corporations in Brazil, China, and India as holding the "key to future success,"[112] although these would always represent a tiny minority of the company's modest customer base. In addition, throughout this period of crisis at UNext, Rosenfield kept busy with significant outside business interests. In addition to his continuing association with Lexecon, he worked on establishing a venture capital accelerator with the Pritzkers[113] and later became a founding partner in the Chicago office of investment bank Gleacher & Company, another UNext investor.[114]

By late 2001, UNext began to significantly shift its focus. It first decided to "lower its brow" and push short, two-hour corporate training courses, leading its hometown business rag to suggest that the "Harvard of the Internet is morphing into something more like DeVry."[115] The following year, the company began to market the MBA directly to consumers online, competing head to head with businesses like not just DeVry but also Apollo and the entire established sector.[116] At the time, the market capitalizations of those companies were in the billions, and each had marketing budgets in the hundreds of millions.

The last significant strategic move during Rosenfield's tenure as CEO was the 2003 launch of an entirely new online nonprofit university called Ellis College, which was part of New York Institute of Technology (NYIT). NYIT is a well-established nonprofit technical training institute, and Ellis College would serve as NYIT's online arm, enabling them to extend their reach to "serve working adults worldwide with excellence," according to NYIT president Edward Guiliano.[117] NYIT essentially outsourced the bulk of the Ellis operations to UNext. Structured not unlike the earlier deals with the five prestigious business schools, NYIT received a cut of the revenues and stock options in Cardean. In the press announcement, Rosenfield appeared to repudiate the previous business model for which he had raised nearly $200 million: "Students want to be associated with a recognized accredited site-based university via distance" to provide "the best of both worlds."[118]

By the time UNext had established this alliance, it no longer referenced any association with the five prestigious business schools that had once been central to its identity.[119] Thomson, the educational publisher who had invested in 2001, would also soon negotiate an exit from the unfruitful alliance in which it would sell back its entire stake in the company in return for the promise of no future legal entanglements.[120] When Rosenfield stepped down a few months later, he pointed to the management of the rapid growth of Ellis College as the new CEO's primary task.[121]

Not until the court filings in the ugly litigation between Cardean Learning Group (UNext officially changed its name to this in 2005) and NYIT were released, five years after the launch of Ellis, did it become clear just how important this venture had been to UNext. NYIT filed suit when it realized that its options were worthless and Cardean had failed to pay the $2 million owed to NYIT. In its countersuit, Cardean conceded that it had staked its entire future on Ellis. "Without a services agreement with Ellis University," the documents stated, "Cardean will have no business function and cease to exist as a going concern."[122] In 2010, Cardean's few remaining assets were quietly sold for scrap to K12 Inc., another Milken-affiliated company, where they still sit, unbeknownst to most shareholders, in a subsidiary called Capital Education LLC.[123]

It is striking how different the enterprise begun a decade earlier was from the one that emerged from reading the court filings in the ultimately settled lawsuit. Rosenfield had once bragged to the *New York Times* that he had spent nearly $100 million on developing courses before receiving a single dollar of tuition[124] and that he was focused exclusively on developing relationships with high-profile institutions, academics, corporations, and investors. By the end, however, the company had focused on developing relationships with poor working adults dreaming of a better life. How Cardean established and managed those relationships would become an issue not just for NYIT but also for accrediting bodies and federal prosecutors.

In its lawsuit, NYIT complained about privacy breaches of student records, and accreditors cited "substantive and pervasive problems" related to "administrative oversight, integrity," and "quality issues" more generally.[125] But the most serious problem that attracted the attention of the federal authorities was Cardean's illegal use of recruiters to attract poor students eligible for federal loans and grants. The problem was that Cardean paid these recruiters a bounty—a practice clearly banned under federal law as "incentive compensation"—based on how many students they enrolled. Although NYIT was unaware of the activity, it shared in a $4 million government settlement with Cardean for failure to provide oversight.[126]

Cardean was not the only degree-granting online learning venture to end ignominiously over this period. Caliber, the Wharton School's e-partner, filed for bankruptcy. Fathom, a for-profit online consortium launched in 2000 by Columbia and a dozen university partners, shut down in 2003. A variety of other individual universities announced their own online plans with much fanfare, only to pull the plug as losses mounted.[127]

In 2008, just as what was left of Cardean was collapsing, along with its relationship to NYIT, a researcher at the University of Prince Edward Island coined the term MOOC, or massive open online courses. There continues to be much debate over the distinguishing features of MOOCs, but the characteristic that most differentiates these courses from the many distance-learning efforts that had preceded them is the emphasis on "openness." Although even the meaning of this term has been the subject of controversy, it broadly refers to the notion that content should be free or almost free. This idea is consistent with the key tenets of the open educational resource movement, which is the spiritual inspiration for MOOCs. Such was the momentum behind this idea that the *New York Times* declared 2012 "the Year of the MOOC."[128]

Given how difficult it was to build a sustainable, pure distance-learning model when charging for the service, the insistence on "free" can only be expected to make it an even harder slog. This does not mean that MOOCs will not be able to provide socially valuable services. A number of nonprofits and public entities, from Khan Academy to edX, have already done so. That said, however, these organizations have not found permanent solutions to the challenges long faced by the for-profit distance-learning market—that is, low completion rates, an often less-than-rich educational experience, an inability to achieve the social objectives of the educational experience, and weak acceptance of the credential by employers and traditional universities. To these long-standing obstacles are now added, of course, increased competition from the nonprofit entities serving the same markets. But these are still relatively early days.

For the for-profit enterprises, however, the huge obstacle to any MOOC business model is the structural tension between the high cost of curriculum creation and the inability to charge for it.[129] The two largest for-profit MOOCs—Coursera and Udacity—have attracted high-profile investors and leaders.[130] Coursera hired former Yale University president Richard Levin, another leader without business operating experience, as CEO. At least his tenure at Yale was more successful than Benno Schmidt's had been. In addition, the business Levin is running is in the same general domain as his university career—unlike Schmidt, who moved from Yale into K–12 education.

That said, these are very different businesses—one an established long-time leader with prodigious barriers to entry, the other a start-up with new well-financed competitors emerging all the time. The disclosure in 2015 that Levin had been given an $8.5 million payout as an "additional retirement benefit" from Yale on stepping down—more revenues than Coursera had at the time—was a reminder of just how different the businesses are.[131] Despite the fundamental challenges faced by these business models, Udacity has now graduated to "unicorn"-level valuations.[132]

Both Udacity and Coursera have had to change their revenue model and pursue somewhat different paths, though both charge for certification and various premium services. Udacity has focused on getting corporates to pay for development of nano-degree courses that will pre-certify students for specific jobs at those companies.[133] Coursera is also working with corporates, but its aim is to develop "capstone projects" that it hopes will encourage more students to obtain certificates.[134] Both companies have modest revenues and remain unprofitable.

It is at least arguable that the broader aims of the open educational resource movement would be better served by being a bit less religious on the "openness" requirement. The evidence suggests that MOOCs are overwhelmingly taken advantage of by a well-heeled population that could afford to pay, thus undermining the basic democratization objectives that animate the movement. Presumably, payments by those who can afford it could subsidize outreach to those who cannot. Without a sustainable business model, however, everyone will need to rely on the kindness and continued financial capacity of nonprofits or public sources. This in itself, however, raises serious policy questions distinct from the issue of sustainability. Escalating costs of higher education at public and nonprofit institutions have been an increasing focus due to the magnitude of the resulting financial burden on students. The evidence suggests that these institutions are subsidizing the development of MOOCs, which in turn puts additional pressure on tuition costs. If the financial profile of those taking advantage of MOOCs is demonstrably stronger than those on campus, then the ideology of the open educational resource movement may be having the perverse effect of having the world's less-well-off fund the educational aspirations of their wealthier counterparts.

As the next chapter shows, there are some sustainable distance-learning models, but they violate the extreme version of the principle of openness. At some point, the movement and these companies may need to decide which principle is more important—actually educating people or the principle of openness. Of course, as the experience of UNext demonstrates, even if the lack of openness may be a necessary condition for a robust distance-learning business model, it is far from a sufficient condition.

Milken's efforts in the digital realm suffered from many of the same infirmities that hamstrung his efforts in more traditional education businesses. In addition to the consistent lack of focus, the contrast between Milken's financial sophistication and his naivety when it came to market structure and execution is striking. Timing the market opportunistically can yield superior results, but Milken remained a long-term holder of most of these investments far beyond their sell-by dates. His continued commitment to these enterprises is in some sense laudable. However, without an understanding of how to build sustainable value in education, that commitment is self-destructive. We now turn to the topic of the shared characteristics of the most successful education businesses.

CHAPTER FIVE

What Makes a Good Education Business?

THE PRECEDING CHAPTERS examined a wide range of high-profile investments in education that ended badly. Not all educational investments end disastrously, though more than their fair share have done so. Before trying to turn these cautionary tales into teaching moments, it is worth standing back and asking, more broadly, which characteristics successful education businesses share. A few attractive education businesses have briefly appeared as supporting characters in the dramas surrounding the failed undertakings that have been the primary focus of this book so far. These businesses will now take center stage, as we examine the key attributes of the most lucrative educational undertakings.

The question of what makes a good educational business is not fundamentally different from what makes a good business in general. Investors who believe there is a difference are likely to experience poor returns. Businesses do consistently well when they can do something that others cannot. Being uniquely positioned to perform a particular activity is unusual but essential for sustainable superior performance. If others can do the same thing, it is a sure bet they will. Performance then, by definition, will no longer be superior. The term for this relatively rare quality is *competitive advantage*. Although often mistakenly assigned to any number of attractive business characteristics, competitive advantage refers to something very specific: a structural barrier that prevents competitors from simply replicating the results of a successful business.

It should not be surprising that the terms *competitive advantage* and *barriers to entry* are interchangeable. Without barriers to entry, a business cannot long enjoy an advantage over competitors that will quickly do the obvious—enter. This process of new entry will hurt not only relative performance but also absolute performance, as competition for customers dampens revenues, and competition for resources raises costs. These generic observations are true for all businesses, but their application in the context of particular industry sectors can look very different. It is not that the general categories of relevant competitive advantage are different. Rather, it is that industry structure determines which categories are most likely to manifest themselves and in what form.

In *The Curse of the Mogul: What's Wrong with the World's Leading Media Companies*, my coauthors and I applied the framework of competitive advantage to the media industries.[1] That framework, however, was largely lifted from an earlier work by one of my coauthors, *Competition Demystified: A Radically Simplified Approach to Business Strategy*, which applies to all industries.[2] It is a testament to the consistency of the key categories of competitive advantage that they are so readily adaptable across sectors. In *Curse*, we broadly defined the media industry as "the production and distribution of information and entertainment."[3] The education industry, however, represents a small subset of the sector so defined—namely, the facilitation of the portion of "information and entertainment" that is directed toward personal or professional development. As this chapter shows, although the key categories of competitive advantage are still the same, important lessons can be drawn from seeing their successful application within the educational ecosystem.

A more detailed discussion of the landscape of competitive advantage can be found in either of the two books referenced. For our purposes, it will suffice to highlight the four sources of advantage most pertinent to education—scale, demand, supply, and regulation—and then quickly turn to examples of prosperous educational businesses that have built and continue to reinforce these advantages. These four advantages can all be supercharged by efficient operations, though efficiency does not constitute a structural advantage. Because operating effectiveness—and the absence of it—has played such an important role in the outcome of investments in the educational sector, it is treated separately.

Size Doesn't Matter, but Scale Does

Michael Milken pursued a strategy of putting together the largest collection of assets dedicated to the increase of human capital.

University of Chicago Nobel Laureate Gary Becker, who also sat on the UNext advisory board, popularized the theory of human capital.[4] The obstacle to Milken's success was not any flaw in that theory; rather, it was the fact that human capital is not an industry. Industries are made up of companies related to each other in terms of their primary business activities, not their overarching objective. Amalgamating subscale businesses in different industries cannot establish an enterprise of scale, no matter its ultimate size in absolute terms.

Scale is a relative concept, not an absolute one. The benefits it bestows are relative to peers within the relevant competitive set. No matter how large Edison Schools had gotten elsewhere, no number of private plane trips by Benno Schmidt to Hawaii to establish a beachhead would have detracted from the structural disadvantage vis-à-vis any larger private school networks already operating in Hawaii. Yet, this may not seem obvious—why wouldn't a global network of K–12 schools be able to do everything cheaper and better than a small but dense cluster of institutions limited to Hawaii? The answer goes to the real source of the scale advantage at the heart of most great historic educational franchises: fixed costs. Scale matters most when fixed costs matter most relative to the business's overall cost structure. With large fixed costs, the operator serving the most customers will have a significant advantage due to its ability to spread those costs over more unit sales. If the costs of a business were entirely variable and increased proportionally as it grew, there would be absolutely no advantage to scale. The extent of the advantage is determined by how relatively important fixed costs are and how relatively large the business is compared to the next competitor.

The problem with Edison was twofold. First, the cost structure of the K–12 school business is largely variable. The majority of the costs are specific to the individual school—that is, the teachers and staff, the real estate and maintenance, the student materials and equipment. There are some advantages from absolute size— in procurement, for instance, volume discounts would undoubtedly be available on chalk and iPads. And definitely some back- and mid-office functions can and should be effectively centralized. These aspects of the business, however, still represent a tiny fraction of the cost base. Although Schmidt's outlandish salary was clearly a fixed cost, the private aircraft to Hawaii was a variable cost. Second, much of what is thought of as traditional fixed costs in school management—administration, school relations and lobbying, and even curriculum development—has a significant variable component. It is simply not practical to manage many key functions centrally in a geographically dispersed organization, which is why even Edison established a number of regional administrative hubs to deal with everything from teacher recruitment and relations to marketing to parents and bureaucrats. The staff or consultants Schmidt left behind in Hawaii needed to have local relationships and expertise to succeed.

In the K–12 educational realm, even domains such as curriculum, which conceptually would seem to lend itself to exclusively central investment, actually require meaningful local customization. A major textbook publisher must produce literally hundreds of thousands of SKUs of its core products to respond to local requirements. The impact of the much-touted national "common core" standards initiative has reduced this task, but only at the margin. In fact, after publishers and other curriculum developers collectively invested hundreds of millions of dollars to align their products in anticipation of common core implementation, the political backlash at the state level over a perceived federal takeover of local educational prerogatives has meant that much of those expenditures were wasted.

In recent years, a number of international chains of for-profit K–12 schools have emerged, attracting significant capital from sophisticated investors and high valuations as public companies. Surely, it could be argued, this emergence demonstrates the folly of the assertion that there is little advantage from global, rather than local or regional, scale. Three of the highest-profile international chains are Nord Anglia Education, GEMS Education, and Cognita Schools. A closer look at all three of these businesses reveals the opposite.

Nord Anglia is a Hong Kong–based company that went public in 2013. GEMS is a Dubai-based business, controlled by Sunny Varkey, that recently attracted expansion capital from Blackstone and two Middle Eastern sovereign wealth funds. GEMS also had a brief and highly unprofitable association with Whittle (see chapter 1). Cognita—now backed by Kohlberg Kravis Roberts, along with its original funder Bregal Capital—started as a roll-up of independent UK schools under the leadership of a controversial former chief inspector of schools in England.

Both GEMS and Nord Anglia offer the International Baccalaureate (IB) course of study to standardize curriculum development across schools in its far-flung operations around the world. In practice, both have had to adopt a variety of other tailored curricula to operate effectively in certain countries. In addition, as Nord Anglia notes on its website, whichever curriculum is being used must be adapted "to embrace local culture and conditions." GEMS offers eight curricula across seventy schools in fourteen countries. Nord Anglia offers four curricula across forty-two schools in fifteen countries. Cognita, by contrast, though also offering the IB, emphasizes the benefits of a *lack* of standardization: "Our non-prescriptive, market-driven and agnostic approach to curricula allows us to identify and then invest in any projected imbalance between supply and demand for a curriculum in any market."5

The most significant commonality among Nord Anglia, GEMS, and Cognita is that their profits all come disproportionately from a small number of countries or regions in which they have a structural advantage, such as scale or a preferred regulatory position locally. When Nord Anglia went public in 2014 for the second time in its history, it touted its global network, even though more than half of its profitability (which was still less than 40 percent of its revenues) came from its operations in China. Until a major acquisition made the previous year, more than two-thirds of the profit had come from China. Thus, Nord Anglia had secured a unique position in the expatriate market (the only potentially available market for foreign operators in China) with multiple schools in the three largest cities and tuition typically paid by employers.

Although GEMS has not gone public, those who have seen its financials note that it generates most of its revenues—and maybe all of its profits—from its base operations in the Middle East. Almost fifty of the network's seventy schools are based in the United Arab Emirates, including twenty-nine in Dubai, the company's headquarters. The flagship school there is the most expensive in Dubai, another market with unusual characteristics in terms of a supply/demand imbalance for high-quality K–12 schools serving the expatriate community.6 Similarly, while Cognita operates sixty-seven schools across seven countries in Europe, Latin America, and Southeast Asia, fully forty-three of those schools are in the UK.

The downside of failing to have an adequate local focus is demonstrated in the experience of another international school group, Meritas. After a ten-year global roll-up strategy backed by private equity firm Sterling Partners, it was unable to find a buyer for the entirety of the business.[7] In the end, Sterling was forced to sell to Nord Anglia selected assets of Meritas that fit well into its geographic footprint but keep a handful of those that did not.[8]

The diversity and fragmentation of the private K–12 school market around the world suggests that scale is not the dominant characteristic of these businesses—except potentially within certain narrow geographic niches. By contrast, the U.S. K–12 school textbook publishing has long been dominated by a handful of players. This difference reflects the continuing value of scale in textbook publishing, though that scale is realized on a country-by-country basis due to differences in language, curricula, and distribution channels. An examination of this sector provides a window into the typical sources of fixed-cost scale in education broadly.

Many people seem to think that scale in textbook publishing comes from the actual manufacturing of the product. This thought is not surprising since, as we saw from the story of Houghton Mifflin, many publishers started life as printers. But printing has long been an outsourced function for all the major players. Distribution of books is still undertaken in part by the publishers themselves, with the large physical warehouse and logistical infrastructure a significant source of fixed costs. But even more and more of this facet of the business has begun to be outsourced and, in any case, is not the biggest source of fixed costs.[9] The two primary sources of fixed-cost scale in education generally are content development on the one hand and sales and marketing on the other.

Before their combination, Houghton and Harcourt were each spending in the neighborhood of $100 million annually on "plate." As explained earlier, the combined business collapsed under the weight of the combined cash needs. This did not mean that the combination wasn't strategically sensible or that there weren't some genuine synergies in content development that rationalized the combined offerings. Rather it reflected that the combined business had far too much debt and weak operating management. Indeed, the need to relentlessly invest that quantum of capital each year in order to be a credible national K–12 competitor is precisely what has made it such an exclusive club and such a profitable business. Although the nature of the investment has shifted more recently toward software, this shift has not dramatically affected the overall level of fixed costs required to compete effectively.

Given the required recurring investment in product, it is critical for any major publisher to put in place the sales and marketing infrastructure required to most effectively monetize that investment nationally. Even with the adoption of national common core standards, states and localities have additional requirements in selecting a curriculum provider. Although this customization introduces a variable element to cost structure, the commonalities are greater than the differences. Without a national sales and marketing footprint, it is difficult to generate enough sales to justify the content investment. In addition, a well-run organization can leverage its national sales and product expertise to the key levers and adaptations required to compete most effectively locally.

Interestingly, although scale in most K–12 content businesses is defined nationally rather than regionally or locally, it is often defined by discipline or by grade. Certain publishers have particular strength in K–8, while others focus on the higher grades. Similarly, each major textbook publisher has focused on specific subjects that is its forte. When Apollo Global Management (the private equity firm, not to be confused with Apollo Education, operator of the University of Phoenix)[10] bought McGraw-Hill Education in a $2.5 billion LBO, the K–12 portion of the business (which was a minority of the overall operation) was actually losing money. Among other things, Apollo identified that McGraw-Hill had felt an obligation to participate across all disciplines and grades, even those in which it was subscale.

After the purchase, Apollo exited those unprofitable pieces and reinvested where the company was a leader, turning the segment solidly profitable. Since the 2012 purchase, Apollo has been able to return its entire original investment, just on the back of the cash flows from the K–12 business. In September 2015, McGraw filed to go public, with Apollo still owning 100 percent of the equity.[11] The contrast with Barry O'Callaghan's financial stewardship of Houghton highlights that the difference between them was not a question of scale. Notably, an even larger LBO of a pure higher education textbook business—Apax Partners's 2007 $7.8 billion buyout of Thomson Learning—also ended in bankruptcy.[12] Although the distribution channel of higher education publishing is completely different, the success of McGraw-Hill Education—whose primary profit source continues to flow from this segment—demonstrates that the problem for Apax was not a lack of scale advantages. Like Houghton, the problem was simply too much debt; it had the wrong capital structure for a business with this level of ongoing and highly seasonal capital requirements.

Scale on the Internet: Network Effects

The initial euphoria around the potential for the digital revolution to quickly expand the reach and effectiveness of educational products reflected a variety of misconceptions regarding the structure of educational markets and the Internet's economic impact. The Internet radically increases product and pricing transparency for the consumer and can significantly reduce the fixed costs entailed in production, marketing, and distribution for the producer. This is great news for the user; for the operating business, however, the benefits of any reduction in fixed costs are overwhelmed by the increased competition that comes with the corresponding reduction in barriers to entry. As a result, fixed-costs scale—historically the major source of competitive advantage in education—has become less strong and less prevalent than it once was. This does not mean, however, that scale does not continue to be highly relevant. With the diminution of the prevalence of fixed-cost scale has come an increase in the frequency of an entirely different kind of scale: network effects.[13]

The Internet is itself a network of networks linked by a common language. Although in many instances the killer app of the Internet feels like it is the destruction of competitive advantage, its structure facilitates the possibility of network effects in a variety of contexts that were previously impossible. The benefit of network effects comes not so much from lowering unit costs with every new customer but from every new customer actually making the product better. As a result, the biggest network delivers the best product, which is an inherent characteristic of any marketplace—a new buyer makes it a better place for the sellers, and every new seller makes it a better place for every buyer.[14] The virtuous circle of network effects is why eBay has 30 percent margins, whereas straight e-commerce businesses like Amazon struggle to achieve any margin. With every new buyer and seller, the eBay ecosystem becomes more valuable to all participants. Amazon has a traditional consumer retail business model that unquestionably provides a great service, but its value to the customer does not vary in the same way with the number of other users.

Relatively few education businesses have exploited network effects to powerful advantage, though more are emerging to do so. One of the most dramatic and well-established of these is Turnitin,[15] founded in 1998 by four University of California—Berkeley students as an online peer review system. Turnitin's focus shifted, however, to address an exploding problem in both K–12 and higher education. That problem, like its solution, was made possible by the Internet: rampant plagiarism. Developing clever software to detect plagiarism does not feel, by its nature, to be a scale business—whether of the fixed cost or the network effects variety. Indeed, intuitively, one might imagine that a handful of smart coders with adequate caffeine (or harder stuff) could create a serviceable product in a relatively short time. But Turnitin has both varieties of scale in abundance.

The possibility of powerful competitive advantage in plagiarism software is made possible by the way people cheat. If the primary culprit were the copying and pasting of Wikipedia entries, then barriers to entry would be few. In practice, however, cheating in the digital age happens like it did in the analog age—copying off a friend. That said, how you communicate with a friend and what constitutes a friend have changed radically. Craning one's neck or late-night "study" sessions with a classmate have been replaced with texts and visits to anonymous sharing sites.

The danger of these developments for the detection business is obvious: there is no central repository of the material being plagiarized. But this is where network effects come in. Turnitin is an institutional subscription sale, and all students submit their work electronically for analysis. Turnitin is the sole source of submitted work to compare against other submissions anywhere on the network. Every new institution on the network makes the product better. Current customers have every incentive to encourage their peers to join, which is the best and cheapest marketing a company could wish for.

Luckily for Turnitin, despite its overwhelming relative scale advantage built as it added new clients around the world over almost twenty years, there is still plenty of white space filled with institutions in denial. That space gets smaller with every predictable high school or university plagiarism scandal (or with every scandal involving U.S. presidential candidates or a German minister). Once the decision is made to address the problem, the choice is between the product that has the relevant database to check and a variety of lower-priced competitors that do not.

It was observed that the Internet is generally the enemy of fixed-cost scale economies. Exceptions to this observation are cloud-based distributed software businesses like Turnitin. Unlike traditional software businesses, which require significant variable implementation and maintenance for each customer, software-as-a-service (SaaS) models are much more reliant on central fixed costs. The trick, of course, is to develop a product that gets customer traction quickly enough to establish enough relative scale to have a significant advantage. Turnitin's continuous software investment since 1998 and its corresponding huge customer base have clearly created a complementary fixed-cost advantage that could not be easily replicated. The net impact is that Turnitin's profitability is far superior to that of any of the textbook publishers, even in their best years.

A traditional-scale software business but without network effects is eCollege. Developed in the same era as UNext and also targeting the distance-learning market in higher and continuing education, eCollege thrived where UNext failed. By 2007, when it was acquired by Pearson for half a billion dollars, eCollege had become the leading outsourced manager of U.S. distance-learning programs operated by colleges and universities.[16]

The contrast between UNext and eCollege could not be starker. UNext focused on relationships with highly bureaucratic, prestigious brands that were happy to get "money for nothing" but cared far more about preserving their exclusivity and reputation than about expanding their reach. eCollege focused on relationships with commercially oriented institutions—not just for-profit, but public and nonprofit as well—whose mission was delivering skills to precisely the populations of working adults for whom distance learning provided essential flexibility. "Our model student got home from work, fed the kids, put them to bed and then went to school online," said early investor and eCollege CEO Oakleigh Thorne. "That created a set of needs that we focused hard on serving, namely the system had to be dependable, it had to be easy to use (even at low connection speeds) and it had to be engaging enough to keep a tired mom awake."[17]

UNext structured its institutional relationships with large upfront payments and minimum payment commitments, irrespective of actual enrollments. In contrast, eCollege was structured under long-term relationships, with incentives aligned and payments tied exclusively to the number of students in courses using the platform. Most relevantly, eCollege identified a narrow domain that structurally lent itself to the existence of a small number of industry utilities, which, once adopted effectively, would be costly to switch—namely, a software and service platform on which to run an institution's distance-learning programs. UNext focused its investment on developing "better" versions of online MBA courses that were already developed by many others and that a long list of newer entrants had also committed to developing. Even worse, rather than using a scale platform like eCollege to deliver the courses, UNext decided to develop its own proprietary learning management system (LMS), which was as foolish as it would have been for eCollege to decide to develop its own courses.

Ultimately Pearson folded eCollege into a new initiative to grab a piece of an emerging adjacent opportunity—online program management (OPM).[18] Where LMS providers focus on delivering a scalable platform to institutions, OPM operators are the comprehensive outsourced provider of everything needed to establish an online program other than instruction—not just technology but everything from student recruiting, on-boarding, and retention to sometimes even curriculum development and tutoring.[19] Like the original UNext business model, OPMs take a share of the overall tuition bill in return for the services and for footing the bill for the upfront cost of establishing the program—which can run into the many millions of dollars. The attraction of the OPM sector, however, was clear: it was large and growing fast. By 2015, after only a few short years, OPM had established itself as a billion dollar industry with half of colleges surveyed either customers or planning to be.[20]

Pearson's commitment to this sector was reflected in the $650 million acquisition of EmbanetCompass in 2012, five years after the purchase of eCollege.[21] Growth aside, given the diversity of services provided and types of institutions and programs served, there is at least a question as to whether the OPM sector has the same scale characteristics as the LMS sector. Indeed, a college survey revealed that the industry included not just Pearson, but thirty-five other competitors ranging from established companies to start ups, suggesting that barriers to entry are not high. The anemic level of profits reported, while not dispositive given the early stage and investments required, also gives pause. 2U, an OPM company founded in 2008 that went public in 2014 and focuses on serving elite universities, remains unprofitable.[22] Deltak.edu, an early OPM founded in 1997 was purchased by educational publisher John Wiley in 2012.[23] Although the business has continued to grow, it was still unprofitable in 2015.

Outside of software, most Internet businesses—both in education and otherwise—do not benefit significantly from fixed-cost scale. However, a number of such businesses in the educational realm do benefit purely from network effects. One exciting early-stage educational business that follows a traditional "marketplace" model is Teachers Pay Teachers (TpT). The business was founded by a New York City public school teacher who saw the benefits of facilitating the sharing of original educational materials among educators. Today, educators not only share but also sell and buy resources, with TpT taking a small fee on any transactions. Although only aggressively developed as an independent business in the past few years, TpT already has 3.5 million active members—about the same number as total K–12 schoolteachers in the United States. Those teachers have already earned close to $200 million by selling their materials on the site.

Many educational investors have lost money following the siren song of getting in early to benefit from the so-called first mover advantage. That advantage, however, does not come from being first—it comes from gaining scale. More often than not, being first is charity work for whoever comes later and is able to take advantage of your generous, free market research. Just ask the unhappy investors in Edison, UNext, or Amplify. The ability to gain scale quickly requires a level of stability in the structure of both market demand and delivery technology. If either is in significant flux, it is simply not possible to gain enough traction to swiftly corner the market. In online marketplace businesses, being first has often—though by no means universally—yielded scale. The basic technology of e-commerce is well accepted; if someone identifies a niche market in desperate need of transparency, the opportunity is there. It is early days, but TpT could be a kind of unicorn upon which venture capitalists should be far more focused—a business with an actual first mover advantage.

Demand Advantages: Keeping Customers Captive

As with all structural advantages, scale can be fragile. A deep-pocketed investor or new potential competitor who sees your success can always try to replicate it to split the market. The most effective way to protect a competitive advantage is to have a second one. All great business franchises have more than one competitive advantage. The competitive advantage most frequently paired with scale is on the demand side of the market—*customer captivity.*

Customer captivity can be as simple as habit or as complex as the switching costs involved in removing a product that has been integrated into a client's work flow. It provides important added protection for incumbents in battling insurgents hungry for its customers. A new entrant who is successful at perfectly copying an existing scale business and offering an identical product at an identical price may succeed at splitting new customers, but it won't get a single existing "captive" customer. Starting a price war won't help, because all the incumbent needs to do is announce that it will match any price and wait it out.

Every one of the scale education businesses profiled in this chapter has some element of customer captivity. In K–12 textbooks, the state adoption process ensures that, once selected, a publisher is protected until at least the next adoption cycle. In higher education textbooks, the protection for publishers is less formal but even more powerful: just try to get a tenured professor who has been using the same book for decades in an introductory calculus or economics class to change the text used. If a community college has successfully implemented the eCollege platform and is successfully growing the number of distance-learning classes it offers, the potential risks of replacing it with a new platform will loom very large indeed.

A number of the businesses we examined without significant competitive advantages could have been altered to facilitate their development. The core child-care business of Knowledge Universe had little customer captivity—a drop-off center in a strip mall may be the best alternative in a pinch, but it faces significant competition as a longer-term day-care solution—as almost half of the care provided for children up to four years of age is by a family member.[24] Even among the less than a quarter of children who are in some kind of center-based care, a variety of public and private options are usually available. The permanently crowded nature of the market and the often ad hoc nature of the need make customer captivity unlikely.

But what if the business model were turned on its head and the customer was an employer under a long-term arrangement to provide employees with a benefit of day care in a facility at or near the workplace?

In this case, captivity comes not only from the long-term nature of the contractual relationship but also from the potential backlash from employees if the benefit is removed or if the service provider is switched—particularly given the unique convenience that proximity provides. Starting in 1986, Bright Horizons, founded by a Bain consultant and his wife, pioneered the on-site child-care model. In 1987, the company was one of the first to receive funding from the new Bain Capital and used the capital to build its first twenty centers or so in the Boston area. Bain did very well on its investment when Bright Horizons went public in 1997.[25] A decade later, Bain took the company private again in a $1.3 billion LBO, which once more yielded stellar returns when the company went public a second time in 2013.

Although today Bright Horizons operates child-care and early learning centers for almost 150 of the Fortune 500, it took many years for it to secure its current market position. It did so through a combination of consistent organic growth, complemented by acquisitions that cemented regional dominance, established dominance in a new region, or added an important national complementary corporate client base across regions. Although the strongest barriers to entry remain local, the large corporate client focus made a strong national footprint a competitive differentiator in some instances.

In contrast, the first acquisition the Knowledge Universe undertook in this space was called Children's Discovery Centers of America (CDC), which itself had been rolling up child-care centers since 1983. A few years before Knowledge Universe purchased CDC in 1998, it had acquired a business called Prodigy that specialized in employer-sponsored child-care centers for blue-chip clients like General Motors and IBM. Knowledge Universe could have become the company Bright Horizons is today if it had done fewer acquisitions and focused on this part of the business, instead of pursuing a misguided strategy of trying to create scale and captivity in the part of the industry where structurally little exists. Even after decades of rolling up competitors, Knowledge Universe represents only 2.5 percent of the national child-care market, with dozens of competitors of comparable scale in the relevant local markets. Bright Horizons, by contrast, has 10X the share of the next largest competitor in the employer-sponsored market. Bright Horizons' valuation was more than three times what Knowledge Universe sold for in 2015.

Renaissance Learning, one of the earliest businesses to introduce technology into the classroom, also came to benefit from intense customer captivity. More than thirty years ago, a mother who wanted to be more involved in tracking her children's reading skills developed a series of multiple-choice tests based on popular titles by grade level. This became the computer-based reading assessment product Accelerated Reader, which continues to attract a fervent following among educators. Even before numerous studies established the product's efficacy in increasing children's interest in reading and skill level, it attracted enthusiastic teacher support because of the "unprecedented level of flexibility, control and time"[26] it afforded them.

Renaissance grew through sales to teachers and principals, supported by word of mouth. Its resulting footprint and credibility allowed it to launch not just an Accelerated Math product but also a broader formative reading and math assessment product, called STAR, that is sold primarily at the district, rather than school, level. STAR is now the most widely used assessment in K–12 schools, as the resulting scale across almost twenty million students supports development of predictive models and allows Renaissance to validly norm reference data across an unprecedented number of relevant dimensions and demographics. Teachers usually obtain results in fewer than twenty minutes. The intensity of loyalty to product has resulted in extraordinarily high renewal rates, even during inevitable periods of budget cuts, sometimes supported by heavy lobbying from local Parent Teacher Associations.

Supply Advantages: Leveraging the Learning Curve

The power of habit is such that many incumbent businesses enjoy at least some customer captivity. Alone and without meaningful switching costs, this advantage is unlikely to stand up long to a better or cheaper alternative; in conjunction with scale, however, it can be part of a formidable franchise. It is much more unusual to find corresponding sustainable advantages on the cost or supply side of the education market equation.

Many educational technology products tout their "proprietary technology," and yet the ability to deliver better and cheaper educational outcomes turns out to be a difficult thing to prove. It is not that all customers wait for proof—in fact, many institutional buyers of educational product appear to be driven by a need to own "the new shiny one."[27] In addition, the speed of innovation is such that, once proven, a plethora of promising and "shiny," if as yet unproven, alternatives will have emerged. Not withstanding the overblown claims and the challenges of measurement, digital technologies have enabled a much greater level of continuous product improvement of the kind that is a hallmark of "learning curve" advantages.

Businesses that are first down the learning curve are able to deliver superior product for less than those who come behind simply by virtue of their experience. This phenomenon has long been observed in a variety of low-tech businesses, but it is the ability to get continuous user feedback for the first time that has magnified the potential. Google describes learning curve advantages as the "secret sauce" that fills its ever-expanding competitive moat in the search engine industry.[28] The so-called data exhaust from educational SaaS platforms is a tool not just for improving the core product but also for strengthening customer captivity. It also often offers the opportunity to build entirely new revenue streams by separately selling the data or building new products on the back of it. Turnitin has benefited from the learning curve in precisely these ways. Its core plagiarism software algorithms are adjusted regularly to reflect institutional feedback. It has also been able to use its data to more inexpensively develop and introduce broader grading and writing effectiveness products.

Like many other buzzwords, however, the promise of "big data" has been far oversold compared with what has been delivered to date. In addition, as Joel Klein painfully learned, privacy and regulatory concerns will continue to be a check on the speed with which the promise can be translated into product. That said, "big data," particularly within domains in which the breadth and depth of information collected over time demonstrably improves the ability to deliver actionable insights, will undoubtedly move to the forefront of these supply advantages that are still a barrier-to-entry backwater in education.

Not just high-tech pure digital education businesses benefit from the learning curve. A modest student coaching business called InsideTrack has been shown to be remarkably effective at reducing dropout rates at the universities it serves.[29] In addition to these results on outcomes, over time, InsideTrack becomes better and better at delivering the same results with fewer and fewer resources. InsideTrack "learns" over time how to most effectively coach students facing the particular requirements needed to thrive at that particular institution. Although other coaching services exist, replacing InsideTrack with another after it has this advantage will be tough—the incumbent should be able to deliver the same or better results for less.

Regulation: We're Here to Help

The idea of regulation as a potential source of competitive advantage may seem counterintuitive given how much businesses complain about the pervasive influence of government on their operations. A recent survey of more than 1,300 "participants in the education ecosystem" cited regulation at the state and federal level as the first and second largest challenges, respectively, to successful sector investments.[30] On closer inspection, however, there is something often quite disingenuous, or at least misguided, about many of these grievances. Meeting regulatory requirements, although a financial burden, often has the effect of protecting scale incumbents from new competition by increasing the minimum level of fixed cost that must be incurred to enter the industry.

Many media industries are built on the back of exclusive licenses provided by federal or local government—the right to use a portion of the federal broadcast spectrum or being awarded a local cable franchise, for instance. Government intervention and oversight in these markets are designed to pursue a variety of public policy objectives, but it can sometimes affect market structure in ways that are at odds with these laudable aims. For instance, the Securities and Exchange Commission's creation of a limited number of nationally recognized statistical rating organizations was to ensure adequate transparency of the increasing complexity in financial markets. In the end, however, this system merely facilitated the establishment of three mega-agencies with well-documented failures during the financial crisis. The incremental regulations placed on the agencies in the aftermath will have the perverse effect of further entrenching their unassailable incumbent status.

No less impactful is the structure of the current high-stakes state adoption process in K–12 education. Although the large K–12 publishers complain about the huge financial outlays required to participate in these crucial competitions, it is precisely this government-imposed method of selection that has driven the industry's consolidation. As aggravating as it may be, the fact that there are only three remaining significant market participants, rather than the dozen that operated not so long ago, is certainly a preferable market structure from a share-holder perspective.

The pervasiveness of regulation in the educational sector specifi-cally flows from the simple fact that most of the money feeding the industry comes directly or indirectly from the government. In K–12 education, only about 10 percent of students attend a private school of any kind. Although prestigious private nonprofits may be what come to mind when one imagines the iconic symbols of American higher education, almost three-quarters of students attend public colleges. The balance—both for-profit and nonprofit—rely heavily on access to government funds for their survival. Even corporate training is often the result of specific regulatory certification requirements and is more broadly the subject of a complex web of government incentives.

The largest single chunk of federal government support for higher education comes in the form of loans and grants to low-income stu-dents. Although public universities still receive more funding from state than federal government, the explosion in these programs has resulted in federal funding overall now overtaking state funding for the first time.[31] These programs underpin access to a college educa-tion and historically have been made available to anyone meeting the applicable income thresholds who has been admitted to an accredited institution, regardless of whether it is public, nonprofit, or for-profit.

For-profit colleges have been a part of the landscape since the colonial era and were championed by Benjamin Franklin. Although a founder of the nonprofit University of Pennsylvania, Franklin was a fervent advocate of the kind of practical vocational instruction that would one day be a hallmark of for-profit education.[32] Until relatively recently, however, for-profit institutions served fewer than 1 percent of college graduates.[33] The modern era of for-profit education is usu-ally credited to John Sperling, who founded the University of Phoenix in 1976 as part of the Apollo Education Group, which he had started three years earlier. Like most of these schools, Phoenix was focused on working adults whose life responsibilities made the rigid sched-ules of traditional colleges impractical. In addition, initially at least, the University of Phoenix focused on selected vocational programs at campuses in Arizona and California.

When Apollo Education went public in 1994, it was not the first to do so—DeVry University had already gone public in 1991—but it opened the floodgates for a steady stream of IPOs in the sector that continued until the sector's collapse in 2010. The Apollo offering also signaled the beginning of an unprecedented bull run in the sector over the next fifteen years. At the beginning of 2010, there were more than a dozen public companies with a combined market capitalization approaching $25 billion. By then, the number of students enrolled at for-profit colleges had grown to almost 2 million, from just over 200,000 in 1995.[34]

This explosion in the number of students at for-profit colleges was not simply a testament to the power of Sperling's vision. It also reflected a series of government programs put into place beginning with the 1965 Higher Education Act and significantly expanded over the subsequent decades. These programs ultimately made it possible for anyone meeting the eligibility requirements to attend any eligible program at any eligible university using a combination of grants and federally subsidized loans. The result was that a key competitive differentiator became a for-profit school's effectiveness at convincing prospective students to tap these programs to enroll. The most significant fixed-cost scale advantage from being a large for-profit university had nothing to do with curriculum or outcomes—it was the marketing budget.

The result was that many of these for-profit institutions that once focused on a narrow set of vocational programs regionally now moved into a broad range of general topics, such as business, and sought to establish a national footprint. At the time of the 1994 offering, the University of Phoenix still operated in only six states in the Southwest plus Hawaii; by 2010, however, it was operating in forty states. Notably, although both student enrollment and the number of campuses operated by Apollo doubled between 2004 and 2010, profit margins were actually lower—suggesting limited scale benefits from this unfocused growth.

Aggressive industry expansion efforts were coupled with a variety of aggressive marketing efforts, many of which were subsequently shown to be at least unsavory and, in some cases, illegal. The level of loan defaults rose as student completion rates fell. The beginning of the end came with the announcement in July 2010 of proposed federal rules to significantly restrict the access of for-profit institutions to federal educational programs.[35] Although it took years before these rules were actually finalized,[36] the impact on the stocks of these companies was immediate. By the time the rules went into effect, enrollments at for-profit colleges had fallen dramatically, with more to come at most of these companies. Apollo's University of Phoenix, for instance, lost more than half of its nearly half a million students during this time.[37] In touting his success in getting the rules put in place over objections and court challenges from the industry, U.S. secretary of education Arne Duncan estimated that another 840,000 students were attending for-profit institutions that would currently fail the standards.

The rules would bar federal funding from programs in which graduates' loan payments exceed 12 percent of their total earnings. The articulated objective of the "gainful employment" regulations was to protect students "from becoming burdened by student loan debt they cannot repay" and was designed "to complement" a variety of other initiatives to prevent "fraud, waste and abuse, particularly at for-profit colleges."

Although these public policy aims sound laudable in themselves, two related aspects of this new regulatory regime are worth highlighting. First is that the rules apply exclusively to "career-oriented" vocational programs. Students who decide to pursue a degree in liberal arts—English literature, history, and general humanities remain top choices[38]—rather than focus on a specific marketable skill face no risk of not being able to use government loans and grants for their chosen institution. They can max out, regardless of their repayment prospects. The notion may be that because these programs do not aspire to provide preparation for gainful employment, they should not be judged by this standard. Interestingly, however, they are not judged by any standard. The absence of incentive for traditional public and nonprofit universities to measure their own performance manifests itself in a complete lack of interest by many in keeping track of any relevant metrics. They focus intensively on the number of applications and "yield" from acceptances, but little after that and almost nothing related to either skills acquisition or postgraduation success. This indifference has a number of follow-on effects, particularly in undermining broader efforts to study the impact of different pedagogical approaches. For example, one of the biggest problems in conducting research on the relative effectiveness of MOOCs is that there is no baseline to which it can be compared.

It would be wrong to conclude from this narrow focus, however, that the government is hostile to vocational training. Indeed, the recently announced proposal to make community colleges—the historic focus of which has been career-oriented training—absolutely free suggests quite the opposite.[39] Notably, if community college were free, the gainful employment regulations would never apply to their vocational programs, because there would be presumably no debt required to pay tuition. This fact foreshadows the second anomaly in the rules: they simply do not apply to public and nonprofit institutions (which together make up around 90 percent of U.S. college student enrollment) in the same way. Unlike for-profit universities, associate's and bachelor's degree programs at these schools are exempted from the gainful employment rules. Only their certificate programs are subject to the same review.

An argument can be made that for-profits have earned this heightened relative scrutiny. After all, almost half of student loan defaults are from students at for-profits. The government points out that the average tuition at a two-year for-profit institution is four times as much as at a public community college.[40] But the very fact that for-profit enrollments exploded in the face of this overwhelming price disadvantage suggests that maybe something is wrong at community colleges.[41] Although unsavory marketing practices certainly played some role, it is hard to believe that for-profit's responsiveness to the complex needs of this difficult-to-serve population was not a critical element of their growth. The data in fact suggest that student completion rates at community colleges are actually lower than for similar programs serving comparable student populations at for-profits.[42] Although it is true that default rates are much higher at for-profits, this is not that surprising given the relative price and resulting debt load. In addition, from a taxpayer perspective, it probably doesn't matter much whether their money is being wasted through direct state and local subsidies to bad public community colleges that keep the price low or through indirect federal subsidies to fund tuition for bad for-profit universities. The real question is how to most effectively—from both a cost and outcomes perspective—serve these nontraditional students.

Notably, when the gainful employment regulations were finalized in 2014, a key requirement of earlier draft proposals was mysteriously dropped. Under previously circulated draft regulations, schools would also be judged by an independent standard related to the frequency of student loan defaults. When pressed for an explanation for dropping this requirement, the government said, unconvincingly, that it was looking to "streamline" the regulations. For-profits, however, suspected that "the change was mostly about protecting community colleges," whose students consistently fell afoul of the rules despite having much lower borrowings.[43] What's more, the gainful employment calculations are made only for those who actually graduate, creating a potential incentive to encourage those considered likely to harm the statistics to drop out (much like the charge that charter schools manage low performers out to show high average test scores[44]).

Regardless of how one feels about the wisdom of the current approach to for-profit regulation, from a public policy and industrial logic perspective, the correct answer is the same: consolidation. From a public policy perspective, having the better-run schools buy the weaker-run schools would seem the most effective way to improve program effectiveness. Such combinations have the added advantage of providing continuity to the existing student populations. From an industrial logic perspective, the increased regulatory burden adds significant fixed costs of both tracking and reporting. The increasing importance of technology—both for compliance and for delivering hybrid and full-distance-learning programs—also heightens the central cost requirements. In addition to the resulting advantages of absolute scale, certain combinations would provide scale in regional geographies or specific degree programs, where one or another of the institutions lack the needed heft to be competitive.

Unfortunately, the new rules have resulted in transactions of very different kinds: bankruptcies, restructurings, go-privates, and reorganizations from for-profit to nonprofit simply to avoid the application of the rules. Corinthian Colleges, with 72,000 students, filed for bankruptcy. Education Management Corporation (EDMC) succeeded in restructuring its debt out of court but quickly announced plans to close a quarter of its Art Institutes.[45] Grand Canyon University is the largest for-profit so far to look to change its status to nonprofit to avoid the additional regulatory scrutiny.[46]

The lack of significant strategic combinations is a function of a number of obstacles. Chief among them is the lack of any mechanism to obtain prior approval from the U.S. Department of Education to ensure continued eligibility for federal programs after the ownership change. Some believe that the government's failure to facilitate sensible combinations is a function of its general hostility to the for-profit sector. Indeed, as a practical matter, most well-run schools would be loath to take on the regulatory risk to their existing business of becoming associated with a poorly run one, even if they were in a position to meaningfully improve its performance. Former university president and U.S. Senator Bob Kerrey charged that the government's "incoherent public policy" in this regard "betrays a bias against private enterprise."[47] These critics view the regulatory initiative as driven not by a desire to improve vocational education opportunities but by an ideological desire to have public community colleges replace the entire for-profit industry. If this was their hope, the data are not encouraging. For-profit enrollment fell by more than 500,000 between 2010 and 2015, and community college enrollment fell by almost as much.[48] Indeed, the data suggest that when he leaves office in 2017, Obama may become the first president since data began being collected in 1869 to have presided over a decline in total enrollments at degree-granting institutions.[49] More disturbing given the policy objectives is the fact that the declines have been greatest among low-income students.[50]

Regardless of the motivations and justifications for the radically changed regulatory landscape for for-profit higher education, it is worth looking at which for-profit educational institutions have performed relatively well in the face of it. In short, the institutions that have best averted the extended sector downturn are the niche players who stuck to their respective defensible market positions. Notably, they resisted the temptation to be all things to all people and avoided pressure to pursue growth at all costs.

All of the public for-profit universities lost between almost 50 percent and close to 100 percent of their value during the five-year period ending at the start of 2016—the sole exception is Grand Canyon University. The other distinguishing characteristics of Grand Canyon are that (1) it is the only for-profit that eschewed geographic expansion, and (2) it boasts the highest operating margins in the sector. The school has the same single base campus in Phoenix that it began with in 1949, when it was founded as a Christian university. Today that campus has grown to 205 acres from the original modest facility. The school has also leveraged its full-service campus—including a Division I sports program—serving 8,200 traditional students to build a highly profitable business serving more than 50,000 evening and online learners. This approach has made the business significantly less reliant on government aid programs than

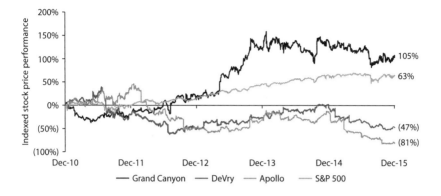

Figure 5.1 Grand Canyon University indexed stock price performance, five years ending December 31, 2015

Data Points: Grand Canyon University, DeVry University, Apollo Education Group, S&P 500

the for-profit peer schools because of the parental support afforded its traditional on-campus students. In addition, the Christian affinity represents a psychographic niche within which it is less costly to build scale and strengthen captivity.

More recently, two other institutions also stand out: Strayer University and Capella University (see Figure 5.2). Along with Grand Canyon, these are the only major public for-profit universities whose revenues are actually anticipated to grow in 2016. Strayer has managed to stabilize enrollments, even as the rest of the industry has continued to decline significantly. It has tied its business model to corporate partnerships and has established relationships with community colleges. The corporate relationships strengthen the stability of enrollments and the likelihood of "gainful employment." The community college relationships are the kind of legal cooperation that minimizes destructive competition, improves the nature of possible integrated offerings available for students, and inexpensively expands Strayer's footprint.

Capella is a pure distance-learning provider that has long focused on a narrow range of graduate degree programs in high-demand sectors. It has actually reversed enrollment declines and returned to levels above those achieved in 2010. Capella has avoided the certificate courses that have been a mainstay of the original explosion in for-profit enrollments generally. The school's online programs attract students

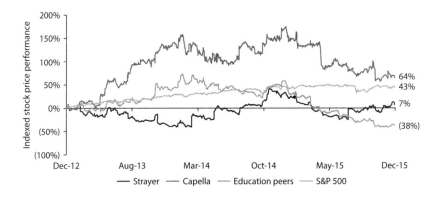

Figure 5.2: Strayer and Capella Universities indexed stock price performance, three years ending December 31, 2015

Data Points: Strayer University, Capella University, Education Peers, S&P 500

with a significantly higher probability of completion. Founded in 1993 by the former president of Central Michigan University and the former CEO of Tonka, the company went public in 2006 and, in 2007, received the National Centers of Academic Excellence in Information Assurance Education designation from the National Security Agency.

Even in the ashes of the restructuring of EDMC is further evidence of what makes a good education business in highly regulated markets. The company's first acquisition was of the fifty-year-old Art Institute of Pittsburgh in 1970. Although the strategy of focusing on a vertical subject expertise by leveraging an established local franchise made sense, the mismatch between the cost of delivering a high-quality product on the one hand and the attractiveness of employment opportunities in art and design outside selected major markets on the other doomed the aggressive national expansion in the face of gainful employment rules. The jewel in EDMC ended up being an entirely unrelated business acquired in 2003 called South University—a regionally focused provider of degrees in a wide range of health-related professions with a heritage dating back to 1899. South grew largely by launching new schools in the region and expanding the accredited health-related programs it offered, up to the doctoral level in some cases, in areas such as nursing, pharmacy, physician assistant, and health sciences. Although enrollments at the Art Institutes, which by then numbered in the many dozens, began to decline precipitously in 2010, South's enrollment has increased since then, with strong profitability well above that achieved by any other part of EDMC.

Although South represents a solid franchise, there is no evidence that it was made more valuable in EDMC's hands. South simply continued to operate independently under Chancellor John T. South III after the acquisition. The error in EDMC's strategy was not the acquisition of South in itself, but the fact that the transaction was part of a much broader effort to simply get larger as fast as possible. For the twenty-five years leading up to its IPO in 1996, EDMC had added only eight art schools. It had instead focused on building and investing in the existing core franchise. The same year that EDMC purchased South, it also bought the far more generic American Education Centers, with eighteen schools scattered among far-flung states and offering a wide range of business programs. Changing the AEC schools' names to Brown Mackie College the following year did not make the business any more compelling.

From its IPO as a focused, well-regarded art and design school in fewer than twenty markets with less than 25,000 students, by 2010 EDMC had become the second largest for-profit, with more than 150,000 students around the country. By aggressively exploiting the unfettered availability of federal student grants and loans, EDMC rapidly built absolute size without reinforcing actual scale in more durable relevant market segments. The result was a missed opportunity to use the extended period of misguided regulatory largesse to build a more sustainable franchise.

Operating Efficiency: Running It Well

Across industries, the performance gap between best and worst in class is massive. For all the rhetoric about the potential productivity gains from the introduction of new technologies, the reality is that over any reasonable time horizon, these could be dwarfed by low-tech operating improvements. Just bringing industry laggards up to the standards of industry leaders represents low-hanging and plentiful fruit.

Strategy is about reinforcing competitive advantages. Operating efficiency is about performing optimally with or without barriers to entry. In businesses without competitive advantages, superior operations are the only way to deliver superior performance. In businesses with competitive advantages, efficient operations can provide a multiplier effect to the superior returns afforded by industry structure, just as inefficient operations can be a powerful impediment to superior returns.

The strategic importance of efficient operations is that even the most seemingly insurmountable competitive advantage is not forever. When strong barriers to entry become weak or nonexistent, the lack of a culture of efficiency leaves a business dangerously exposed. This is precisely what happened in the newspaper industry, when the Internet robbed the sector of its wildly profitable classified advertising franchises. Generations of indifferent management made the resulting transition much more wrenching than it needed to be. Newspaper proprietors, with very few exceptions, have largely become observers in the transformation of the broader news and information sector as they have played catch-up and focused on internal restructuring that should have been undertaken years earlier.

Contrasting the performance of Nobel Learning over time—both before and after the installation of CEO George Bernstein and before and after Milken's ownership—demonstrates the potential power of operating excellence. Nobel itself is in the school and preschool sectors, both of which have modest barriers to entry. And yet, the business has managed to combine these businesses in a way that strengthened the operations of both. When Bernstein took over from CEO Jack Clegg and his family-dominated management team in 2003, the stock had fallen since Milken had first invested, delivering a meager annualized return of 3.5 percent since its IPO. This result was achieved during a period when the overall stock market had delivered greater than 10 percent returns. Bernstein quickly exited a number of noncore ventures and implemented a variety of retail-like processes to streamline operations. In addition, he closed underperforming schools and organized the business in critical mass clusters—adding both organically and inorganically to optimize the footprint—under regional managers.

Almost half of the cost structure of these businesses is local wages. From a revenue perspective, the key to effectively managing schools— both preschools and K–12—is to ensure that those personnel (and the facilities they are working in) are being optimized. A few points of capacity utilization can make the difference between a poor and a satisfactorily performing facility or between a good and a great one. It is here that Nobel really excelled in designing its product and targeting its markets.

On the product front, Nobel provides a wide variety of services under the moniker of "early learning"—everything from essentially babysitting for toddlers to a serious nursery program for four year olds. Bernstein invested in developing a branded curriculum—Links to Learning—that goes from six weeks to kindergarten (five years old). Parents are given monthly reports highlighting progress across key developmental stages. This approach keeps the family engaged and justifies refusing to accept children on an ad hoc, drop-off basis as opposed to committing to a schedule that permits effective curriculum delivery. In addition, by eschewing government support and focusing on educated families with a median income around $150,000, the business avoids the operating challenges associated with managing transient populations and volatile funding regimes.

Furthermore, Bernstein instituted best practices on the teacher training and development front that have yielded high Net Promoter Scores and parent satisfaction rates—critical in a market where 60–70 percent of customers come from local word-of-mouth referrals. Among the early innovations was an intranet portal for sharing lesson plans across the network, not unlike what TpT has built. The combined impact of a high-quality, integrated product and corresponding payment plans structured to encourage student continuity has resulted in lower customer "churn" than in typical childcare settings. This, in turn, supports meaningfully higher capacity utilization.

Although operating K–8 schools and child-care centers is not intrinsically synergistic, the Links to Learning curriculum feeds into the core curriculum of the early years at the elementary schools. About half of Nobel's revenues are from clusters of stand-alone preschools; the other half comes mostly from linked clusters of preschools and K–8 schools. All the Nobel K–8 schools benefit from a significant percentage of their enrollment coming through the linked preschools, which supports their capacity utilization as well. Notably, each cluster typically operates under its own, often long-established local brands rather than under the Nobel banner.

From the time that Bernstein joined the business until the buyout, the share price grew at a compounded rate of 12 percent, even as the stock market was growing at just 2 percent. As mentioned in chapter 4, however, the real benefits came once Milken exited and Bernstein was able to focus exclusively on operations rather than governance.

Growing and Protecting the Franchise

Having a good education business is one thing; keeping it good and growing it is another. Often, however, protecting and further developing the franchise are deeply intertwined activities. Defending and growing both require the same activity: investing.

The key to smart investing is a keen sense of the specific source of competitive advantage that supports an enterprise. Investment in growth is only good for shareholders when the expected returns are greater than the corporate cost of capital. It is only in the face of a barrier to entry—that is, an ability to invest in an opportunity not open to others—that investment results excel. It may be that all children in Lake Wobegon are above average, but corporate investments in the absence of competitive advantage are destined to just be average.

Having a barrier to entry is a necessary but not sufficient condition to being better than average when it comes to investing for growth. Simply spending more—particularly on venture investments or entirely new business lines designed as a "hedge" against risks to the core business—should not be expected to yield superior returns. It is only when the investing specifically reinforces an existing advantage that others cannot follow suit. Possible, but much more rare, is the situation in which aggressive early investing allows the establishment of an advantage—typically, scale—where none existed before. The critical point, however, is that different competitive advantages are bolstered by different kinds of investments (Table 5.1).

Economies of scale are reinforced by investing to ensure that relative scale is maintained or extended—whether reflected in the size of the customer base over which fixed costs are being spread or in the size of the network that delivers superior value to participants. Fixed-cost scale is also enhanced by continually raising the ante in terms of the extent of fixed costs that need to be incurred to play. Aggressive investment in product research and development is a key fixed-cost category, but so are lower-tech functions, such as the sales infrastructure.

Many acquisitions are justified based on the ability to deliver scale. These scale advantages can result in real "synergies"—both cost synergies from eliminating duplicative fixed infrastructure and revenue synergies from selecting the most productive infrastructure to keep and leveraging that across the entire combined business. But whether

TABLE 5.1
Sources of competetive advantage

	SCALE		CUSTOMER CAPTIVITY			COST		GOVERNMENT PROTECTION
	Fixed Cost	Network Effects	Habit	Switching Cost	Search Cost	Proprietary Technology	Learning	Various
Optimal Reinforcing Strategies	Reinvest in fixed-cost base	Broaden network	Enforce product consistency, encourage usage frequency	Focus on complexity and embedding into core processes	Invest in complexity and comprehensiveness	Invest in rapidly changing environment and get a patent	Generate relentless production improvements	Hire a good lobbyist
Key Threat	Growth, patient, well-financed new entrants, adjacent niche players		Battle for new customers, execution failure in quality or consistency			New better technology	More relevant lessons elsewhere	A better lobbyist
Education Examples	Textbook Publishers	Turnitin	Renaissance Learning	PowerSchool	Bright Horizons	?	InsideTrack	For-Profit Universities

such synergies actually deliver benefits to the shareholders is a separate question. If multiple strategic suitors would benefit from the same synergies, however, it is likely that competition will force the winning bid to price in all of the potential synergy value. The only circumstance in which the buyer will be able to retain some of this value for itself is when either the buyer is uniquely positioned to benefit or when the other similarly situated competitors have some constraint—financial or otherwise—that impedes their ability to participate. As an example, if an existing K–8 school becomes available in an area where Nobel has a cluster of preschools, then Nobel is uniquely positioned to pay the top price while still retaining benefits for its shareholders. However, when a textbook publisher outbids all the other textbook publishers for a synergistic product or service, it is likely that very little of the strategic benefits will accrue to its shareholders rather than the sellers.

Customer captivity comes in a variety of flavors, and the investments required are distinct, if sometimes related, for each. Habit is enhanced by frequency of use; switching costs, by integrating product into the customer work flow; and search costs, by providing a uniquely comprehensive suite of products. As Coca-Cola learned the hard way with its 1985 introduction of New Coke, product consistency is critical for maintaining all manner of customer captivity. The art of building the moat is to make continuous improvements that are subtle enough to not rock the captivity boat.

In education, the subsector that exhibits the strongest customer captivity is the market for student information systems (SIS). A public school system of any size simply cannot operate without an SIS, which serves as a central data repository for managing everything from student grades, assignments, attendance, and scheduling to all the school's core daily operating activities. The importance of an SIS relates not just to its role in ensuring effective operations; it is also essential for being able to satisfy the myriad regulatory requirements of the many federal, state, and local authorities that provide funding.

The PowerSchool Group, founded in 1997 as the first web-based platform, is the largest SIS, with more than twice the market share of its nearest competitor—giving it scale as well as captivity. In any given year, however, due to the power of all the dimensions of captivity, very few customers are in the market for a new SIS. Renewal rates at PowerSchool average 99 percent, and the balance of the industry is not far behind. The PowerSchool Group achieved most of its market share the old-fashioned way: it bought it.

In 2006, Pearson bought both PowerSchool, which had been owned by Apple for the previous five years, and Chancery SMS (another SIS that focused on large urban districts) and combined both with its existing system. Although all new sales are made on the PowerSchool platform, such is the importance of consistency to maintaining customer captivity that Pearson never pushed its Chancery customers to migrate to PowerSchool. A decade after the acquisitions, almost two million students remain on Chancery. Although financially "inefficient," the decision reflected Pearson's appreciation of the true source of competitive advantage and the sensible desire to not make PowerSchool the New Coke of the SIS market.

Cost advantage is most frequently best pressed by hurtling down the learning curve. Although obtaining truly proprietary technology that provides a sustainable cost advantage is rare, it doesn't mean you shouldn't try. Indeed, the process of continuous technological improvement and investment helpfully increases the fixed-cost table stakes, regardless of whether a defensible proprietary technology results.

Regulation in education is pervasive but also highly unstable. Local and national preferences shift with the political winds, making it dangerous to count on a specific regulatory regime or funding paradigm to permanently buttress a business model. From for-profit colleges to online charter school managers, the thrill of government largesse and protection can quickly be overwhelmed by the realization that the business is going down the drain once the authorities decide to pull the plug.

Lobbying can be money well spent, but it is often money badly spent. Given the inherently volatile nature of politics, if it is the only money being spent, the benefits of regulatory advantage are likely to be short lived. The trick is to use the temporary protection of government to build a more permanent moat that will survive regime change. Just as a studio executive spends his days scheming to stay on top, while simultaneously planning for life after his inevitable downfall, a business built on the back of a specific government program, contract, or law must prepare, from its earliest days, for an afterlife.

Contrast Wireless Generation, which never managed to turn the windfall of the New York City ARIS contract into a commercializable product, with SchoolNet's ability to leverage its early relationship with

Philadelphia into a business operating well beyond "the city that loves you back." Similarly, Strayer's aggressive partnerships with private businesses as a central part of its business model explain its relatively muted recent enrollment declines, as compared with Apollo, in the face of the dramatic changes to the federal rules. Or consider that the fastest-growing and most profitable part of Nobel, a company that generally eschews any government ties, is the white labeling of its online Laurel Springs AP classes to private schools—a market that K–12 should have cornered long before Nobel had a chance.

Even when the regulatory framework endures, it is often the other structural competitive advantages built up behind it that drive long-term value. In the case of the ratings agencies, the initial government designation allowed them to build scale so that, if the government now allowed anyone to issue ratings, it would make no real difference to the strength of the core franchises. Similarly, the scale that Grand Canyon built around its core geography and demography will endure in a way that those for-profits that simply sought to grow enrollment at all costs will not.

Cooperation Without Incarceration

Reinforcing and growing barriers to entry must not be undertaken in a vacuum. As many sources of competitive advantage as a business may be blessed with, nothing is forever. The aim should be to ensure that the full potential benefits of competitive advantage are enjoyed and that they endure as long as possible. These objectives are not in conflict, but they do require a willingness to temper any testosterone-fueled inclination to destroy all competitors and ruthlessly press an advantage against customers and suppliers.

The two theoretical extremes of industry structure are intense competition among many competitors with free entry and exit and a single dominant player whose competitive advantages are so many and so profound that none dare challenge. The former yields relatively modest returns for even the best operators, whereas even the slothful may enjoy great bounty in the latter environment. Far more typical, however, are industries in which a handful of participants have roughly comparable competitive advantages vis-à-vis all others. How an individual player fares in such circumstances will be driven not only by their operating prowess but also, and more important, by how they decide to interact with their peers. More than anything else, how market leaders with shared competitive advantage manage competition among themselves determines whether the industry thrives or suffers. The decision to engage in no-holds-barred, hand-to-hand combat across every potential dimension of competition is unlikely to deliver world domination to a single victor. Rather, prolonged, shared misery—akin to life in sectors without any barriers to entry—is the almost certain outcome.

By choosing cooperation over competition, however, those with competitive advantage open up the possibility of re-creating a market structure that operates precisely like one in which a single firm dominates. There are two obstacles to achieving such an outcome. First, to make sure such a strategy endures, the nature of the arrangement must provide for a fair sharing of the benefits. Any lopsided division will not last long and will inevitably collapse into an orgy of mindless competition. Second, those cooperating need to be very careful to avoid criminal or civil prosecution under the antitrust laws.

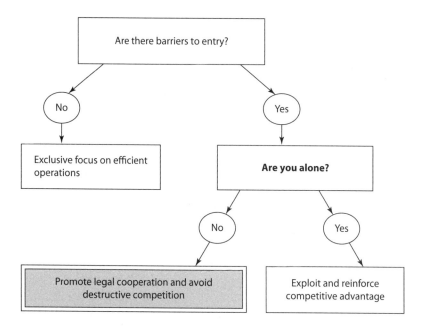

Figure 5.3 Industry structure and strategy

Legal cooperation takes many forms, but the outcome is an industry structure that optimizes returns. Today, three major basal K–12 publishers remain. In chapter 3, we described how competition for a major state adoption involves large capital investment in plate. If all three competed aggressively for each adoption in every subject at every grade level, returns would be poor. If, however, each publisher let its areas of specialization be widely known—whether through public statements or simply through marketing materials—it is likely that competition for any particular adoptions would not involve all three. One publisher may focus on earlier grades, and another, on later ones. One may come to be known for its strength in soft subjects, and another, hard. Even in critical areas like reading and math, where all major publishers need to participate on some basis, important subspecialties are likely to develop. All of this can come about without publishers actually speaking to each other about how they should split up the market—which would be the kind of formal agreement that would fall afoul of the antitrust authorities.

As counterintuitive as it may sound, such cooperation for the benefit of shareholders can also benefit society. This behavior is likely to result in both a higher absolute level of investment and more effective investment in educational product. The level of investment that can be justified by a publisher on any individual adoption decreases as the number of competitors increases. Similarly, by emphasizing subject matter domains in which a publisher has relative scale, the returns from incremental investment are likely to be higher. It should not be surprising, therefore, that society is better off when each publisher invests heavily in its area of relative expertise rather than modestly across the board. Cooperation inevitably yields specialization, which in turn generates unparalleled efficiency.

A danger of private equity participation in education sectors is that short-term focus can lead companies to abandon a cooperative paradigm designed to maximize long-term value—particularly if burdened with an unsustainable capital structure. The higher education publishing sector had, by 2000, consolidated into an oligopolistic structure similar to K–12 publishing: in this case, the three market leaders were Pearson, Thomson, and McGraw-Hill. When Thomson sold its business in an overly leveraged private equity transaction just before the 2008 market downturn, the new owners had trouble meeting their obligations.[51] Competitors were quietly furious when Cengage significantly raised textbook prices beyond typical historical increases. Their view was that Cengage's short-term cash needs were driving decisions that undermined the sector's long-term institutional relationships and that accelerated the growth of used book and other emerging competitive products.[52]

It is not only through informal market signaling that cooperation can legally be encouraged. The nature of a wide range of standard industry practices—from the nature of contracts with suppliers to employment arrangements—can also reinforce the value of cooperation. In addition, industry trade associations can legally be used to establish such standards. They can also be used to encourage broader public policies that facilitate the efficient operation of the industry. Establishing national common core standards, for instance, allows the reduction of literally hundreds of pedagogically pointless variations in basic K–12 texts. In addition to the financial benefit to publishers, children—particularly poor children who are more likely to have transient living arrangements—are less likely to face confusing new curricula when moving from one public school to another.

Even in an industry with a single clear industry leader, cooperation—not so much with now irrelevant minor competitors, but with the broader ecosystem in which a company operates—is equally critical. An unwillingness to share the spoils of one's structural good fortune is to dangerously tempt fate. If the current industry structure is not in the interest of the other industry participants, they will eventually find a way to change it—maybe not today, maybe not tomorrow, but soon enough and in a way that will leave the once dominant player on the wrong side of history. For example, suppliers being unreasonably squeezed will offer extremely attractive terms to new entrants. Likewise, institutional customers being gouged financially or taken for granted commercially may band together to establish a new competitor.

The lesson is that it is as important to play nice when you find yourself alone at the top of the industry hill as it is in the sandbox—maybe even more so, as there is so much more to lose. Playing nice means doing everything possible to make the maintenance of the current industry structure feel equally vital to those with whom you do business. Achieving this outcome requires not just fair terms and responsiveness to their needs but also continuous investment in product innovation.

One education company that was dominant in its sector until relatively recently, but which has failed to protect its perch, is Blackboard. Blackboard was the leading LMS in higher education. Unlike eCollege, which focused on the niche of managing university's distance-learning offerings, Blackboard provided a comprehensive suite of software products for managing the classroom. Blackboard allowed itself to become the company that students, faculty, and administrators loved to hate. Once established as the overwhelming leader in the space, it was known primarily for its aggressive litigation, acquisition, and pricing strategies—everything other than product development and customer service. Few would dispute that Blackboard was "one of the most disliked—even detested—companies in education."[53]

The company went public in 2004 and quickly announced the acquisition of its largest competitor, WebCT, the following year. The next largest remaining competitor, a venture-backed insurgent founded at the University of Indiana, was ANGEL Learning. With barely $20 million in revenues and little cash flow, ANGEL could not offer all that Blackboard did, but it was growing rapidly off the back of Blackboard customers that had had enough. Rather than see ANGEL as the canary in the coalmine and change its ways, Blackboard had aggressively tried to buy ANGEL for years. When they finally succeeded in 2009, the blogosphere and twitterverse lit up in horror. With this transaction, one college instructor wrote, "denizens of Alderon" (misspelling the name of Princess Leia's home planet destroyed in *Star Wars* by the Death Star) could be heard "screaming [their] last breath."[54]

To its credit, Blackboard hired ANGEL's chief technology officer to begin the process of repairing its customer relationships. But this was too little, too late. Within a few short years, other new, innovative entrants leveraged developments in SaaS technology to develop less-expensive, more-responsive offerings that quickly chipped away at Blackboard's once overwhelming market share. Blackboard's CEO, Michael Chasen, was responsible for the culture, but apparently he could see the writing on the wall: he cashed out to a private equity firm in 2011[55] and left the company in 2012.[56]

Today, Blackboard, which once boasted a 90 percent market share in the United States, has less than half that position. The next three competitors—Moodle, a free open source LMS used in 200 countries; Instructure, a venture-backed company that went public late in 2015; and D2L a Canadian-based competitor founded in 1999—all barely registered back in 2009. Indeed, Instructure was founded by two Brigham Young University students in 2008. Together these three now represent more of the U.S. market than Blackboard. But disruptive new entrants are not a new phenomenon.[57] The speed with which Blackboard lost its commanding position suggests that the company would have done well to invest at least as much in innovation and collaboration as it did in buying up its smaller competitors. If you leave yourself open to attack by failing to do the former, the latter will inevitably degenerate into a futile game of whack-a-mole.

CHAPTER SIX

Lessons from Clown School

THESE TALES FROM the frontlines of educational enterprise span a wide range of subsectors, business models, and ambitions. What they mostly share is a bleak ending. We have seen, however, that in many cases, these endings were not forgone conclusions. Some investors have managed to do just fine operating in precisely the same domains as others who fared poorly.

Chapter 5 focused on the structural commonalities of the best educational businesses and the strategies for ensuring their enduring success. Considered alongside the preceding detailed case studies of financial catastrophe, this framework provides a critical context for distinguishing the avoidable from the inevitable. The perspective provided facilitates the identification of consistent themes from the ashes of the diverse failures. The dozen lessons that emerge are mostly subjective observations rather than fundamental imperatives. They take the form of cautionary reminders, empirical observations, and hopeful exhortations. The themes relate as much to the recurring behaviors and attitudes of education investors as to the industry structures that define the ultimate outcomes. Some of these lessons are education specific, while others are broader principles. Even when the concept is more general, however, its application to the educational domain is colored by the idiosyncrasies of both the structure of the sector and the aims of those who invest there.

The Road to Disastrous Educational Businesses Is Paved with Good Intentions

The idea of doing well by doing good has intuitive appeal and is a venerable American tradition.[1] Although true motives are often difficult to discern, most of the money-losing ventures profiled here were animated in part by a genuine desire to improve education. There is good reason to question the sincerity of the distressed debt hedge funds that took control of Houghton expressing only a desire to "educate children in innovative and thoughtful ways."[2] But this is one of the outliers in our pantheon of money losers, and even those funds felt an obligation to articulate high-minded ideals.

There is no reason, however, to question the intentions of controversial figures like Michael Milken and Rupert Murdoch. The former may have been inspired by a quest for redemption and the latter by an unhealthy preoccupation with unions of all kinds, but both had a sincere belief that their investments could profitably increase the productive potential of the population. One could argue whether Chris Whittle and Barry O'Callaghan were just con men. In neither case is such a conclusion fully justified by the facts, although in both cases, the money involved was not mostly theirs. Nonetheless, their pitches to those who parted permanently with their cash tightly tied the ability to generate personal wealth with the ability to improve social outcomes.

Less clear is whether good intentions in general tend to lead to bad results. A review of 167 studies of any link between corporate social performance and corporate financial performance found little relationship,[3] but it also did not find that doing good actually led to doing bad. There may, however, lurk a deeper structural danger from actually mixing an investment decision with nonfinancial objectives.

It is hard enough making good investment decisions in the complex education sector without burdening them with additional considerations. As educational philanthropists from Bill Gates to Mark Zuckerberg have learned, it is even difficult to make successful "investments" in education with no expectation of any financial return. In reviewing the anecdotal evidence presented in this book, one gets the strong impression that the personal life experiences of the investors and entrepreneurs present an additional obstacle to clear-eyed thinking. Life experience is often a useful source of investment ideas.

This is merely speculation, but it may be that the intensity and transformative nature of youthful educational experiences has often made it difficult for investors to draw the proper business inferences.

Many of the otherwise successful investors and businesspeople who made bad education investments went to elite private universities, aspired to do so, or seemed otherwise preoccupied with securing their imprimatur. These institutions have a number of exceptional qualities, but they are not great organizations with which to do business. First, they represent a tiny fraction of the overall market, which is dominated by heavily subsidized public universities. Second, these institutes are far more interested in protecting their exclusivity than growing and their nonprofit ethos and bureaucratic decision making are a significant additional barrier to finding common cause. Third, and most important, although they are nonprofits, these enterprises themselves have overwhelming barriers to entry, making the outcome of any commercial arrangements ultimately consummated likely to be lopsided in the schools' favor.

The best evidence of barriers to entry is lack of entry. In the past fifty years, only Stanford University has broken into the top tier of elite U.S. universities.[4] First Japan and more recently China and a number of Middle Eastern countries invested hundreds of millions over many decades to establish universities of this caliber, only to discover how deep the moat around this elite group is. The network effect of current and former students and faculty continuing to attract the best and the brightest is an enduring legacy that even bad management, indifferent teaching, and plagiarism scandals cannot undermine.

And yet, educational ventures consistently aspire to secure a pact—or worse, to compete—with a top-tier university at all costs. Like most deals that an investor wants in the worst way, that is precisely the way it comes to pass. As Michael Milken and Andrew Rosenfield learned, when the price of "success" is to provide their prestigious partners with "money for nothing," failure is actually a better option. The argument that these kinds of deals are loss leaders that will accelerate the ability to attract other, more profitable customers is simply not borne out by the facts. Indeed, as painful as it is to negotiate an agreement with a leading nonprofit university, it is a walk in the park compared to actually working with one on an ongoing basis. Interestingly, the businesses interacting with these institutions that have done well are those that have managed to capture the loyalty of the most powerful decision makers: the faculty. If a tenured professor has grown accustomed to teaching out of the same textbook, no administrator or procurement officer will ever even try to get that professor to change.

The relative unattractiveness of this end of the market is also reflected in the relative performance of players in the OPM market discussed in chapter 5. 2U has seen its stock flourish as it delivered $150 million in 2015 revenues managing online programs for top-tier universities like Yale and Northwestern. Academic Partnerships, a private OPM company with an investment from Insight Ventures, by contrast, had just under $100 million in total revenues, but more than 2U in the market segment that is its exclusive focus: public universities. The difference in target customer base translates into a very big difference on the bottom line. Academic Partnerships is highly profitable while 2U continues to bleed money.[5]

Besides the generally unappealing nature of leading private universities as customers, this result is driven in part by two significant aspects of the respective cost structures. First, the upfront costs incurred by 2U on behalf of their demanding clients with myriad bespoke requirements dwarf those of Academic Partnerships, which benefits from the strong similarities in the needs of public institutions. Second, student recruitment—a key component of the overall OPM value proposition—represents a much more manageable cost where students (typically working adults) are overwhelmingly drawn from the local geography. Tuition at public institutions is a relative bargain and the university brand is strong among both students and their prospective employers locally.

An even more recent venture backed by Benchmark, one of the most respected venture capital firms in Silicon Valley,[6] actually wants to compete with the Ivy League head on. Minerva Project's well-meaning conceit is that the path to a great education is for students to live in rented housing in a rotating series of major international cities each semester and take their classes through computers.[7] Like UNext fifteen years earlier, it boasts a world-class cognitive psychologist responsible for the pedagogy, big-name academics as advisors, and a hyperconfident leader, without much relevant experience, who serves as the "principal evangelist."[8] Much of the diagnosis of the ills of the current system of higher education that Minerva CEO Ben Nelson relates at conferences and in interviews rings true. The noble objectives of focusing on actual learning to solve real-world problems rather than grades and credentials are inspiring. But there is no evidence that these objectives produce better outcomes, and there is plenty of reason to suspect, declarations of "brilliance" by commentators aside,[9] that the business model—classes limited to nineteen students, tuition half of competitors', competing directly with the most selective universities, eschewing all federal funding, building the enterprise on a bespoke learning platform—is not sustainable.

———————

Regardless of any actual correlation between doing good and doing well, with respect to the management of or investment in for-profit ventures, one basic fact is incontrovertible: one cannot do good for very long if the business does not do well enough to survive. Yet there is a sense that some of the investors and operators profiled in this book thought that the mere fact of pursuing a high-minded ideal should allow them to be given a pass on rigorous financial standards. If one truly believes in the ideal, however, that argues for a higher, not a lower, financial standard. Given the risk of business failure to both the ideal and the investors, operating close to the line is foolhardy. Doing well is a necessary but not sufficient condition of doing sustainable good. The possibility of doing good would expand exponentially if more investors and managers shifted their focus even incrementally toward the fundamental question of what qualities are most important in building successful educational franchises.

Beware of Bankers Bearing Gifts

Jean-Marie Messier became a symbol of just how much damage could be done with an investment banker actually running a company.[10] His ownership of Houghton Mifflin was brief and represented a tiny fraction of the ultimate value destruction. Notwithstanding that cautionary tale, a surprising number of failed pure education ventures were entrusted to bankers, lawyers, or consultants with big ideas and little business operating experience. Michael Milken put Ron Packard, veteran of McKinsey and Goldman Sachs's merger department, in charge of online charter school operator K12 Inc. and put Andrew Rosenfield, a university law lecturer, in charge of what started as Knowledge University. Rupert Murdoch gave brilliant litigator Joel Klein carte blanche and a blank check (and a News Corp. board seat) to reshape elementary education. Investors in Edison Schools let impresario

Chris Whittle surround himself with lawyers rather than operators—First Amendment expert Benno Schmidt as chair and former White House counsel Chris Cerf as president. In the case of former banker Barry O'Callaghan at Houghton, he at least had some self-awareness—possibly pressed on him by lenders and investors—that he needed to augment his team with a senior operating executive. The problem was that he then appointed his corporate lawyer as president.

As a banker and recovering lawyer myself, I would never diminish the many talents that the finest service professionals exhibit. But running a company well is not one of them. Good lawyers in particular have one notable dangerous quality in business: they are effective advocates for their client, even when their client is guilty. That talent makes the world go round in our system of justice, but when the "client" is a misguided business idea, investors inevitably lose. When I asked a frustrated former executive of UNext to describe the company's single biggest obstacle to success, he identified the fact that lawyer-CEO Rosenfield "could win any argument." The exec said that unfortunately, "it didn't mean he was right."

There is nothing that makes individuals who began their careers in these various professional roles incapable of one day becoming a CEO. It is just that the functional skills required to excel in each are dramatically different. In addition to raw intelligence and a command of the technical aspects of their chosen profession, the most successful service industry executives shine where it matters most—in sales. Unless you make the cash register ring, the chances of eventual partnership for even the most brilliant professional remain bleak. Salesmanship is certainly useful in a CEO—we have seen how these skills enabled the executives mentioned to successfully attract capital and manage investors. The problem is that this is not the CEO's core function; managing the operating performance of the business is. To transition successfully from a service role to a leadership role requires development of these very different capabilities, which are only obtainable through operating experience. It is for this reason that public companies almost never appoint a CEO without a track record either in the field or in running another organization—even CFOs rarely get the nod without first being given divisional profit and loss responsibility.

In education, not just good intentions are overrated; so is the ability to compellingly articulate and effectively sell a vision to realize those good intentions. It is in this role that the best lawyers, bankers, and consultants particularly outperform. Instilling a shared mission to the troops is a genuinely important task for a CEO. But no matter how effective at this he or she may be, without the basic tools and capabilities to deliver on that promise, a CEO is destined to breed a culture of cynicism and, ultimately, failure.

It's the Industry Structure, Stupid

Chapter 5 emphasized the importance of industry structure to building and growing successful education businesses. Warren Buffet famously said, "When a manager with a reputation for brilliance tackles a business with a reputation for poor fundamental economics, it is the reputation of the business that remains intact."[11] The failed efforts that populate this book repeatedly ignored this fundamental truth in ways big and small.

To be fair, the structures of the various sectors of the education industry profiled are diverse and complex. Getting one's arms around industry structure in the first place is not for the faint of heart. In typical media industries, it is not unusual to confront two-sided (consumers and advertisers) or even three-sided (buyers, sellers, and advertisers) markets. In education, twice as many constituencies may have a role in buying decisions: students, parents, teachers, and administrators (at the local, district, state, and federal levels), as well as various political entities. The actual and potential competitive set often includes not only other for-profit businesses but also both public and nonprofit entities and even DIY solutions. Difficulty, however, does not suggest impossibility, though it does reinforce the importance of closely aligning strategies with the nuance of industry structure. All forms of hubris are particularly misplaced in a sector characterized by a multiplicity of anachronisms. At the end of the day, although a convoluted industry structure may be challenging, it is far more likely to yield attractive business opportunities than are straightforward ones. Transparency is the friend of the consumer, not the producer, and barriers to entry are exceedingly difficult to enforce when information flows freely and evenly through the ecosystem.

No amount of brilliance or good intentions can overcome an unwillingness to accept the predominant role of understanding industry structure in achieving superior outcomes. The best evidence of this deep strategic infirmity is the tendency to blame the market itself rather than the inability to effectively serve it. Those responsible for failed businesses often continue to insist that the problem was not the product but the failure of the marketplace to appreciate the wisdom of their approach. This excuse is not unlike the student who brags that he could have achieved a perfect score if only he had studied. In business, being "ahead of your time" is not a legitimate justification but an embarrassing admission. As discussed in chapter 5, there is no such thing as a "first mover advantage." The relevant question is, When can a significant infusion of investment spending facilitate the acquisition of scale? The evidence is overwhelming that scale is rarely achieved by going first. The strategic challenge is to identify the moment when the market and technology will allow a product to move from serving early adopters to being one of mass adoption. It is not easy to recover from either going too early or waiting too long.

Even great businesspeople suffer great business failures. Taking a risk that doesn't pan out is not necessarily a sign of incompetence or foolishness. The greatest businesspeople learn from their past mistakes to build their most successful enterprises. Conversely, investors in individuals who misdiagnose or refuse to acknowledge the source of their previous failures get what they deserve. Whether it's Barry O'Callaghan's post-bankruptcy confidence in the wisdom of his pre-bankruptcy investment thesis or Joel Klein's insistence that he should get extra credit points just for being "innovative and transformative" after a billion dollars had been lost, these constitute "tells" of the kind that could have saved many of the unhappy investors profiled.

Execution Matters

The importance of the principles pursued by the highest-minded educational ventures has consistently led investors to lose focus on the importance of execution. We have seen one manifestation of this in the decision to place salespeople, rather than operators, at the head of the organizations. Mission-driven organizations may have a structural tendency to devalue execution and overvalue the virtues of being a true believer. What else could explain the ability of Chris Whittle to continue to attract capital in the face of serial financial implosions or the ability of his failed Edison leadership team to easily find high-profile, education-related positions in businesses, government, and NGOs?

Another challenge to effective execution has been to place an entirely different kind of executive at the top of these businesses: the education expert. Former educators or executives involved in curriculum development have a special caché that has frequently led to their elevation to roles for which they are ill equipped. Tony Lucki began his education career as many industry executives did—as an assistant editor. He worked his way up the publishing ladder and was eventually put in charge of the entire education division at conglomerate Harcourt General, before jumping ship to Houghton Mifflin under Bain/Lee after Reed bought Harcourt and passed Lucki over for the top education job. Although Lucki was well regarded as a publisher, he had no experience as a CEO of an independent, private equity–backed company. The complex seasonal working capital dynamics and cash flow drain from plate capital expenditure require careful management in the best of times, and in the context of a business with a substantial debt burden, it is a matter of life and death. The point is not that developing effective publishing programs is not an important part of being a successful educational executive; it is that, like sales expertise, it represents a small part of the CEO's overall responsibilities.

Although Bain/Lee did well on their investment because of the outlandish price paid by O'Callaghan, the business was absolutely stagnant and paid down no debt under the years of Lucki's leadership. Lucki had no experience in, nor did he show any apparent aptitude for, managing a highly leveraged educational publisher. O'Callaghan then added both more debt and a series of new, even more significant management challenges. The integration of Houghton first into Riverdeep and then into Harcourt entailed a massive restructuring of both the cost base and the organizational structure. Experience with developing strong publishing programs is of little help in these often-painful exercises. Lucki stepped down from his CEO role less than eighteen months after the Harcourt acquisition closed.

Educational specialists have been responsible for some fantastic products, but ensuring that that those products achieve their full potential usually requires professional management. The parents who founded Renaissance Learning in the mid-1980s did a spectacular job of spreading the word and building the product. After going public in 1997, Renaissance looked like it was poised to hit $100 million in revenues in 2000 and grow to more than $130 million the following year. The business did grow to over $130 million in revenues—but not until a decade later. In the interim, the company was plagued with missed earnings that could wipe out half of its value in a day based on not just the unpredictability of school funding cycles but also poor product rollout planning.

In 2011, private equity firm Permira purchased the business, whose margins had declined over the course of the previous decade. Permira installed Jack Lynch Jr., a respected operating executive hired from Wolters Kluwer, as CEO. Although Wolters is not in the education business, it is a global provider of information, software, and services to law, tax, finance, and health-care professionals. Once installed, Lynch quickly completed the transition to a 100 percent SaaS model, closed a hardware division that had been established through a misguided acquisition by the founders, and focused on managing the core reading and math products effectively. Revenues grew more over the next three years than they had in the previous decade, and profit margins hit all-time highs. After receiving an investment from Google at a $1 billion valuation, Permira quadrupled its original investment when it sold the business in 2014.[12]

This pattern has repeated itself in many of the more successful education investments profiled. George Bernstein had no significant experience in the education sector when he took over Nobel Learning. Although he had graduated from law school and started his business career as a consultant, Bernstein had held a series of relevant retail operating jobs—most recently as president of Pearle Vision. Current Turnitin CEO Chris Caren was similarly bereft of educational bona fides when he joined the company in 2009 after a career in a variety of relevant management roles at other software businesses, including Microsoft and Oracle. When Apollo looked for a CEO to lead McGraw-Hill Education after the successful completion of its LBO in 2013, they turned to David Levin, a seasoned executive who had run a range of public media and technology companies, but none in education.[13]

Continuity Counts

The importance of continuity in education manifests itself in a wide range of diverse contexts. Continuity matters in everything from how students actually learn to how school districts make product adoption decisions. As such, accounting for continuity is essential both to building robust educational business models and designing sensible educational public policy. The critical role continuity plays in business resiliency and product effectiveness is inconsistent with a relentless focus on identifying "revolutionary" approaches to education. Indeed, there is a strong correlation between the magnitude of the failure of the ventures profiled in these pages and the extent to which their business propositions required a fundamental transformation of the existing order.

Continuity is central to both establishing and maintaining competitive advantage in business. The key to reinforcing customer captivity is the constant focus on product quality and consistency. Conversely, the fastest way to lose a preferred position is by falling down along these competitive dimensions. Particularly in education markets, in which the teachers and administrators who dominate purchase decision making are notoriously resistant to change, it is always far safer to implement regular, modest product improvements rather than undertaking anything dramatic.

This is true even if the proposed modification would represent a significant upgrade. As an example, even though the legacy Chancery software serving major urban school districts represented a far less robust offering than the PowerSchool product, Pearson (which owned both) made no concerted effort to migrate customers. Distinct from the inherent intransigence of the customer base, more radical changes have a number of other practical obstacles to effective implementation. For example, fundamental retraining of the teaching force responsible for delivering an entirely new educational approach can be fraught with difficulty.

Similarly, the best way to grow a strong existing business is to add adjacent products and functionality that build on the customer's strong product connection to the core. Nobel Learning has lower customer churn in its early learning business than many peers, and it uses this loyalty to feed its elementary school operations. This task is achieved in part by establishing a consistent overarching curricular framework as well as a continuous mechanism to track students and communicate with parents.

For a new business trying to ultimately displace an incumbent, a Trojan horse strategy almost always beats a revolutionary one—even if revolution is the ultimate objective. Initially offering something to enhance or augment, rather than completely replace, the existing way of doing things is far more likely to secure a hearing. If product consistency is imperative for captivity of current customers, it is even more important to attract new customers. A devoted client may forgive an unusual disappointment, but an unhappy first-time user is unlikely to offer a second chance.

Chapter 2 focused on Amplify's overly broad ambitions rather than the relative virtues of its various products. Regardless of these possible merits, Amplify consistently underestimated the structural challenges to convincing teachers, principals, districts, and states to quickly commit to the wholesale adoption of new, untested products. Amplify developed, at great expense, a pure digital-reading middle school curriculum—along with some hybrid reading products for earlier grades and digital supplemental products for math and science—which it introduced in 2014 at the South by Southwest education conference in Austin, Texas. The previous year, it had introduced its custom-built tablets at the same conference, only to have to reimburse its largest customer almost $5 million shortly thereafter due to broken screens and melted chargers. Amplify was thus forced to introduce the new curriculum product at the same time as it announced "a do-over for its brand image" as a provider of "device agnostic" digital content.[14]

As hungry as some educators are for high-quality digital content, many students don't have computers, and many schools don't have broadband access. Even in the best-funded districts with both hardware and network availability, administrators need a solution flexible enough to respond to the inevitable computer system outages. Amplify, however, initially did not have a print companion to its digital curriculum, making it impractical for some of those favorably inclined to adopt it. Amplify suggested to some that teachers should simply print out the interactive digital product, an obviously unsatisfactory solution. Although the company scrambled to develop a hybrid print/ digital solution, as one Amplify executive described it, they were "half way along the journey" before they realized they needed to "build print back-up for every lesson."[15] The belated realization of the necessity to design and manufacture a parallel print curriculum for the "revolutionary" digital product had a variety of significant implications. The need to ensure the availability of a ubiquitous "off ramp" from the digital to the print had a huge impact on the anticipated cost. More important, Amplify already had developed a mixed reputation at best for consistency in anticipating schools' needs. Taking a chance on the company began to look foolhardy.

Finally, teachers themselves are a key constituency in adopting new curricular products. Renaissance Learning succeeded by anticipating teacher needs and providing comprehensive professional development to demonstrate how the products would make their job easier. The teachers became the biggest advocates for the product. Amplify's product, however, fundamentally changed the teacher's role in language instruction. One commentator noted that the ability to simply "put their classes on autopilot" with a product that "'choreograph[s]' every five minutes of instruction, and often delivers it along with feedback, directly to the student" would, at a minimum, "raise eyebrows" among teachers. Furthermore, Amplify's sales strategy was focused on the state and district levels, rather than the school level, making it unlikely to attract grassroots support from educators and local administrators.

Some of this, of course, was just poor execution. But much of it reflected a failure to appreciate the importance of all aspects of continuity in attracting and keeping customers. According to an industry trade association leader, "Schools tend to stay with companies and products that they've been successful with," and Amplify "just came in too late to make any real impact."[16] The schools were already using "tablets they liked from tech companies they liked," and the "curriculum publishers they'd already been working with had started transitioning with them to digital."

This is not to say that there was no opportunity for disruptive new entrants, but it is useful to contrast News Corp.'s approach to the more successful introduction at around the same time of a pure digital curriculum by another media company, Discovery Communications.[17] Discovery had long sold a supplemental science video product, called United Streaming, as a subscription product to schools through its education division founded in 2004. Rebranded Discovery Education Streaming Plus in 2007, the company grew its penetration in schools from 20 to 40 percent nationwide as the product incorporated not just video but also a variety of broader interactive multimedia capabilities. In deciding to enter the core curriculum market, Discovery positioned itself as a solutions provider to help districts manage the transition to digital over time. The company's initial product launch in 2011 was limited to middle school science, where its brand credibility was highest, using the existing sales force and leveraging its existing content. In addition to embedding significant teacher professional development into the product introduction, the company established the Discovery

Educator Network (DEN), an online "global community of education professionals that are passionate about teaching with digital media, sharing resources, collaborating and networking."[18] DEN became an important ally and source of ongoing feedback as Discovery expanded into additional grades and, ultimately, other subjects. The professional development efforts were so successful that these ultimately became an independent source of revenue. Today, Discovery's science curriculum spans all grades and has been adopted in all fourteen states in which it has competed. It introduced social science curricular product in 2013 and math in 2015. Notably, the overall business is profitable, and the payback on the initial investment in science curriculum was two years.

It is not only in the corporate realm that the significance of continuity in achieving educational success has been underestimated. Although somewhat beyond the scope of this book, educational public policy has also often shortchanged the value of continuity in the effort to achieve laudable goals. The most disturbing aspect of the recent expensive reform efforts in Newark public schools, discussed in more detail later, was their failure to acknowledge the special impact of continuity on the children served, who have suffered unspeakable trauma from exposure to a combination of violent crime, family turmoil, and deep poverty. With all the well-meaning, high-minded talk that accompanied the reforms, remarkably little thought went into the actual effect these policies might have on this population in desperate need of stability.[19]

The poster child for successful educational reform is the State of Massachusetts. By most accepted measures, student results in the Bay State are not just the best in the nation in reading, math, and science—if it were a country, Massachusetts would be "at the top of the pack."[20] Massachusetts instituted wide-ranging reforms n 1993, and to this day, there is deep disagreement over which aspect, or what combination of aspects, has driven the stunning outcomes.[21] What is indisputable is that a central leg of the legislation was the establishment of clear curriculum frameworks in each subject. Well over a decade before national Common Core State Standards were developed, the state provided its own consistent standards. Although a number of factors, both pedagogical and financial, undoubtedly supported the effort's overall success, it is hard to imagine that the clarity and continuity of expectations for teachers and students did not also play important roles.

Specialization Is the Mother of Invention

McGraw-Hill's sale of its educational business was not just successful for Apollo; it was also wildly successful for McGraw-Hill. McGraw shareholders valued the company more after the sale of the educational business—not counting any proceeds of the sale. How can a business that Apollo paid $2.5 billion for (and that has grown in value since) have been effectively valued by the public markets *negatively* inside McGraw-Hill? The answer is the remarkable power of focus. McGraw itself was a professional information conglomerate whose other businesses were characterized by extremely high renewal rates and low capital requirements. Education, with its inherent seasonality and hit-driven adoption cycle, sat uneasily within the portfolio. Although representing less than 25 percent of McGraw's profit, education was responsible for more than half of the company's capital expenditures. In addition, the division was a disproportionate source of earnings disappointment and a drain on management's time.

Management's time and attention are uniquely scarce and valuable corporate resources. Thus, it was perfectly rational for investors to value the McGraw portfolio more without education than with it, simply on the basis that management was liberated to focus on the remaining, more closely linked businesses. In the three years after McGraw's announcement of its intention to separate its education business, the company's stock price more than doubled, and its profits soared.

For an independent McGraw-Hill Education, the benefits were even greater. No longer the ugly stepchild that had to beg for a crust of bread, the business was the main event and had the complete attention of senior management and the new shareholders. The impact on its ability to attract and retain talent and reinvest in the most promising areas of growth were immediate and dramatic. The company filed in September 2015 to go public. EBITDA less plate grew from barely $400 million in 2012 when Apollo bought it to almost $500 million in 2015. Revenue, which had been flat, also grew.

It was noted earlier that mission-driven organizations often fail to adequately recognize the importance of operational effectiveness. There are, however, a number of tangible benefits of being a mission-driven organization, particularly in the area of talent management. The more focused the mission, the more powerful these effects. Even the ability to entice attractive educational assets to become part of the company at reasonable prices can be enhanced. Soon after becoming independent, McGraw was able to buy out its long-time partners at ALEKS and Area9 Learning, two adaptive learning companies. McGraw had worked with both companies for a decade, but only after becoming independent was it able to interest the private companies in combining their businesses on acceptable terms.

Specialization also matters for achieving operational efficiency and competitive advantage. The education sector encompasses a vast range of products and services, distribution channels, and end markets. Defining the target market as anything that expands the store of "human capital," as Milken did, cannot be practically translated into an effective operating model or an effective business strategy. Even focusing simply on the K–12 sector with the objective of becoming a leader in curriculum, software, and hardware, as Murdoch did, is far too broad. Many areas that may seem highly specialized from afar appear much less so close-up. Educational publishing, for instance, is really a collection of smaller markets. Although Pearson and McGraw-Hill operate in both the higher and K–12 education markets, Cengage and Houghton Mifflin do not appear to operate at a disadvantage by virtue of focusing exclusively on one or another of the segments. Although certain advance placement programs and emerging adaptive learning technologies may span the two markets, the core product and distribution infrastructure are quite discrete. Indeed, success is often determined by strength within distinct geographic regions, academic disciplines, or product sets.

The best businesses start by dominating a niche and systematically building around that core franchise. Turnitin started by focusing exclusively on plagiarism software. Once that position was established, the company began to layer additional capabilities around writing effectiveness, online grading and assessment, and long-term progress tracking for students and institutions. But such is the power of specialization that even the most entrenched established franchises remain at risk of being "niched" at the margin, which opens the door to broader attack.

eCollege came out of nowhere to dominate a niche within the LMS market of serving the needs of managing full distance-learning programs. At the time, Blackboard already had relationships with almost all of those who would become eCollege's core customers. But Blackboard was focused on the much larger market of managing what was going on in the classroom and on various "hybrid" programs. eCollege, in contrast, realized that institutions operating entirely online programs had a wide range of unique needs that required a platform specifically designed for that purpose. Blackboard may have dominated the overall LMS market, but every single public for-profit school that used an outside vendor hired eCollege to manage its online program. More broadly, more than half of the online programs that enrolled over 10,000 students—eCollege's core target market, which encompassed public and nonprofit universities as well—used the eCollege e-learning platform.

The success of eCollege was possible because specialization facilitates both developing and reinforcing all key aspects of competitive advantage. Scale is more easily established and reinforced within the narrowly defined boundaries of specialization. Deep domain expertise allows the cultivation of intense customer relationships and corresponding captivity through product and service innovation. Focusing one's energies on a single activity accelerates movement down the learning curve in a way not possible when those energies are dispersed across multiple initiatives.

Finally, from an investing perspective, specialization also matters. Even Warren Buffett's track record is less than stellar when he strayed into industries in which he did not have deep knowledge of the structure and dynamics—airlines and energy, for example, in contrast to financials and consumer staples. A look at the major LBO restructurings in the education sector just since 2010 reveals billions of losses shared across most key segments of the industry. The investors represent a veritable who's who of international private equity, hedge, pension, and sovereign wealth funds (see Table 6.1). What most had in common, however, was little expertise in the industry.

Relatively few private equity firms have actually specialized in the education sector. One that has is Leeds Equity Partners, which was founded in 1993 to focus on investments in education and which raised its first fund in 1995. Leeds is now on its fifth fund, which was raised in 2010. Although not all of Leeds's nearly fifty investments have been as successful as Nobel—they partnered with Goldman and Providence in the unsuccessful EDMC investment noted earlier—overall the industry-dedicated strategy appears to have outperformed. The latest fund was around $500 million and has achieved returns well above most comparable vintage funds, according to the benchmarks used by Cambridge Associates.[22] Leeds is currently raising a new fund that will likely be significantly larger. The spectacular early

TABLE 6.1
Major LBO restructurings in education sector since 2010

Company	Sector	Date	Key Investor	Type
Houghton I	K–12 publishing	2010	Istithmar World (Dubai)	Sovereign wealth
Houghton II	K–12 publishing	2012	Paulson et al.	Hedge
Cengage	Higher ed publishing (Thomson Learning)	2013	Apax/OMERS	Private equity/Pension
ATI	For-profit university	2013	BC Partners	Private equity
Education Holdings	Test prep (Princeton Review)	2013	Bain Capital	Private equity
EDMC	For-profit university	2014	Goldman Sachs/Providence	Private equity
Edmentum	Supplemental materials	2015	GTCR	Private equity
Nelson Education	Canadian textbooks	2015	Apax/OMERS	Private equity/Pension

returns of Rethink Education suggest that specialization is equally valuable in venture investing.[23]

A number of other broader and larger private equity funds—notably Apollo, Insight, Providence, Spectrum and Warburg Pincus—have also developed significant expertise within the sector. Although it is not possible to identify the returns associated with just their education investments—and, to be sure, not all of them have been winners—a disproportionate number of the most successful private education investments seem to have come from firms with a substantial specialization in the sector.

All Strategy Is Local—Especially in Education

The term *specialization* generally refers to expertise in a certain product or customer "space." Of continuing and even greater importance in most contexts is specialization in physical space.[24] The power of local competitive advantage, particularly in the ability to build scale, continues to be a key determinant of success in education.

Many treat geography as a passé strategic concept in the emerging global digital economy in which customers, partners, and purchases are all a click away. It is true that digital tools and capabilities have in many cases reduced the impact of local scale or have at least broadened the boundaries of the relevant locality. Thus, for instance, Nobel can now manage most of its marketing budget centrally using various online technologies and services to target the relevant demographics and localities with the right messages. But such examples overstate the impact on local competitive advantage. For Nobel, the marketing budget represents a tiny portion of the cost structure. For any business that relies on expensive mass consumer outreach requiring the use of television, newspapers, billboards, and the like, the cost effectiveness remains primarily a function of local scale. Even for Nobel, whose business (like the sector as a whole) relies overwhelmingly on word-of-mouth referrals for marketing, local density of operations is as important as ever. Being recommended to a family who does not live within a few miles of the facility is a wasted referral.

Even in purely digital businesses operating internationally, local scale often remains the prevalent industry characteristic. Turnitin is a "global" leader in antiplagiarism software. The network effect, however, derives from the tendency of students to rely on unpublished materials submitted elsewhere by a friend or online acquaintance. It is accordingly not surprising that the company's global footprint is over-whelmingly an English-language one. In higher education, where the lingua franca of many academic disciplines is English, the proprietary database will still be valuable, but overall it will pale in comparison to the worth of a scale database of local language submissions.

Not surprisingly, the global giant Turnitin has few tools to attack markets in which a relatively small, incumbent, local competitor has been able to build a local network, even with far inferior technol-ogy. Luckily for Turnitin, this is precisely where inorganic acquisitions can actually create value for shareholders. When Turnitin purchased the leading local European competitor in Scandinavia, the company was able to realize significant fixed-cost consolidation opportunities around technology, sales, and marketing combined, as well as revenue opportunities related to its much deeper product set. What's more, because Turnitin is uniquely positioned to benefit from these syner-gies, a reasonable sharing of these will result. For Turnitin's sharehold-ers, this outcome contrasts quite favorably with a more typical auction dynamic with multiple similarly situated suitors in which the seller is able to capture all of this incremental value creation for itself.

The desire for national or international expansion can lead investors to forget the extent to which local scale barriers are often the stron-gest. The tendency of digital developments to expand the borders of the relevant competitive markets is generally bad news for competitive advantage. A simple mathematical example demonstrates the point. In a given local market with some barriers, it is typical that a competitor would need to have at least a 15–25 percent market share to operate at an efficient scale, and only a few could achieve this. Once that mar-ket becomes national, however, local scale players from around the country can all become credible competitors. The scale requirement in this much-expanded marketplace could easily fall to 5 percent or less. This has two implications. First, one is likely to go from a world of a handful of competitors—with whom the chances of developing a con-structive cooperative ecosystem is markedly greater—to one in which twenty or more can profitably be sustained. Second, if it is a sector in which market shares can move 2–3 percent annually, a potential new entrant in a national market could imagine a path to breakeven within a couple of years. In a local market, they would need to expect a cash drain for at least five and maybe as many as ten years.

These observations do not suggest that incumbents should ignore national and international opportunities as the industry structure makes them economically viable. Rather the point is to continue to reinforce local advantages while remaining acutely aware of others to ensure that any new markets provide a viable path to scale. Investing aggressively in adjacencies, whether geographic or in the product or customer space, can play effective offensive and defensive strategic roles. But it can also represent a costly distraction from a core franchise under threat. Which it is in any particular instance requires a nuanced understanding of the sources of incumbent competitive advantage and the potential path for establishing competitive advantage in each relevant market.

Breakups Do Better Than Roll-ups

Chapter 5 noted that acquisitions that build scale can create value for investors if multiple parties that share the same benefits don't bid against each other for the scale-building target. In practice, however, value is destroyed most often not from overpaying for scale but from misunderstanding what constitutes scale. These kinds of strategic errors take two forms.

First, where variable costs predominate and where competitors can operate profitably at "scale" at relatively low market shares, businesses do not have relevant "scale," regardless of their size. There are prices at which bulking up is still worthwhile, but it makes no sense to pay a meaningful "strategic" premium for a competitor in a sector in which scale is not a structurally relevant characteristic. The new private equity owners of Knowledge Learning can continue to buy child-care centers, as Milken did for twenty years, but doing so is unlikely to create any more value over the next twenty years than it did in the last.

Second, when one business buys another business, it is not scale enhancing if the two businesses do fundamentally different things. This is true regardless of whether one or the other or both of the businesses has scale on its own. This may seem obvious, but it is the source of much of the foolish deal making in the sector. Somehow owners manage to convince themselves that the relevant boundaries of the sectors within which they play are far broader than in reality. The private equity buyers of Plato Learning thought it was a good idea to buy Archipelago Learning to create a scale provider of computer-based K–12 supplemental learning products. Neither company ever gained much traction on its own in the public markets. The problem was that the specific products were sold through entirely different sales channels—one sold primarily to districts and the other to individual schools. In addition, from a product perspective, they were entirely distinct. The resulting combination took on more debt than it could support and filed for bankruptcy in 2015. It would not be surprising if the new owners, predominantly distressed-debt investors, ultimately decide to sell off the business in pieces.

A number of even less obvious expansions into educational domains have also had poor outcomes. In early 2015, the Advisory Board Company, a health-care research and consulting business, spent $850 million for Royall, a consultant to the higher education sector focusing on enrollment management. The Advisory Board lost almost a third of its overall value after it reported disappointing results for the acquisition only six months later.

Also in 2015, LinkedIn bought Lynda.com, an online video training platform, for $1.5 billion. LinkedIn shareholders should have had a heavy degree of skepticism, even before the disappointing guidance that quickly followed the acquisition announcement.[25] The transactions that represent the closest precedents ended badly. In the 1990s, Monster.com, the leading online jobs platform for the previous generation, spent over $1 billion on more than a dozen off-line staffing and training businesses. When it announced the spin-off of these in 2002, in an admission that the combination of businesses made no strategic sense, the stock skyrocketed.[26]

A year after making the acquisition, LinkedIn shareholders received an unexpected windfall when Microsoft paid a 50% premium to buy the entire company.[27] Unfortunately, however, because the company had performed so poorly in the interim, the price was still far below where LinkedIn had traded before buying Lynda.com. Microsoft shareholders should be skeptical of the "big dreams" articulated by management to "transform education" through the acquisition.[28]

As with the spin-off of McGraw-Hill's education business and the education separations by Reed, Wolters, Viacom, and others before it, the track record for shareholders from spinning off and slimming down is far better than for bulking up and broadening out. In 2015, Pearson decided to sell PowerSchool for $350 million in a hotly contested auction won by Vista Equity Partners, one of the most successful private equity firms of recent years.[29] This decision was not driven by Pearson's view that this was a bad business. On the contrary, PowerSchool has some of the highest competitive advantages in the sector. Rather it was from the realization of the obstacles to connecting the management of school administration functions to Pearson's overarching focus on improving student outcomes.

Content Is Not King, and It Is Really Expensive to Develop

In education, as in media, great content and brands are hugely valuable. Unfortunately, there is no barrier to spending large sums of money to try to create such content. As a result, the business of spending money to create great content has never been a very good one. If a movie studio only produced hits or a basal publisher was always ensured its curriculum would be universally adopted, these enterprises would spout unending streams of money. Sadly, although there are anecdotal cases of studios and publishers that had a historic run of success at some point or other, these have all come to an end. And when they do end, no one knows how to replicate those rare periods of uninterrupted prosperity.

The fact that these are both fundamentally hit-driven enterprises does not mean there are not best practices to follow—indeed, the margin disparity between the best and worst run industry players is substantial in both the entertainment and educational sectors. Nor does it mean there is not value in specialization in these businesses—studios do better when they stick to genres in which they have experience, and educational publishers do better when they stick to disciplines in which they are the leader. But the core scale advantage in both of these content-creation enterprises comes from the substantial fixed-cost infrastructure required to market and distribute the product, not from the content creation itself.

To be fair, education publishing is consistently a better business than movie making, in part because there are greater fixed-cost requirements to the content-creation side of educational publishing. Making a new movie is almost entirely a variable-cost undertaking. New curriculum product development, whether for a basal adoption or a new online course, does build on the previous fixed-cost investment in tools and content. That said, hold your wallet close whenever an educational company touts the ability to throw bodies at new content development as its unique competitive advantage—whether it is UNext spending a million dollars per course, K12 Inc. developing an entirely new basal curriculum, or Amplify hiring hundreds of developers in its hip Dumbo offices.

The cost of developing educational content has come down due to the availability of new technology. Although, for a time, the additional requirements of creating hybrid products actually increased costs, the long-term trend is clearly in the other direction. This fact is not good news but bad news for these businesses. The historic strength of educational content businesses relative to pure entertainment ones was precisely the fixed-cost requirements that are becoming increasingly insignificant. Indeed, the explosion of small new entrants on the content side is reflective of this new economic reality.

As the fixed-cost scale components of these businesses decline, the attractiveness of pure educational content businesses will also diminish. Although learning curve cost benefits should be theoretically available to educational content businesses with personalized adaptive learning models, the evidence of these is still scant. Both new entrants and incumbents would do better to look outside of content for opportunities either to establish network effects, as Teachers Pay Teachers or Turnitin have, or for more traditional scale businesses. Such businesses are the ones that provide tools and capabilities—learning management systems and predictive analytic software, for instance—to improve the effective distribution reach of the now relatively less attractive pure curriculum content players.

You Can't Win If You Don't Play—Nice

"World domination. The same old dream."
—JAMES BOND IN *DR. NO* (1962)

The prospect of total victory can be an inspirational objective for the troops, but it rarely guides a successful strategy. Although natural monopolies exist in sectors with overwhelming scale advantages, few educational verticals appear to have such characteristics. In any market in which profitable scale can be achieved at less than a 50 percent market share, the best strategies revolve around peaceful coexistence, not endless war. Finding a successful equilibrium in educational markets involves identifying the sources of one's own relative advantages and pressing these, while avoiding those in which others have the advantage. The relevant dimensions of competition can be by geography, product, discipline, customer segment, or some combination thereof. When a competitor violates this unspoken rule, one must retaliate hard in the aggressor's own most profitable niche—not in anger, but in sadness. It is also critical to signal a willingness to return to the status quo ante by designing a path for a mutually dignified retreat from the unprofitable battlefield.

Achieving some stability and balance in relation to one's horizontal competitors is only part of the battle. When Pearson, the leading textbook publisher, bought eCollege, the leading manager of online courses for universities, some at the company advocated requiring eCollege customers to now use only Pearson-developed curriculum. Wisely, Pearson leadership realized that the continued success of eCollege hinged on its ability to work effectively with as wide a range of course and curriculum developers as possible. If Pearson had limited access to the eCollege platform, as some proposed internally, Pearson's acquisition would have created dis-synergies and improved the competitive prospects for all the alternative learning management systems operating without such restrictions. More problematic, such a move would have likely led other publishers and platforms to establish competing exclusive alliances. The result would have been both less profitable businesses and less useful products.

Educational companies operate in a complex, multilayered ecosystem that includes institutional and individual customers, competitors and suppliers, public and private entities, for-profit and nonprofit organizations, current and prospective employers, and parents and interest groups of various stripes. Given the structurally conflicting objectives of many of these constituencies, keeping them all happy all of the time is neither sensible nor possible. Just the same, doing what one can to keep peace in the broader educational cosmos is as important as keeping peace among peers. Blackboard's failure to do this is what created such an opportunity for Instructure, Desire2Learn, and Moodle. All commercial equilibriums are fragile, and there is nothing like externally imposed tensions to shatter an informal armistice. As Blackboard learned the hard way, it is worse than just bad karma when everyone in your ecosystem is giving you the evil eye. It really is a sign that the end is nigh.

Regulation Is a Fickle Benefactor

Given how much of the educational universe is directly or indirectly funded by public sources, the avoidance of regulation is not feasible. Even a business like Nobel, which has studiously avoided government funds, cannot help but be deeply affected by the regulatory environment. The quality of competing local public schools and preschool funding will necessarily affect their business. Similarly the particular local licensing requirements are likely to circumscribe the possible cost structure, including minimum staffing ratios. The optimal strategies are to use any period of government largesse to build a business model that is robust enough to thrive under a wide range of funding and regulatory regimes. The total collapse of the for-profit university sector suggests that not enough was done in anticipation of changes to the Title IV programs on which the sector relies. Only Grand Canyon University seems to have avoided the temptation to engage in an orgy of unfocused growth in programs, locations, and acquisitions.

Public authorities can offer a business more than cash. The imposition of license requirements on all industry participants that track investments made by a particular incumbent clearly benefit that player. Indeed, incumbents have every incentive to encourage ever more costly regulatory burdens that are consistent with their own investment strategy to both give themselves a head start and eliminate the possibility of low-cost competitors. More broadly, compliance requirements typically define the magnitude of fixed-cost investment needed to participate in an industry and accordingly imply the level of scale needed to operate profitably. In the extreme, it could ensure a "natural" monopoly or even make it impossible to economically provide the particular service.

But any educational business lucky enough to benefit from the protection provided by regulatory requirements that constrain competition should prepare for a change in regime or, potentially worse, complete liberalization. The best defense for such an eventuality—in addition to aggressive lobbying—is to build not just relevant scale but also customer captivity in every way possible in the interim: contractually, by integrating the product into the customer work flow, and by creating such a uniquely comprehensive integrated package of products and services that finding an alternative provider (or even a group of providers) would be difficult. In short, rather than letting the protection provided by the high government barriers lull management into a false sense of security, the time should be used to establish the business an indispensable partner to its customers. If successful, the loss of those government barriers will only reveal a more permanent set of competitive advantages.

When the Facts Change, Change Your Mind

"Humility is really important because it keeps you fresh and new."
—STEVEN TYLER

"It ain't the heat, it's the humility."
—YOGI BERRA

Everyone comes to the subject of education with deep preconceptions from their own formative life experiences. Distinguishing which aspects of these personal epiphanies, if any, provide a useful source of investment ideas is a complicated process. To be successful, the underlying analysis must be grounded in an appreciation for the nature of of competitive advantage, on the one hand, and an understanding of the structure of the targeted educational industry sector, on the other. Failing to take either into account is a recipe for financial disaster.

The hallmark of successful investment decision making is to approach an opportunity with an openness to new information. It is perfectly acceptable and indeed useful to begin with an investment thesis regarding a particular asset class. But the trick is to be willing to alter the nuances of the thesis as new data arise. Starting out with immovable biases undermines the integrity of the process and will inevitably lead to a flawed outcome. The profound emotional connection many of the profiled investors had to a particular educational investment thesis led to two related "bias" problems.

First, initial investment decisions were made that not only had apparent flaws but were structured to make shifting course later difficult. Both the design of the university "partnerships" and the decision to invest tens of millions in course development before understanding the market appetite made it difficult for UNext to effectively change direction later. This troubling tendency to double down on one's own preconceptions reflects the millions in other people's money spent by

Whittle to design the "optimal" K–12 school model—which magically produced exactly the model that Whittle thought made the most sense before the expensive masturbatory exercise started.

Second, even when the initial structure does not prove an obstacle, the intensity of belief in the thesis being pursued can lead investors to be dangerously slow in shifting their approach, even in the face of overwhelming evidence of its flaws. Successful entrepreneurs and innovators of all kinds consistently demonstrate the ability to undertake a "strategic pivot" at the right moment.[30] To their credit, both of the leading commercial MOOCs—Udacity and Coursera—have undertaken significant pivots to their initially flawed business models. Time will tell whether these changes were too little, too late.

Even in established businesses, particularly those that have a hit-driven aspect, as many educational content businesses do, the distinguishing characteristics of the best-run businesses are the ability to quickly and mercilessly cut off investment in failed product and to redeploy the capital into more promising ones. The slow, five-year, billion-dollar death march of Amplify could have ended differently if the company had decisively refocused and redeployed its investments in a single domain built around the core Wireless Generation assessment products. The fact that new owner Laurene Powell Jobs insisted that News Corp. fire almost half the staff and reinstall Larry Berger as overall CEO before taking it on—and has continued to refocus the business since—provides some hope for a more modest but more successful future.

Adherents of particular educational business models and advocates of particular educational public policy approaches have a tendency to use very similar language in promoting their views. Their favored instrumentality of change is typically described alternatively as "transformational" or "revolutionary." In both cases, the evidence suggests that a narrowing of focus, a nuanced appreciation of the particular market structure and context, and an emphasis on the importance of effective execution would go a long way toward improving the probability of successful outcomes.

But this is easier said than done. In general, revolutionaries are not known for their humility. Scaling back ambitions and moving from high-minded rhetoric to the gritty operational challenges can have the feel of selling out. When the principles involved are viewed as fundamental, compromise—whether to a business model or to a policy platform—can be anathema. Yet the failure to do so in both instances not only makes the perfect the enemy of the good, but it also threatens to more permanently undermine the potential long-term benefits to both shareholders and the public.

In the public policy arena, there is no better example of this phenomenon than the failed efforts of well-meaning reform advocates to use Facebook CEO Mark Zuckerberg's $100 million gift to Newark's public schools to revolutionize urban public education more broadly. As documented by Dale Russakoff in her compelling 2015 book *The Prize*, the Newark initiative was disastrous, leaving little to show for the massive investment. In seeking transformational results that could be used as a template elsewhere, leaders misjudged the political environment, ignored the specific needs of the traumatized local population, and entrusted execution to true believers who did not have the required skills. It would be hard to argue that the magnitude of this failure has not set back even better-conceived reform efforts. Those most responsible for the Newark debacle frequently invoked jargon plucked from business best sellers to justify their misguided efforts. Given the embarrassing results of many of the "transformative" educational business initiatives—including a number with which the same executives involved in Newark were associated—it is unclear how compelling these references were. More broadly, the failure of these business ventures has given credible fodder to those who resist the active participation of for-profit enterprises in the educational sphere.

The education ecosystem will always comprise a complex network of public and both for-profit and nonprofit institutions. The public sector is subject to political whims, and the nonprofit sector typically relies on uncertain funding from public and private sources. Advocates of for-profit education often understandably emphasize the invisible hand of market forces in improving quality and efficiency. The most constructive role that the for-profit segment may play in the overall educational environment is the unique level of stability provided when it establishes defensible business models.

The most aspirational educational ventures have the virtue of good intentions but often come at the cost of a lack of sustainability. The strongest education franchises benefit from multiple competitive advantages reinforced by a consistent operational focus. These characteristics are structurally difficult to achieve in broad-based revolutionary business models. As frustrating as it may be to an education visionary, both investors and the public will be better off if the innovative ideas are applied to a narrow product or geographic space in which scale, customer captivity, and learning can be practically achieved. Such modest successes can serve as both a platform and an inspiration for broader transformation to come. Without a sustainable business model, however, even the most inspirational educational investors and entrepreneurs will ultimately build only a legacy of disillusionment.

Notes

Acknowledgments

1. Alasdair MacIntyre, *After Virtue: A Study in Moral Theory* (Notre Dame, IN: University of Notre Dame Press, 1981).
2. Jerome Karabel, *The Chosen: The Hidden History of Admission and Exclusion at Harvard, Yale, and Princeton* (New York: Houghton Mifflin, 2005).
3. Nicholas Lemann, *The Big Test: The Secret History of the American Meritocracy* (New York: Farrar, Straus and Giroux, 1999).

Introduction

1. Although this quote is widely attributed to Dewey, like much conventional wisdom in education, there is scant evidence for its truth. According to the Center for Dewey Studies, the closest sentiment for which written attribution can be found is "Cease conceiving of education as mere preparation for later life, and make it the full meaning of the present life." http://deweycenter .siu.edu/faq.html, retrieved May 17, 2016. The actual quote may be from a 1912 book by a professor of education at the State University of Iowa. See Irving King, *Social Aspects of Education: A Book of Sources and Original Discussions with Annotated Bibliographies* (New York: MacMillan, 1912), 274.
2. Edward Wyatt, "Investors See Room for Profit in the Demand for Education," *New York Times*, November 4, 1999, 1A.
3. Chris Whittle, interview in "Privatizing Public Education," *60 Minutes*, CBS, November 14, 1999.
4. Joseph Kahn, "Wall Street's Banks Kept to Hierarchy During 1998," *New York Times*, January 1, 1999.

5. Terzah Ewing and Suzanne McGee, "Deals and Dealmakers: Venture Capitalist Allen Gains from as Many as 3 IPOs in a Week," *Wall Street Journal,* November 15, 1999, C27.

6. DLJ held shares through the Sprout group, its venture arm.

7. The National Commission on Excellence in Education, *A Nation at Risk: The Imperative for Educational Reform* (Washington, D.C. U.S. Government Publishing Office, 1983).

8. Alexis de Toqueville, *Democracy in America* (1835; New York: Library of America, 2004), 46.

9. The field of education has spawned multiple genres of literature, spanning both academic and popular formats. Within academia, serious research has moved well beyond traditional areas of study within "soft sciences," such as education, law, and sociology, to encompass highly specialized realms, such as advanced economics and neuroscience. See Joseph Stiglitz and Bruce Greenwald, *Creating a Learning Society: A New Approach to Growth Development and Social Progress* (New York: Columbia University Press, 2014). Popular formats include memoirs from the front lines; policy tracts from long-time sector scholars; and chronicles of scandal, history, political combat, and even scientific research across the full landscape of educational activity from thoughtful journalists. See Benedict Carey, *How We Learn: The Surprising Truth About When, Where, and Why It Happens* (New York: Random House, 2014); Elizabeth Green, *Building a Better Teacher: How Teaching Works (and How to Teach It to Everyone)* (New York: Norton, 2014); Dana Goldstein, *The Teacher Wars: A History of America's Most Embattled Profession* (New York: Doubleday, 2014); Amanda Ripley, *The Smartest Kids in the World and How They Got That Way* (New York: Simon & Schuster, 2013); Paul Tough, *How Children Succeed: Grit, Curiosity, and the Hidden Power of Character* (New York: Houghton Mifflin Harcourt, 2013); and Jeffrey Selingo, *College Unbound: The Future of Higher Education and What It Means for Students* (New Harvest, 2013).

10. "Foundation States," Foundation Center, http://data.foundationcenter .org.

11. George Joseph, "9 Billionaires Are About to Remake New York's Public Schools—Here's Their Story," *The Nation*, March 19, 2015.

12. Walter Isaacson, *Steve Jobs* (New York: Simon & Schuster, 2011), chapter 18.

13. Jeffrey Silber et al., *BMO Capital Markets 2015 Education and Training Yearbook,* September 2015, 6. http://bmocm-archives.com/uploads /Education_&_Training_Report_File.pdf.

14. James Surowiecki, "Better All the Time," *New Yorker*, November 10, 2014.

15. Early childhood learning represents only 5 percent of overall K–12 spending, or $37.6 billion. Unlike the rest of K–12 education, however, most

of the providers are private, not public, so that it represents just over half of for-profit K–12 revenues. This category encompasses activities both in and out of school, from infancy until the early grades.

1. The Wizard of Ed

1. Michael Cannell, "Bicoastal Romance," *Architectural Digest* 69, 8 (August 2012): 68–75. The firm also designed Karan's majestic retail stores.

2. See Deborah Sontag, "Yale President Quitting to Lead National Private School Venture," *New York Times*, May 26, 1992, A1.

3. Fourth Annual Avenues New Year Letter, January 7, 2014.

4. All subheading quotes are from *The Wonderful Wizard of Oz*. Frank Lyman Baum, William Wallace Denslow, and Michael Patrick Hearn, *The Annotated Wizard of Oz: The Wonderful Wizard of Oz* (New York: Norton, 2000).

5. Unless otherwise specified, the details on Whittle's early years are from Vance H. Trimble, *An Empire Undone: The Wild Ride and Hard Fall of Chris Whittle* (New York: Birch Lane, 1995) and James Stewart, "Grand Illusion," *New Yorker*, October 21, 1994.

6. In a 1990 *Vanity Fair* profile, Lynn Hirschberg describes the rupture with Whittle's one-time mentor as the culmination of five years of "Oedipal combat." Lynn Hirschberg, "Is Chris Whittle the Devil?," *Vanity Fair*, March 1990, 233.

7. Hirschberg, "Is Chris Whittle the Devil?", 198.

8. Stewart, "Grand Illusion," 71.

9. Trimble, *Empire Undone*, 288.

10. Ibid., 326.

11. Whittle initially sought as much as $30 million; the amount he ultimately settled for has been reported as between $7.5 and $11.25 million. Compare Stewart, "Grand Illusion," 79 ($7.5 million) to Trimble, *Empire Undone*, 327 (claiming that Whittle received three $1.25 million annual payments on top of the $7.5 million).

12. Stewart, "Grand Illusion," 64.

13. Trimble, *Empire Undone*, 327.

14. Ibid., 293.

15. Ibid., 275.

16. The seminal modern case is *United States v. Jewell*, 532 F.2d 697 (CA9 1976). The Supreme Court recently extended the doctrine to civil as well as criminal cases, in *Global-Tech Appliances v. SEB*, 563 U.S. 754 (2011). See also Edwards, "The Criminal Degrees of Knowledge," *Modern Law Review* 17, 4 (July 1954): 294.

17. Stewart and I teach together at Columbia Journalism School, and he generously shared some of his background notes collected in preparing the 1994 article.

18. Stewart, "Grand Illusion," 80.

19. Whittle wrote a regular column for *Tennessee Illustrated*. Trimble, *Empire Undone*, 262.

20. *Yale Alumni Magazine*, October 1992.

21. Sontag, "Yale President Quitting."

22. Jordan later said, "I wasted three years with Whittle Communications. They were the most unproductive years of my life." Stewart, "Grand Illusion," 74.

23. Commenting on the stream of "million dollar men" pouring into Knoxville at Whittle Communications by the early 1990s one observer said, "They look to me like 'trophies.' I don't know how he can use all of them." Trimble, *Empire Undone*, 234.

24. Richard Bernstein, "The Yale Schmidt Leaves Behind," *New York Times*, June 14, 1992.

25. See Benno Schmidt, *Wall Street Journal*, June 5, 1992 ("The problem, I think, is the system itself . . . The system virtually cries out for radical change.").

26. Interview with former K-III executive.

27. Interview with Peter Haje.

28. Stewart, "Grand Illusion," 74.

29. Trimble, *Empire Undone*, 350–51.

30. Ibid., 352.

31. Diane Brady, "Commentary: Chris Whittle's New IPO Deserves a D-," *Businessweek*, September 5, 1999.

32. Trimble, *Empire Undone*, 343.

33. Ibid., 270.

34. Morley Safer, "Privatizing Public Education," *60 Minutes*, November 14, 1999.

35. Edison Schools Inc., IPO Prospectus, November 10, 1999, 41.

36. Stewart, "Grand Illusion," 76.

37. See Prospectus. Years later, in 2005, Hawaii would finally hire the company for selected turnaround services.

38. Many of the technology IPOs of the same era faced analogous valuation challenges. See Jonathan A. Knee, *The Accidental Investment Banker: Inside the Decade That Transformed Wall Street* (Oxford: Oxford University Press, 2006), 123–126.

39. The precise calculation of the WACC is $E \times Re + D \times Rd \times (1{-}corporate$ tax rate). E and D are the proportion of the company's total value reflected in its equity and debt, respectively. Re and Rd are the respective rates of

return required to attract that equity and debt—usually referred to as the cost of equity and the cost of debt. Although the cost of debt can usually be calculated with reasonable precision based on rates at which companies with comparable credit profiles have borrowed money, the cost of equity is always subject to disagreement among bankers and economists. The cost of equity is a function of the size of the risk premium investors would require to invest in a particular company. This in turn is a function of two always controversial variables: the risk premium embedded in the stock market as a whole, and the extent to which the particular company's returns are correlated with the market as a whole (the latter is known as Beta, the coefficient of market risk for a particular security or portfolio).

40. From 2000 to 2002, more schools (27) dropped Edison than decided to renew their contracts. Heidi Steffens and Peter W. Cookson, Jr., "Limitations of the Market Model," *Education Week*, August 7, 2002.

41. Terry Webster, "Protesters Complain About Edison at School Board," *Las Vegas Sun*, August 24, 2001.

42. Mark Walsh, "Still in the Red, Edison Now Hit with Case of 'Enronitis'," *Education Week*, February 20, 2002.

43. Diana Henriques and Jacques Steinberg, "Operator of Public Schools in Settlement with SEC," *New York Times*, May 15, 2002. Although many stocks fared poorly after 9/11, Edison shares actually experienced a brief renaissance, breaking $20/share in January 2002.

44. "Edison Schools Announces Additions to the Management Team, *PR Newswire*, August. 7, 2002.

45. "Edison Announces Four New Nominees for Board of Directors," *PR Newswire*, November 19, 2002. The fourth independent was necessitated by Delaney's appointment as a company officer. One of these independents was replaced several months later. "Edison Schools Welcomes Edward S. Harris to Board of Directors.," *PR Newswire*, April 30, 2003.

46. Dorothy's response to the observation that she had "some queer friends." I was part of the team at Evercore Partners that advised the Special Committee of the Board that considered the Edison go-private transaction. All of the key dates and facts described here are as detailed in the shareholder communication of October 10, 2003. Additional color is provided from interviews with participants in preparation for this book.

47. Michael Gross, "Whittling Away Debt," *New York Daily News*, November 10, 2002. Although not included in the agreed terms, some suspected an informal understanding that a new buyer would forgive these company loans. See Nelson Schwartz, "The Nine Lives of Chris Whittle," *Fortune*, October 27, 2003.

48. Although he ended up with less than he had hoped, Whittle did just fine. "Chris Whittle came out of the deal with about $21 million dollars [sic],

a 42 percent raise, a loan of $1.68 million, and eligibility for a bonus of 245 percent of his base salary." Kenneth Saltman, *The Edison Schools: Corporate Schooling and the Assault on Public Education* (New York: Routledge, 2005), 64.

49. Diana B. Henriques, "A Learning Curve for Whittle Venture," *New York Times*, May 25, 2002.

50. Trace Urban et al., "Thoughts on the Deal: Adding Insult to Injury," ThinkEquity Partners, July 17, 2003.

51. Trace Urban et al., "Arbs Likely to Make Money Here," ThinkEquity Partners, September 15, 2003.

52. Carmen McCollum, "Edison Learning Official Takes New Job," *Times of Northwest Indiana*, December 31, 2013.

53. Kris Hudley, "State Pays $180 Million in Fees, Gets Little from Long-Term Investment," *Tampa Bay Times*, October 17, 2010.

54. Kate Nelson, "Florida Teachers Say They Want No Part of Edison Buyout," *The Notebook*, November 1, 2003. The union had leaked a copy of the "scathing critique" of Liberty Partners by the outside consultant just days before the shareholder vote on the deal. Vineeta Anand, "Scathing critique: Consultant gives failing grade to Florida's private equity manager," *Pensions & Investments*, November 10, 2003.

55. A sinister interpretation of events and a broader critique of Edison performance can be found in Kenneth Saltman, *The Edison Schools*, 57–64.

56. Kris Hudley, "State Pays $180 Million in Fees."

57. "Edison Schools Partners with Essex County to Develop and Launch New School Design in the United Kingdom," *PR Newswire*, June 13, 2003.

58. From the Nations Academy website, quoted in Dana Rubenstein, "School's Out Forever as Durst, Whittle Part Ways on Private 57th Street Academy," *New York Observer*, September 9, 2008.

59. Thomas Toch, "Super-Special Ed," *New York Magazine*, July 20, 2008.

60. The capital contribution and corresponding ownership of Nations Academy is included as Exhibit A in the fraud complaint filed by Lynn Tilton.

61. Steve Hendrix, "Buyers of Montgomery Estate Plan a 'Global' Private School," *Washington Post*, December 8, 2007. Whittle was typically vague on the price and terms: "Let's just say that we have an agreement and that some money has changed hands."

62. Eliot Brown, "Durst to Build Private School on 11th Avenue," *New York Observer*, February 19, 2008.

63. Jon Boone, "Global Network of Schools Planned," *Financial Times*, June 23, 2007.

64. Jenna Goudreau, "Lynn Tilton: Is She the Richest Self-Made Woman in America?" *Forbes*, April 6, 2011. Tilton herself has become the subject of SEC fraud charges. See Sheelah Kolhatkar, "How Lynn Tilton Went from Company Savior to SEC Target," *BloombergBusiness*, July 16, 2015.

65. *Emet v. Nations Academy et al.*, SDNY, August 23, 2010. A settlement in which Varkey agreed to pay Tilton her $5 million back was reached before the end of the year.

66. Steve Hendrix, "New York Firm Ends Bid to Build School," *Washington Post*, September 25, 2008. Although the development plan had drawn some local criticism, one of the opponents conceded that their efforts had not been dispositive: "It just might not be the best time to build a 1,600-student private school in an area that already has plenty of private schools."

67. Dana Rubenstein, "Durst Files Plans for Off-Again, On-Again Esquire Private School," *New York Observer*, September 18, 2009.

68. Shelly Banjo, "Whittle Starts a City School," *Wall Street Journal*, January 31, 2011. Although not publicly revealed, a portion of Liberty's share was off-loaded to a group of wealthy individuals.

69. Although originally planned as a division of Edison, the new funding partners necessitated the creation of a new investment vehicle, Edison School Holdings.

70. David Kaplan, "Chris Whittle's Plan to Make a World-Class Private School," *Fortune*, April 6, 2011.

71. Jenny Anderson, "The Best School $75 Million Can Buy," *New York Times*, July 8, 2011.

72. Aaron Gell, "Has Avenues Mastermind Chris Whittle Learned His Lesson?" *New York Observer*, June 13, 2012.

73. Richard Bradley, "The New School," *Worth* (August/September 2011).

74. See Kaplan, "Chris Whittle's plan." Teachers were said to make over $100,000 on average. See also Carl Swanson, "How Do You Say 'Early Admission' in Mandarin?," *New York Magazine*, September 9, 2012.

75. Sophia Hollander, "Private School Goes All In with Tech," *Wall Street Journal*, November 18, 2012.

76. Amanda M. Fairbanks, "Whittle Is Seeking a Global Audience for His New Ed Venture," *Education Week*, September 26, 2012.

77. In 2011 and 2012, Whittle asserted the availability of, alternatively, $4 million in scholarship money (see "Move Over, Dalton," *Economist*, September 1, 2012), but this was reduced to $3 million by 2013 (Jenny Andersen, "Is This the Best Education Money Can Buy?" *New York Times*, May 2, 2013). This corresponded to the equivalent of less than 70 full scholarships, or under 5 percent of reported full capacity of 1635 students. A typical New York City private school gives 12–18 percent in scholarships.

78. See Gell, "Has Whittle Learned His Lesson?"

79. Celia Walden, "World Class: a superschool for the global age," *Daily Telegraph*, February 4, 2013.

80. Sometimes, but not always, the claim of one additional round of financing is couched with the caveat this would cover the first two of the schools. See Anderson, "Best School $75 Million Can Buy."

81. According to Whittle, the schools will be on average as large or larger than the New York one, with an anticipated 30,000 to 40,000 students. See Dan Wolfman and Chris Beier, "How I Did It: How Education Entrepreneur Chris Whittle Disproved Skeptics," *Inc.com*, November 12, 2012.

82. Anderson, "Best School $75 Million Can Buy."

83. The teaching of the French national curriculum by these schools is overseen by the Agency for French Teaching Abroad, which is part of the Ministry of Foreign Affairs.

84. Lycée aside, there has been an explosion of international chains of profit-driven private schools with which Avenues will be competing (discussed in chapter 5). See Ian Wylie, "Education goes global," *Financial Times*, December 12, 2012.

85. Fairbanks, "Whittle Is Seeking a Global Audience."

86. Sophia Hollander, "Education Entrepreneur Chris Whittle Resigns From Avenues School," *Wall Street Journal*, March 5, 2015.

87. See Carl Swanson, "How Do You Say 'Early Admission'?"

88. Nelson Schwartz, "Nine Lives of Chris Whittle."

89. Hollander, "Education Entrepreneur Chris Whittle Resigns."

90. "NJ Acting Schools Chief Faces Questions About Transparency, Imperiling His Confirmation," *Star-Ledger*, March 13, 2011.

91. Maura Waltz, "Chris Cerf returns to the education private sector—but in Brazil," *Chalkbeat*, March 10, 2010.

92. Arianna Prothero, "John E. Chubb, Education Researcher and National Private School Leader, Dies," *Education Week Blog*, November 13, 2015.

93. See "GSV Capital Corp. Reports First Quarter 2013 Results of Operations," *Global Newswire*, May 8 2013. Current holdings at http://gsv-cap.com/charts/.

94. Consistent research results since the 1970s confirm that people arrive at desired but erroneous conclusions by emphasizing consistent evidence at the expense of any inconsistent evidence. See C. G. Lord, L. Ross, and M. R. Lepper (1979). "Biased Assimilation and Attitude Polarization: The Effects of Prior Theories on Subsequently Considered Evidence," *Journal of Personality and Social Psychology*, 37 (1979): 2098–2109; or, more recently, P. H. Ditto and D. F. Lopez, "Motivated Skepticism: Use of Differential Decision Criteria for Preferred and Nonpreferred Conclusions," *Journal of Personality and Social Psychology*, 63 (1992): 568–84.

2. Rupert and the Chancellor: A Tragic Love Story

1. See Matt Richtel, "In Classroom of Future, Stagnant Scores," *New York Times*, September 3, 2011.

2. See Trip Gabriel and Matt Richtel, "Inflating the Software Report Card," *New York Times*, October 8, 2011.

3. Lee Wilson, "Apple's iPad Textbooks Cost 5X More Than Print," *The Education Business Blog* (February 23, 2012).

4. Phil Wahba, "Archipelago Learning IPO Prices Within Range," *Reuters*, November 19, 2009.

5. Clayton M. Christensen, *The Innovator's Dilemma: When New Technologies Cause Great Firms to Fail* (Cambridge, MA: *Harvard Business Review*, 1997).

6. Jill Lepore, "The Disruption Machine," *New Yorker*, June 23, 2014.

7. James Liebman and Jonah Rockoff, "Moving Mountains in New York City: Joel Klein's Legacy by the Numbers," *Education Week*, November 30, 2010.

8. "IAC Announces Intent to Pursue IPO of Match Group," *PR Newswire*, June 25, 2015. This will be the eighth independent company to emerge from this strategy.

9. Jim Edwards, "Why News Corp. Invested $30 Million in Cow and Chicken Farms," *Business Insider*, December 6, 2012.

10. Almost $15 billion of these diverse write-downs had occurred just since 2009, suggesting an acceleration in the pace of bad decisions.

11. Amy Chozick and Michael J. de la Merced, "At News Corp., a Plan to Sever Publishing Arm," *New York Times*, June 26, 2012.

12. Robert MacMillan, "Dow Jones Cost News Corp $2.8 Bln in Writedown," *Reuters*, February 6, 2009.

13. The profit metric used is called EBITDA—earnings before interest, tax depreciation, and amortization—and is discussed in detail in chapter 3.

14. Kenneth Gilpin, "Pearson to Buy a Publisher from News Corp.," *New York Times*, February 10, 1996.

15. News Corp. 8-K, November 24, 2004, 95.

16. "News Corporation to Acquire Technology Company Wireless Generation," *Business Wire*, November 22, 2010.

17. News Corp. spokespeople pointed to the fact that the deal "had been in the works for months" as evidence of Klein's complete lack of involvement. Fernanda Santos, "News Corp., After Hiring Klein, Buys Technology Partner in a City Schools Project," *New York Times*, November 23, 2010.

18. Brian Stetler and Tim Arango, "News Corp. Reels in a Top Educator," *New York Times*, November 9, 2010.

19. Katherine Ward, "Who's the Most Important Living New Yorker?" *New York Magazine*, September 26, 2010.

20. Julie Petersen, "For Educational Entrepreneurs, Innovation Yields High Returns," *Education Next*, Spring 2014.

21. Valerie Strauss, "DIBELS Test: A Question of Validity," *Washington Post*, March 26, 2007; Alan Dessoff, "DIBELS Draws Doers & Doubters," *District Administration*, August 2007.

22. The Children First initiative, from which the Accountability Initiative grew, was funded in part with outside contributions from the Broad and Robertson Foundations. "Klein Announces Children First: A New Agenda for Public Education in New York," *NYC Department of Education Press Release*, October 3, 2002.

23. Carl Campanile, "Schools Striking Up the Bandwidth," *New York Post*, October 24, 2003.

24. Precedent examples are detailed in "ARIS on the Side of Caution: A Survey of New York City Principals on the City's Accountability Computer System," a report by Public Advocate Betsy Gotbaum, August 2009, 12–16.

25. Anastasia Gornick, "Law Professor Accepts Post at DOE," *Columbia Spectator*, February 6, 2006. Professor Liebman had also written a handful of law review articles on educational policy topics.

26. "Schools Chancellor Joel I. Klein Announces Selection of IBM to Develop Achievement Reporting System for Educators and Parents" (press release), NYC Department of Education, March 3, 2007. Between CIOs Kroot and Brodheim, an internal staff person served in an acting capacity. McKinsey consulting was also hired to assist the department in assessing the competing proposals.

27. "ARIS on the Side of Caution: A Survey of New York City Principals on the City's Accountability Computer System," a report by public advocate Betsy Gotbaum, August 2009, 6.

28. IBM had also earlier donated a million dollars worth of computers to the public schools. Elisa Gootman, "Equipment Donated to Convention is Passed to Schools," *New York Times*, September 3, 2004. Liebman denied that IBM played any role in designing the specifications.

29. At around $5 million, Wireless Generation's contribution represented less than 10 percent of the overall contract value.

30. Elissa Gootman, "As Schools Face Cuts, Delays on Data System Bring More Frustration," *New York Times*, October 24, 2008.

31. Javier Hernandez, "Chief Accountability Officer for City Schools Resigns," *New York Times*, July 8, 2009.

32. Interview with Professor James Liebman.

33. Race to the Top Program Executive Summary, U.S. Department of Education, November 2009.

34. This is how an Amplify spokesperson characterized it role. Ben Chapman, "City Schools Dumping $95 Million Computer System for Tracking Student Data," *New York Daily News*, November 16, 2014.

35. Anna Phillips, "Murdoch Buys Education Tech Company Wireless Generation," *Chalkbeat NY*, November 22, 2010.

36. Even after early mixed results, former Teacher's College President Arthur Levine, who subsequently became president of the Woodrow Wilson

Foundation, continued to champion the program. Arthur Levine, "Teachers + Tech = Better Learning," *New York Daily News*, September 12, 2012.

37. Georgina Prodham, "Private Equity to Buy Pearson's IDC for $3.4 Billion," *Reuters*, May 4, 2010.

38. Roi Carthy, "Israel's Time to Know Aims to Revolutionize the Classroom," *TechCrunch*, February 2, 2010.

39. Rafael Corrales, "News Corp. Deal for Wireless Generation Is Great, but It Doesn't Make Sense," *Fortune*, November 23, 2010.

40. Through a friend whose brother, a former editor-in-chief of the *Harvard Law Review*, was a partner, I got my first summer law school internship at the firm, Onek, Klein & Farr. It was immediately clear that I was totally out of my league.

41. Javier Hernandez, "Klein's Waiver and the City's Chief Street Monitor," *New York Times City Room Blog*, November 12, 2010.

42. Steven Brill, *Class Warfare: Inside the Fight to Fix America's Schools* (New York: Simon & Schuster, 2011).

43. Ibid, 87.

44. Edmund Andrews, "Bertelsmann Chief Turns Voting Control Over to a New Board," *New York Times*, July 2, 1999.

45. "Joel Klein to Join Bertelsmann AG as Chairman and CEO of US-Based Bertelsmann, Inc.," *PR Newswire*, January 31, 2001.

46. Matthew Rose and Martin Peers, "Bertelsmann's New Executive May Curb Its Online Presence," *Wall Street Journal*, July 30, 2002.

47. Sharon Otterman and Jennifer Medina, "New York Schools Chancellor Ends 8-Year Run," *New York Times*, November 9, 2010. Kristen Kane, the previous COO, had already departed.

48. Gabriel Sherman, "Elisabeth of the Murdochs," *New York Magazine*, November 4, 2011.

49. John Wilke, "News Corp.'s Plan to Buy Heritage May Be Challenged," *Wall Street Journal*, July 29, 1997.

50. Tim Arango, "An Adviser to Murdoch Is Leaving News Corp.," *New York Times*, November 16, 2009.

51. Barbara Martinez and Michael Saul, "New York City Chancellor Moves On," *Wall Street Journal*, November 11, 2010.

52. Stetler and Arango, "News Corp Reels in a Top Educator."

53. Brett Bulley, "News Corp.'s Education Unit Hires Two Public-School Managers," *Bloomberg*, June 8, 2011.

54. Ben Fenton, "Pearson Buys Schoolnet for $230 Million," *Financial Times*, April 26, 2011.

55. Rachel Monahan, "Dept. of Ed. Awards $27M Contract to News Corp. Company," *New York Daily News*, June 9, 2011.

56. Sharon Otterman, "Subsidiary of News Corp. Loses Deal with State," *New York Times*, August 29, 2011.

57. Ben Chapman, "City Schools Dumping $95 Million Computer System," *New York Daily News*, November 16, 2014.

58. Amy Chozick, "Steering Murdoch in Scandal, Klein Put School Goals Aside," *New York Times*, May 7, 2012.

59. Natasha Singer, "InBloom Student Data Repository to Close," *New York Times*, April 21, 2014.

60. See Fiona Hollands, "Using Cost-effectiveness Analysis to Evaluate School-of-One," paper presented at the 2012 annual meeting of the American Educational Research Association, Vancouver, British Columbia, AERA Online Paper Repository.

61. "News Corporation Unveils Amplify to Bring Digital Innovation to K–12 Education," *Business Wire*, July 23, 2012.

62. Ibid.

63. "UBS to Host 40th Annual Global Media and Communications Conference December 3–5 in New York," *Business Wire*, November 13, 2012.

64. Factset callstreet transcript, UBS Global Media and Communications Conference, December 4, 2012.

65. John Hechinger, "K12 Backed by Milken Suffers Low Scores as States Resist," *Bloomberg*, November 14, 2014.

66. See Stephanie Saul, "Profits and Questions at Online Charter Schools," *New York Times*, December 12, 2011; Morgan Smith, "Cyberschools Grow, Fueling New Concerns," *New York Times*, August 24, 2013.

67. Joel Klein, The new News Corp. Investor Day Presentation, New York City, New York, May 28, 2013.

68. Matt Chesler, News Corp. Initiation of Coverage, "From Deep Dive to Deep Value—Initiating with a Buy," Deutsche Bank, July 2, 2013.

69. Alexia Quadrani, News Corp. Initiation of Coverage, "A Murky Transition into the New News—Initiating with Neutral," JP Morgan, July 1, 2013.

70. Andrew Mcleod, et al., "What if Amplify Was Closed? Sizing the Potential Uplift To Shares," Morgan Stanley, September 30, 2013.

71. Laura Colby, "News Corp.'s $1 Billion Plan to Overhaul Education Is Riddled with Failures", *BloombergBusiness*, April 7, 2015.

72. Tony Wan, "One Amplify: Joel Klein's Plan to Unify News Corp.'s Education Business," *EdSurge*, April 29, 2015.

73. Ibid.

74. Colby, "News Corp.'s $1 Billion Plan."

75. Wan, "One Amplify."

76. Molly Hensley-Clancy, "Amplify Education Tries to Build an Identity Outside of News Corp.'s Shadow," *Buzzfeed*, April 14, 2014.

77. Laura Colby, "News Corp. Is Winding Down School Tablet Sales," *BloombergBusiness*, June 26, 2015.

78. Liana Baker, "Laurene Powell Jobs Back Amplify Education Company Bought from News Corp.," *Reuters*, November 20, 2015.

79. Tony Wan, "It's Official: News Corporation Is Looking to Sell Amplify," *EdSurge*, August 12, 2015.

80. All quotes from interview with Joel Klein.

81. Peter Lattman and Clare Cain Miller, "Steve Job's Widow Steps Onto Philanthropic Stage," *New York Times*, May 17, 2013.

82. Sean Cavanaugh, "Amplify Sold Off to Group of Its Executives, Including Joel Klein," *Education Week*, October 2, 2015.

3. Curious George Schools: John Paulson

1. Suzanne E. Stein and Denny Galindo, "Curious George Gets a Tablet; Initiate at Overweight," Morgan Stanley Research, December 24, 2013.

2. Ellen B. Ballou, *The Building of the House: Houghton Mifflin's Formative Years* (Boston: Houghton Mifflin, 1970), 35–36.

3. Ibid., 503.

4. Ibid., 211–312.

5. The change from partnership to corporate form was driven by concern over the potential need to satisfy multiple capital calls from partners seeking to withdraw money simultaneously. The business was incorporated with George Mifflin as president. Ibid., 493–494.

6. Houghton Mifflin Company 1967 Annual Report, 1.

7. Its cultural conservatism may also have played a role in the successful 1975 suit by the Massachusetts attorney general for discrimination against women in hiring and promotion. Houghton would ultimately pay more than $1 million to settle the claims. Wendy Smith, "Houghton Reaches Accord in Sex Bias Suit," *Publishers Weekly*, January 16, 1981.

8. Herbert Mitgang, "Authors Protest Conglomerate Deal," *New York Times*, April 20, 1978.

9. "Houghton in Pact," *New York Times*, July 8, 1978.

10. Laura Jereski, "Making Book," *Forbes*, March 7, 1988.

11. Ibid.

12. "The Media Business: Publishing; A Growing Acceptance of Goliaths," *New York Times*, February 13, 1989.

13. Robert La Franco, "Passionate Textbook Salesman," *Forbes*, January 11, 1999.

14. Edwin McDowell, "The Media Business: Foreign Flavor for Publishing Leadership," *New York Times*, November 5, 1990.

15. Steve Sherman, "Houghton Mifflin's CEO Hopes to Globalize His Company's Outlook," *Publishers Weekly*, July 12, 1991.

16. John Robinson, "Partying with Pavarotti," *Boston Globe*, November 16, 1993.

17. Steve Sherman, "HM's Chief Urges Futurist Outlook," *Publishers Weekly*, October 31, 1994.

18. Julia Lawlor, "Meditation 'Takes the Edge Off' at Work," *USA Today*, June 18, 1993.

19. Jim Milliot, "Houghton Mifflin Sets Sales Goal of $1 Billion," *Publishers Weekly*, April 25, 1995.

20. Aimee Seles, "eBT Decides to Liquidate After Rejecting Plan to Rebuild," *Providence Business News*, May 28, 2001. By then, the company had changed its name first to INSO and then to eBT International.

21. Tom Nutile, "Houghton to Buy D. C. Heath," *Boston Herald*, September 26, 1995.

22. Steve Bailey and Steven Syre, "One for the Books: While Software Firm Info Corp. Flies, Parent Houghton Mifflin Struggles," *Boston Globe*, February 11, 1996.

23. Barbara Carton, "Houghton Mifflin Is Seeking Ways to Make the Grade—Bad Marks Include Missed Profit Estimates, Lackluster Stock Ratings Cut," *Wall Street Journal*, June 24, 1996.

24. Harold T. Miller, *Publishing: A Leap from Mind to Mind* (Golden, CO: Fulcrum, 2003), 48. For a former textbook editor's perspective on the adoption process, see Tamim Ansary, "A Textbook Example of What's Wrong with Education," *Edutopia*, November 10, 2004.

25. Nikhil Deogun and William Bulkeley, "Reed Elsevier, Thomson Agree to Buy Harcourt for $4.45 Billion Plus Debt," *Wall Street Journal*, October 27, 2000.

26. Peter Appert and Peter Salkowsky, "Snatching Defeat from the Jaws of Victory," *Deutsche Bank Equity Research*, October 10, 2000.

27. See "Houghton Mifflin Could Be Takeover Target," *M2 Best Books*, November 6, 2000; Carole Gould, "Investing with Michael A. Prober," *New York Times*, February 18, 2001.

28. Nikhil Deogun and John Carreyou, "Vivendi Talks to Houghton About Purchase," *Wall Street Journal*, May 22, 2001.

29. David Kirkpatrick and Seth Schiesel, "Vivendi Said to Be in Talks About Acquiring Houghton," *New York Times*, May 23, 2001.

30. See Bruce Wasserstein, *Big Deal: Mergers and Acquisitions in the Digital Age* (New York: Warner, 2000), 262–290.

31. Geraldine Fabrikant, "Simon & Schuster in Sale to British," *New York Times*, May 18, 1998.

32. Jean-Marie Messier, "Group Overview and Strategy," Analysts' Presentation, November 11, 2000.

33. The title is a reference to Messier's nickname from a French comedy show. Jean-Marie Messier, *J6M.com: Faut-il avoir peur de la nouvelle economie?* (Paris: Hachette Litteratures, 2000). The book was followed up with an unapologetic defense of his vision and an angry attack on those who facilitated his ultimate downfall. Jean-Marie Messier and Yves Messarovitch, *Mon Vrai Journal* (Paris: Editions Ballard, 2002).

34. Messier is used as the prototype for bad mogul behavior in Jonathan A. Knee, Bruce C. Greenwald, and Ava Seave, *The Curse of the Mogul: What's Wrong with the World's Leading Media Companies* (New York: Portfolio, 2009).

35. Ibid., 13–14. Exhibits to an instructive Harvard case on Messier provide a partial list of the acquisitions and divestitures. Rakesh Khurana, Vincent Dessain, and Daniela Beyersdorfer, *Messier's Reign at Vivendi Universal* (Harvard Business School Case 9-405-063, exhibits 2 and 4, Cambridge, MA, July 21, 2005).

36. Mathilde Richter, "Vivendi's Messier Enlists Monkey in Convergence Campaign," *Dow Jones International News*, September 24, 2001. See Knee, Greenwald, and Seave, *Curse of the Mogul*, 16.

37. Mark Walsh, "Houghton Mifflin Acquisition Extends Industry Trend," *Education Week*, June 13, 2001.

38. Ibid.

39. Kirkpatrick, "Vivendi Said to Be in Talks About Acquiring Houghton."

40. Sallie Hofmesiter, "Vivendi to Buy U.S. Publisher," *Los Angeles Times*, June 2, 2001.

41. Miller, *Publishing*, 299.

42. Ibid., xiii.

43. John Carreyrou and Martin Peers, "How Messier Kept Cash Crisis at Vivendi Hidden for Months," *Wall Street Journal*, October 31, 2002.

44. Seth Schiesel, "Shake-up at Vivendi: The Ex-chairman a Citizen of the World With Few Allies," *New York Times*, July 2, 2002.

45. Blackstone contributed 20 percent of the equity for the deal.

46. "Houghton Mifflin CEO Retires, Gieskes Named," *Boston Business Journal*, June 13, 2002.

47. Robert Weissman, "Houghton Mifflin to Name CEO Today: Appointment Caps 2 Years of Turmoil for Hub Publisher," *Boston Globe*, August 5, 2003. Shortly after the sale of Houghton was announced, Reed had selected Pat Tierney to lead the educational business it bought from Harcourt in 2001. "Reed Elsevier Appoints Chief Executive for Its Global Educational Business," PRNewswire, December 5, 2002.

48. Robert Weisman, "Reinvigorated Houghton Mifflin Presses Forward: New CEO Makes an Investment in Growth," *Boston Globe*, June 1, 2004.

49. Ibid.

50. Ibid.

51. Ibid.

52. Nicole Bullock, "Houghton Mifflin Increases Junk Bond Deal to $1 Billion," *Dow Jones Business News,* January 24, 2003.

53. Houghton Mifflin 2002 EBITDA and plate were $253 million and $95 million, respectively. With debt of $1.096 billion, the respective leverage multiples, depending on whether one looked at EBITDA or EBITDA less plate, were 4.3x and 6.9x.

54. See Jeremy Adams, "Houghton Mifflin Faces Downgrade," *Financial News,* October 5, 2003.

55. "Moody's Downgrades Ratings of Houghton Mifflin and Assigns SLG-3 Liquidity Rating," Moody's Investor Service, December 23, 2004.

56. Interviews with corporate executives involved with discussions.

57. Thomas Malloy, "Has O'Callaghan Got What It Takes to Top the Terminator?" *Irish Independent,* January 14, 2010.

58. "A Chief Executive at the Age of 30," *Irish Examiner,* January 14, 2010.

59. CBT Group would change its name to SmartForce in 1999 and merge with SkillSoft in 2002.

60. Brian Carey, "Master of the Textbook Takeover; Interview Barry O'Callaghan; Business Person of 2006," *The Sunday Times,* December 31, 2006.

61. "Riverdeep Group plc Raising IPO Price Range," PR Newswire, March 7, 2000; Harry Keaney, "Riverdeep IPO Soars on Nasdaq," *Irish Echo,* March 10, 2000.

62. Aine Coffey and Marion McKone, "Fear of the Rocker Feller," *Sunday Tribune,* November 17, 2002.

63. Conor Brophy, "Riverdeep Mulled Ousting O'Callaghan," *Sunday Tribune,* January 26, 2003.

64. Janine Brewis, "CSFB Takes Riverdeep Private Three Years After Leading IPO," *eFinancial News,* January 20, 2003.

65. Adam Levy, "CSFB's Perks: Casual Dress, Easy Money," *Bloomberg Markets,* August 2001.

66. Mark Paul and Brian Carey, "I'll Be Back: While Investors in EMPG Face an Equity Wipeout, Boss Barry O'Callaghan Is Determined to Emerge from the Group's Latest Crisis as Strong as Ever," *The Sunday Times,* January 17, 2010.

67. See Emmet Oliver, "Quiet Exit for One-Time, High-Flying Publishing Magnate," *Irish Independent,* March 17, 2011: "How Mr. O'Callaghan funded his original stake has never been revealed and which Irish bank was involved is the subject of some conjecture."

68. Nick Web, "Debt-Laden Publisher Is Now a Wage Slave," *Irish Independent,* January 17, 2010.

69. Ciaran Hancock, "Will the Clever Cat Get the Cream?" *The Sunday Times*, October 29, 2006.

70. "Ambition Grows as Riverdeep Deal Moves Forward," *Irish Times*, October 27, 2006.

71. Arthur Beasley, "Merged Riverdeep Group May Float in Two Years," *Irish Times*, October 25, 2006.

72. Riverdeep Houghton Mifflin, Confidential Information Memorandum, J & E Davy, November 17, 2006, p. 8.

73. Christian Berthelsen, "High-Flying Financier on Way Down/Fraud Investigation of Palo Alto Banker," *San Francisco Chronicle*, February 9, 2003.

74. See, "Ambition Grows as Riverdeep Deal Moves Forward." ("So will it work? At one level, O'Callaghan has already convinced the people who really count, investment banking institutions as eminent as Goldman Sachs.").

75. See Alexandra Dawe, "Reed Shares Drop on Lower Education Growth Forecast," *BusinessWeek*, November 17, 2005. See also Robert Lea, "Reed's 'Mr. 10 percent' to Miss Target," *London Evening Standard*, February 19, 2004.

76. Tom McEnaney, "Ernst Quits at Riverdeep," *Irish Independent*, February 15 2007.

77. Michael J. de la Merced, "Houghton Mifflin to Buy Harcourt Units," *New York Times*, July 17, 2007.

78. Education Media & Publishing Group, Confidential Information Memorandum, Credit Suisse, Lehman Brothers and Citigroup, October 2007, p. 77.

79. Joe Brennan, "Dealmaker O'Callaghan Rides Out Choppy Credit Markets," *Irish Independent*, July 3, 2008.

80. Ibid.

81. Ibid.

82. Moody's Investor Service, December 22, 2008; S&P, February 11, 2009.

83. Andrew Edgecliff-Johnson, "Houghton Mifflin Harcourt disputes Moody's Ratings Downgrade," *Financial Times*, January 7, 2009.

84. Jeffrey A. Trachtenberg, "Writer's Block: Houghton Won't Acquire New Books," *Wall Street Journal*, November 28, 2008; Motoko Rich, "Houghton Mifflin Publisher Resigns," *New York Times*, December 3, 2008.

85. Motoko Rich, "Houghton Mifflin Harcourt Abandons Sale of Trade Division," *New York Times*, March 12, 2009.

86. Andrew Johnson and Kate Laughlin, "Education Media Receives Covenant Relief," *Debtwire*, March 17, 2009.

87. "Dubai Royals Back O'Callaghan's EMPG," *Business and Finance Daily News Service*, August 17, 2009.

88. "Houghton Mifflin Riverdeep Group Announces Senior Appointment," *PR Newswire*, April 4, 2007.

89. Jeffrey Trachtenberg, "As Houghton Mifflin CEO Retires, O'Callaghan Will Try to Right the Ship," *Wall Street Journal*, April 3, 2009.

90. See Gregory Zuckerman, *The Greatest Trade Ever: The Behind the Scenes Story of How John Paulson Defied Wall Street and Made Financial History* (New York: Crown, 2010).

91. Andrew Edgecliffe-Johnson, "EMPG Pushes for Financial Shake-up," *Financial Times*, January 14, 2010.

92. Paul and Carey, "I'll Be Back."

93. Paulson had not been publicly involved in the sector from either an investing or policy perspective. There is reason to believe, however, that he viewed the investment as an opportunity to make money while making a contribution to education. A product of Queens public schools, Paulson obviously has strong feelings on the subject of education, having recently donated $8.5 million to the Success Academy charter school network. Carl Campanille, "Hedge-Fund Billionaire Donates $8.5M for New Charter Schools," *New York Post*, July 30, 2015.

94. Milken's involvement does not appear to have been reported in the United States. The UK press, however, had identified Guggenheim as "representing the interests of Michael Milken." See Paul and Carey, "I'll Be Back."

95. In the ultimate settlement reached by Guggenheim with the Securities and Exchange Commission, neither Milken nor Boehly was named. But Charles Gasparino reported that one of the key transactions at issue related to an undisclosed personal loan from Milken to Boehly. Charles Gasparino, "Guggenheim to Pay SEC $20 Million," *FOXBusiness*, August 10, 2015.

96. Edgecliffe-Johnson, "EMPG Pushes for Financial Shake-up."

97. "Aspen Institute to Host 'Education Innovation Forum and Expo,'" *Investment Weekly News*, January 22, 2011.

98. "Riverdeep Auditors Point to Debt Challenge at Publisher," *Irish Independent*, February 12, 2011.

99. Key terms of the arrangement are detailed in the May 9, 2011, Preliminary Offering Memorandum for the Senior Secured Notes Due 2019.

100. For an entire decade prior to joining Houghton as CFO in 2007, interim CEO Michael Muldowney had "served at various times as President, COO, CFO" and a board member for a disastrous Milken-controlled company called Nextera, which is discussed in chapter 4.

101. "Moody's Says Houghton Mifflin's Ratings Not Affected by Revised Refinancing Terms," *Moody's Investor Service*, May 13, 2011.

102. Pricing Term Sheet dated May 13, 2011 to Preliminary Offering Memorandum dated May 9 2011, Houghton Mifflin Harcourt, 10.5% Senior Secured Notes due 2019.

103. "Riverdeep Founder Set for 100M Euro Payday," *Sunday Business Post*, June 19, 2011.

104. John Berke, "Houghton Mifflin Harcourt Reports 67 Percent EBITDA Drop in 2Q11," *Debtwire*, August 18, 2011.

105. Linda K. Zecher, "The Path to Publishing," *New York Times*, January 12, 2013.

106. Andrew Edgecliff-Johnson, "Houghton Mifflin to Cut 10 Percent of Staff," *Financial Times*, November 12, 2011.

107. Jim Milliot, "The Shrinking of Houghton Mifflin Harcourt," *Publishers Weekly*, May 12, 2012.

108. Pearson's stock price actually grew by almost 60 percent from the end of 2005 until the end of 2011 (159.3%) while the overall S&P index remained essentially flat during this period (100.7%).

109. Houghton Mifflin Harcourt Disclosure Statement, Case 12-15610, Doc. 14, filed May 21, 2012.

110. In addition to being unable to calculate the precise amount of Paulson's investment, he is likely to have received some dividends in addition to the proceeds from the share sales. This does not change the conclusion that he cerainly lost hundreds of millions of dollars.

111. Gavin Daly, "Dubai Pulls Out of Deal with EMPGI," *The Sunday Times*, May 12, 2013.

112. "About Us," RISE website, retrieved February 15, 2015.

113. DC Denison, "Bankruptcy Over, Boston's Houghton Mifflin Looks Ahead," *Boston Globe*, June 24, 2012. ("There's a huge market out there for parents. . . . We can now go after that market more aggressively.").

114. Jon Chesto, "Houghton Mifflin Harcourt Embraces the Digital Age," *Boston Business Journal*, July 5, 2013. (Zecher promised to "essentially double the percentage of the company's . . . revenue that come from digital sales" in under two years.) See also Gavin Daly, "I'd Like to Teach the World to Read: The Business Interview," *The Sunday Times*, July 22, 2012.

115. Denison, "Bankruptcy Over."

116. Chris Reidy, "Publisher Buys School News Channel," *Boston Globe*, May 13, 2014.

117. Jeffrey Trachtenberg, "A Reborn Houghton Goes Digital to the Core," *Wall Street Journal*, November 25, 2014.

118. Jeffrey Trachtenberg, "Houghton Mifflin Buys Scholastic's Ed Tech Business for $575 Million," *Wall Street Journal*, April 24, 2014.

119. "Houghton Mifflin Announces Third Quarter 2015 Results," *Business Wire*, November 5, 2015.

120. "Moody's Downgrades Houghton Mifflin Harcourt's CFR to B2," *Moody's Investor Service*, February 5, 2016.

121. Denny Galindo and Toni Kaplan, "Déjà Vu? Guidance Seems Aggressive," *Morgan Stanley Equity Research*, February 26, 2016.

4. Michael Milken: Master of the Knowledge Universe

1. See Mark Walsh, "Education Firm Charts Growth of Its Universe," *Education Week*, August 4, 1999.

2. Milken had previously purchased and, following a brief period, sold an international arm for the early childhood education business.

3. Cale Ottens, "Milkens Sell U.S. Education Business," *Los Angeles Business Journal*, July 9, 2015.

4. Cora Daniels, "The Man Who Changed Medicine," *Fortune*, November 29, 2004.

5. Milken paid a $47 million fine for violating the ban in 1998 in connection with advice he gave on deals involving friends Rupert Murdoch and Ronald Perelman, among others. Michael Schroeder, "Milken Agrees to Pay Fine of $47 Million in SEC Case," *Wall Street Journal*, February 27, 1998. More recently, his relationship with Guggenheim Partners has come under Securities and Exchange Commission scrutiny.

6. Riva D. Atlas, "Milken Sees the Classroom as Profit Center," *New York Times*, December 18, 2004.

7. Ibid.

8. "S&P Cuts Knowledge Universe Rating to CCC," *Reuters*, July 27, 2012.

9. In 2007, Bloomberg reported that Milken had hired Goldman Sachs and First Boston to raise $1 billion to support Knowledge Universe's further growth. At the time, a Milken spokesperson claimed to have already received commitments for more than half of this amount. Miles Weiss, "Milken Plans to Sell $1 Billion Stake in Knowledge Universe," *Bloomberg*, March 20, 2007. As no other public comment—beyond this one related to the apparent $2.25 billion valuation—was ever made regarding this placement, it seems unlikely that much more than the $220 million noted in a public filing at the time was ever raised. See Ottens, "Milkens Sell U.S. Education Business."

10. The international child-care assets Milken had bought out of bankruptcy from ABC Learning and flipped to a Canadian pension fund did yield a gain, but these were relatively small and did not close the massive value gap. Sean Farrell, "Busy Bees Nursery Firm Buys Its First Overseas Childcare Centres," *Guardian*, February 2, 2015.

11. Deborah Vrana, "Education's Pied Piper with a Dark Past," *Los Angeles Times*, September 7, 1998.

12. Ibid.

13. Kathleen Morris, "The Reincarnation of Mike Milken," *BusinessWeek*, May 10, 1999.

14. Amy Feldman, "Milken's New Empire Amasses Education Companies Worth $1B," *New York Daily News*, March 23, 1998.

15. Ibid.

16. Justin Martin, "Lifelong Learning Spells Earnings," *Fortune*, July 6, 1998.

17. Ibid.

18. Preqin, Private Equity Online.

19. "News Corp. Role in Bidding Seen," *New York Times*, May 15, 1998.

20. "Milken, KinderCare Reunited," *CNN/Money*, November 6, 2004.

21. Marvin Harris, "KinderCare Files for Bankruptcy Protection," *Associated Press*, November 10, 1992.

22. "Tax Troubles for Kinder-Care Founder," *Associated Press*, August 3, 1991.

23. Atlas, "Milken Sees the Classroom as Profit Center."

24. Linda Sandler, "Milken Builds New Empire in the Education Industry," *Wall Street Journal*, May 15, 1998.

25. Joseph Nocera " Michael Milken: The Midas of the Eighties Tells Us Where Tomorrow's Wealth Lies," *Fortune*, September 30, 1998.

26. Kathleen Morris and Lisa Sanders, "Professor Milken's Lesson Plan," *BusinessWeek*, August 3, 1997.

27. Ibid.

28. "CRT Group PLC Annual Trading Statement," *PR Newswire*, June 8, 1998.

29. Julia Flynn, "Spring Group Sets Plans to Shift Focus to Information-Technology Professionals," *Wall Street Journal*, May 9, 2000.

30. Ed Bowsher, "Sales Put Bounce in Spring," *Citywire Money*, December 29, 2000.

31. Ruth Sullivan, "Top Management Reshuffle at Spring," *Financial Times*, August 4, 2006.

32. Algernon Hall, "Spring Loses More Bounce," *Citywire Money*, July 29, 2005.

33. "Spring Group PLC Interim Results for the Six Months to 30 June 1999," August 11, 1999.

34. Goran Mijuk, "Adecco Buys MPS for $1.3 Billion," *Wall Street Journal*, October 21, 2009.

35. Josh McHugh, "LeapFrog's Wild Ride," *Wired*, November 2005.

36. Steve Gelsi, "LeapFrog, Hewitt Led '02 IPO Crop," *Marketwatch*, January 3, 2003.

37. Morris, "The Reincarnation of Mike Milken."

38. Hasbro and Mattel generate operating margins in the teens in good years.

39. Matthew Witheiler, "Here's Why It's Tough to Get Investors Excited About Your Toy Startup," *VentureBeat*, October 20, 2013.

40. Kate Kelly, "Milken to Go Ahead with LeapFrog IPO," *Wall Street Journal*, July 25, 2002.

41. Lisa DiCarlo, "LeapFrog Execs Get the Dunce Cap," *Forbes.com*, March 11, 2004, "Technology Briefs," *Wall Street Journal*, November 2, 1999.

42. "Leapfrog Founder Wood Resigns Posts," *Los Angeles Times*, September 2, 2004.

43. "LeapFrog Receives Continued Listing Standard Notice from NYSE," *PR Newswire*, September 4, 2015.

44. "LeapFrog Reports Knowledge Universe Distributes 73 percent of Its LeapFrog Holdings," *PR Newswire*, May 1, 2003; "Leapfrog Reports Knowledge Universe Distribution of LF Shares," *PR Newswire*, April 7, 2004.

45. KU Learning, 13-D filing for Nobel Education Dynamics Inc., January 23, 1988.

46. "Milken, Ellison Invest in Private-Schools Firm," *Los Angeles Times*, January 27, 1998.

47. Public companies with equity value between $300 million and $2 billion are "small cap," $2 billion to $10 billion are "mid cap," and above $10 billion are "large cap."

48. Sandler, "Milken Builds New Empire in the Education Industry."

49. "Nobel Learning Communities, Inc. Clarifies Its Growth Intentions," *PR Newswire*, March 5, 1999.

50. "Management Offers to Buy Nobel Learning for $110 Million," *Associated Press*, August 6, 2002.

51. Reid Kanaley, "Nobel Learning's Shares Drop by One-Third on Buyout Woes," *Philadelphia Inquirer*, November 16, 2002.

52. "Nobel Learning Communities, Inc. Announces Termination of Merger Agreement," *PR Newswire*, February 3, 2003.

53. "Nobel Learning Communities, Inc. and Knowledge Universe Join Forces to Augment NLCI's Future Growth Potential," *PR Newswire*, March 13, 2003.

54. "Related Party Transactions," *NLCI 10-K*, September 19, 2005.

55. "Nobel Learning Communities, Inc. Announces Hiring of Chief Executive Officer," *PR Newswire*, July 25, 2003.

56. "Proxy Statement," *NLCI 14-A*, December 1, 2003.

57. "Michael and Lowell Milken Increase Stake in Nobel Learning Communities to 19.4 Percent," *Associated Press*, March 27, 2007.

58. "Nobel Learning Communities, Inc., Announces Changes to Its Board of Directors," *PR Newswire*, August 11, 2006.

59. Kaja Whitehouse, "Poison Pill Revival Stars Michael Milken," *New York Post*, July 21, 2008.

60. "Nobel Learning Communities, Inc. Adopts Shareholder Rights Plan," *PR Newswire*, July 21, 2008.

61. "Knowledge Learning Corporation Proposes Strategic Acquisition of Nobel Learning Communities, Inc. for $17.00 per Share," *Business Wire*, March 11, 2009.

62. "Nobel Learning Communities Conducting Process to Determine Possible Sale of the Company," *Associated Press*, November 7, 2008.

63. "Knowledge Learning Corporation Proposes Strategic Acquisition of Nobel Learning Communities, Inc. for $13.50 per Share," *Business Wire*, March 11, 2009.

64. "Nobel Learning Communities, Inc. Responds to Proposal," *PR Newswire*, March 11, 2009; "Nobel Learning Communities, Inc. Board Unanimously Rejects Proposal from Knowledge Learning Corporation," *PR Newswire*, March 19, 2009.

65. Milken presumably did better on the distressed loans he made to the company.

66. The price was $405 million plus unspecified indebtedness. "Leeds Equity to Sell Nobel Learning," *Private Equity Professional Digest*, March 30, 2015. In addition, a Swiss private equity group that co-invested with Leeds issued a press release on the sale, touting the 4X return on investment ("Partners Group to Exit Investment in Nobel Learning," *AWP Original Press Release*, March 30, 2015). Interestingly, this group was lead investor in the purchase of Knowledge Universe for $1.465 billion. Given the leverage and nature of the remaining business, it is hard to see them doing this well again.

67. Terzah Ewing, "Milken's Nextera Enterprises Begins Trading with a Dud," *Wall Street Journal*, May 19, 1999.

68. Merton Miller is the Nobel winner most publicly associated with the firm but others include Gary Becker and James Heckman (See "Nextera Leads Prominent Dialogue on Human Capital Management (HCM) During Milken Institute 2001 Global Conference," *PR Newswire*, March 21, 2001) and, much earlier in its history, George Stigler and Kenneth Arrow (See Benjamin Stein, "Don't Blame Us—The New Defense in Shareholder Suits" *Barron's*, June 6, 1988).

69. David Margolick, "The Law: At the Bar," *New York Times*, June 17, 1988.

70. Joseph Cahill, "Milken's Nextera Acquires Consultant for $60 million," *Wall Street Journal*, February 17, 1999.

71. Melody Petersen, "Law Firm to Pay Longtime Foe $50 Million," *New York Times*, April 14, 1999.

72. "Technology Briefs," *Wall Street Journal*, November 2, 1999.

73. Fink was also a long-time associate of Ellison's and was often viewed as Ellison's appointee on the Knowledge Universe company boards on which he sat. He was also Vice Chairman and Treasurer of Knowledge Universe itself and had served as Chair of all the other public companies profiled here— Spring, Leapfrog, and Nobel.

74. Seth Lubove, "Friends and Neighbors," *Forbes*, February 21, 2000.

75. "PricewaterhouseCoopers' David M. Schneider Joins Nextera as President and CEO," *PR Newswire*, October 26, 2000.

76. "Nextera Enterprises Sells Sibson Consulting Unit," *Business Wire*, January 31, 2002.

77. Graef Crystal, "Milken Brothers and Ellison Taken to the Cleaners," *Bloomberg*, November 26, 2003.

78. "Nextera Announces Third Quarter Results," *Business Wire*, October 30, 2003.

79. Nextera proxy statement, October 24, 2003.

80. "Nextera Enterprises Enters Into an Agreement to Sell Lexecon Assets for $130 Million," *PR Newswire*, September 25, 2003. The company had already received its first delisting notice from NASDAQ on May 15, 2003.

81. Patrick McGeehan, "Market Place: Tied to Milken, the Ride Can Still Be Bumpy," *New York Times*, November 12, 2003.

82. Nocera, "Michael Milken."

83. Ibid.

84. Morris, "The Reincarnation of Mike Milken."

85. Ibid.

86. Cyrus Afzali, "Costello Leaves Cadence," *CNNMoney.com*, October 21, 1997.

87. Russ Baker, "The Education of Michael Milken," *The Nation*, May 3, 1999.

88. Peter Lattman, "Perelman Sues Old Friend Milken (Not to Worry. It Isn't Personal)," *New York Times*, July 8, 2013.

89. Patrick Danner, "Harland Clarke Loses Court Fight with Milken," *San Antonio Express News*, March 4, 2015.

90. Morris and Sanders, "Professor Milken's Lesson Plan."

91. "Manhattan U.S. Attorney Announces $4 Million Fraud Settlement with New York Institute of Technology and Cardean Learning Group, LLC" [press release], Southern District of New York, December 27, 2012.

92. Steven Strahler, "One Good Turn May Deserve Another for U of C Trustee," *Crain's Chicago Business*, May 10, 1999.

93. Patrick McGeehan, "Business School Does Its IPO Homework, Links Up with Internet Education Firm," *Wall Street Journal*, April 2, 1999.

94. Goldie Blumenstyk, "A Company Pays Top Universities to Use Their Names and Their Professors," *Chronicle of Higher Education*, June 18, 1999.

95. Columbia may have gotten a slightly better deal than others for being first. Later reports suggest the $20 million due to other universities could be paid over as long as eight years.

96. Jeffrey Pfeffer and Christina T. Fong, "The End of Business Schools? Less Success Than Meets the Eye," *Academy of Management Learning & Education*, September 2002.

97. UNext website, quoted in Harvey Blustain and Phil Goldstein, "Report on UNext and Cardean University," *The E-University Compendium*, October 2001.

98. Stephen P. Pizzo, "Barbarians at the University Gate," *Forbes ASAP*, September 10, 1991.

99. "Corporate Training Goes to the Head of the Class," *Red Herring*, February 25, 2001.

100. Jennifer Renwick, "Private Virtual Universities Challenge Many Assumptions Long Held by Educators: Their Own Challenge: Survival," *Wall Street Journal*, March 12, 2001.

101. Sarah Carr, "Rich in Cash and Prestige, UNext Struggles in Its Search for Sales," *Chronicle of Higher Education*, May 4, 2001.

102. Steven Strahler, "Investors Back Online School Like No Other: Nobel Lineup, Star-Studded Financiers," *Crain's Chicago Business*, March 29, 1999.

103. Keating returned to the nonprofit sector a couple years later. "Keating Is Choice as New Executive Vice President" [press release], Boston of College, July 26, 2001.

104. Sarah Carr, "Amid High Expectations, UNext.com Tests Its First Online Courses," *Chronicle of Higher Education*, April 27, 2000.

105. Abby Ellin, "The Battle in Cyberspace," *New York Times*, August 6, 2000.

106. Renwick, "Private Virtual Universities Challenge Many Assumptions Long Held by Educators."

107. Lisa Bransten, "Something Ventured: Where the Big Money Investors Are Placing Their Bets," *Wall Street Journal*, March 12, 2001.

108. "UNext Forms Strategic Partnership with the Thomson Corporation," *PR Newswire*, March 1, 2001.

109. "UNext Prepares for More Job Cuts," *Crain's Chicago Business*, September 10, 2001.

110. Barbara Rose, "UNext Wants to Alter Deals with Universities," *Chicago Tribune*, August 9, 2001.

111. "A Modern Class Struggle: Distance Learning Is Still a Long Way Off," *Red Herring*, October 1, 2000.

112. Kathryn McCabe, "Online Schools Target Busy Execs: Net Transforming Distance Learning," *Crain's Chicago Business*, November 27, 2000. Rosenfield specifically predicted 200,000 students in India and 300,000 in China. Della Bradshaw, "Why Most Students 'Default to Quality'," *Financial Times*, March 24, 2003.

113. Barbara Rose, "Tech Watch," *Crain's Chicago Business*, February 27, 2000.

114. Steven Strahler, "Chicago Will Get Another Gleacher Center," *Crain's Chicago Business*, December 2, 2002.

115. Julie Johnsson, "Online University Lowering Its Brow: UNext Pushes Corporate Training," *Crain's Chicago Business*, November 5, 2001.

116. Barbara Rose, "UNext to Launch Online MBAs," *Chicago Tribune*, August 6, 2002.

117. "NYIT and UNext Launch Online College for Working Adults," *PR Newswire*, September 16, 2003.

118. Ibid.

119. Apparently the University of Chicago continued to receive royalties from Cardean as late as 2008 for reasons that are unclear. Goldie Blumenstyk, "New Nonprofit Online University Has Unusual Corporate Beginnings," *Chronicle of Higher Education*, August 22, 2008.

120. Interview with former Thomson executive.

121. "UNext Names Cathleen Raffaeli CEO," *PR Newswire*, March 4, 2004.

122. Jack Stripling, "Breaking Up Is Hard to Do," *Inside Higher Ed*, December 9, 2008.

123. K12 Inc., "Form 10-K," October 7, 2011.

124. Jacques Steinberg and Edward Wyatt, "Boola, Boola, E-commerce Comes to the Quad," *New York Times*, February 13, 2000.

125. Steve Kolowich, "Glimpse Into the Future," *Inside Higher Ed*, May 25, 2011.

126. Jason Lewis, "NYIT and Cardean Learning Ordered to Pay $4 Million for Swindling Students," *Village Voice*, December 27, 2012.

127. "Higher Ed, Inc," *Economist*, September 8, 2005.

128. Laura Pappano, "The Year of the MOOC," *New York Times*, November 2, 2012.

129. A recent study by Columbia University's Teachers College found that although MOOCs developed by universities and nonprofit institutions cost far less than the $1 million UNext spent on its full courses, they can still run into the hundreds of thousands of dollars. Fiona Hollands and Devayani Tirthali, "MOOCs: Expectations and Reality," *Center for Benefit-Cost Studies of Education*, May 2014.

130. Liz Gannes, "Education Start-Up Udacity Raises Funds from Andreesen Horowitz," *AllthingsD*, October 25, 2012; Rip Empson, "Online education startup Coursera lands 16M from Kleiner & NEA, adds John Doerr to its board," *TechCrunch*, April 18, 2012.

131. Melissa Korn, "Yale Gives Former Leader $8.5 Million Payout," *Wall Street Journal*, May 19, 2015.

132. Radhika Rukmangadhan, "Google X Cofounder's Udacity Valued at $1 Billion in Latest Funding," *Reuters*, November 11, 2015.

133. Lizetter Chapman, "E-Learning Startup Udacity Raises $35M to Launch 'Nanodegrees,'" *WSJ.D*, September 24, 2014.

134. Claire Zillman, "Coursera teams up with Instagram, Google: The search for a business model continues," *Fortune*, February 11, 2015.

5. What Makes a Good Education Business?

1. Jonathan Knee, Bruce Greenwald, and Ava Seave, *The Curse of the Mogul: What's Wrong with the World's Leading Media Companies* (New York: Portfolio, 2009).

2. Bruce Greenwald and Judd Kahn, *Competition Demystified: A Radically Simplified Approach to Business Strategy* (New York: Portfolio, 2005).

3. Knee, Greenwald, and Seave, *Curse of the Mogul*, 17.

4. Gary Becker, *Human Capital: A Theoretical and Empirical Analysis* (Cambridge, MA: National Bureau of Economic Research, 1964).

5. Ian Wylie, "Education Goes Global," *Financial Times*, December 13, 2012.

6. Matthew Martin, "Blackstone Makes Bet in Dubai Expat School-Place Lottery," *BloombergBusiness*, December 9, 2014.

7. Karla Shores, "Private School President Plans Exchange Network," *Sun Sentinel*, March 17, 2005.

8. "Nord Anglia Education Completes Acquisition of Six Schools from Meritas," *PRNewswire*, June 25, 2015.

9. "GENCO Partners with McGraw-Hill Education to Manage Ohio Distribution Centers," *PRNewswire*, September 22, 2014.

10. Just to make the name game more complex, in early 2016, Apollo Global announced that it had separately reached an agreement to buy Apollo Education as well. Gillian Tan, "Why Apollo Has Eyes for Apollo," *Bloomberg*, January 12, 2016.

11. Chelsea Dulaney, "McGraw-Hill Education Files to Go Public," *Wall Street Journal*, September 4, 2015.

12. "Cengage Learning Files for Bankruptcy," *New York Times DealBook*, July 2, 2013.

13. Network effects are sometimes described as demand-side scale, while fixed cost-based scale is a supply-side phenomenon.

14. These are called "indirect" network effects because the value to buyers comes from the addition of new sellers and vice versa. Direct network effects are present where, for instance, there is a social network aspect to the business. Teachers Pay Teachers, discussed later in this chapter, has both a marketplace and social network dimension and thus displays both direct and indirect network effects.

15. The company was originally called iParadigms, but its core plagiarism detection product was always called Turnitin.

16. "Pearson Agrees to Acquire eCollege for $477 Million," *PRNewswire*, May 14, 2007.

17. Interview with Oakleigh Thorne.

18. Carl Straumsheim, "Pearson to Leave Learning Management System Market by 2018," *Inside Higher Ed*, February 3, 2016.

19. Steve Kolowich, "Outsourcing Plus," *Inside Higher Ed*, October 12, 2010.

20. Carl Straumsheim, "Online Program Management Providers, Now a Billion Dollar Industry, Look Ahead," *Inside Higher Ed*, September 11, 2015.

21. Robert Budden, "Pearson Acquires Embanet Compass for $650m," *Financial Times*, October 16, 2012. The company, which had a troubled early period, was owned by Knowledge Universe.

22. Lora Kolodny, "Education Investors, Startups Hopeful Following Solid IPO by 2U," *Wall Street Journal*, April 3, 2014.

23. Ben Fox Rubin, "Wiley to Buy On-line Education Firm Deltak," *Wall Street Journal*, October 2, 2012.

24. "America's Children: Key National Indicators of Well-Being, 2015," Indicator Fam3.A, Childstats.gov.

25. Peter Lattman, "How Bright Horizons Took Care of Bain Capital Over the Years," *New York Times*, January 25, 2013.

26. Peter Martin, Joseph Sims, and Brian Neigut., "Advantage Learning Systems: Leveraging the Learning Triad," Jeffries & Company Equity Research, March 22, 2000. Advantage Learning Systems changed its name to Renaissance Learning in 2001.

27. Trip Gabriel and Matt Richtel, "Inflating the Software Report Card," *New York Times*, October 8, 2011.

28. Hal Varian, "Our Secret Sauce," *Google* (blog), February 25, 2008. https://googleblog.blogspot.com/2008/02/our-secret-sauce.html.

29. Eric Bettinger and Rachel Baker, "The Effects of Student Coaching in College: An Evaluation of a Randomized Experiment in Student Advising," *Educational Evaluation and Policy Analysis* 36, no. 1 (2014): 3–19.

30. 2012 GSV Advisors Survey.

31. Kellie Woodhouse, "Impact of Pell Surge," *Inside Higher Ed*, June 12, 2015.

32. Richard Ruch, *Higher Ed, Inc.: The Rise of the For-Profit University* (Baltimore, MD: John Hopkins University Press, 2001), 53.

33. In modern times, for-profits only broke 1 percent of enrollments at degree-granting institutions in 1980. National Center for Education Statistics, Digest of Educational Statistics, Table 303.70.

34. Ibid.

35. Tamar Lewin, "Facing Cuts in Federal Aid, For-Profit Colleges Are in a Fight," *New York Times*, June 5, 2010.

36. "Obama Administration Announces Final Rules to Protect Students from Poor-Performing Career College Programs," *U.S. Department of Education*, October 30, 2014. http://www.ed.gov/news/press-releases

/obama-administration-announces-final-rules-protect-students-poor-performing-career-college-programs.

37. Ronald Hansen, "Apollo Sees Its Reach Narrowing, More Enrollment Losses," *Arizona Republic*, July 4, 2015.

38. Carly Stockwell, "Same as It Ever Was: Top 10 Most Popular College Majors," *USA Today*, October 26, 2014.

39. David Hudson, "The President Proposes to Make Community College Free for Responsible Students for 2 Years," White House (blog), January 8, 2015. https://www.whitehouse.gov/blog/2015/01/08/president-proposes -make-community-college-free-responsible-students-2-years.

40. "Fact Sheet: Obama Administration Increases Accountability for Low-Performing For-Profit Institutions," *U.S. Department of Education*, July 1, 2015. http://www.ed.gov/news/press-releases/fact-sheet-obama-administration -increases-accountability-low-performing-profit-institutions.

41. Paul Fain, "Low Bar, High Failure," *Inside Higher Ed*, May 7, 2013.

42. Neal McClusky, "Even For-Profit Universities Are Better Than America's Terrible Community Colleges," *Washington Post*, January 13, 2015.

43. Paul Fain, "Gainful Employment Arrives," *Inside Higher Ed*, October 30, 2014.

44. Kate Taylor, "At a Success Academy Charter School, Singling Out Pupils Who Have 'Got to Go,'" *New York Times*, October 29, 2015.

45. Ann Belser, "EDMC to Close 15 Art Institute Locations," *Pittsburgh Post Gazette*, May 6, 2015.

46. Eric Toll, "IRS Filing Inches Grand Canyon University Closer to Possible Nonprofit Move," *Phoenix Business Journal*, July 31, 2015; Paul Fain, "Dropping Profit," *Inside Higher Ed*, July 17, 2014. Accreditors ultimately blocked Grand Canyon's attempt to convert to a nonprofit. Ronald J. Hansen and Anne Ryman, "Grand Canyon University: Accreditor Blocks Conversion to Non-Profit," *Arizona Republic*, March 4, 2016.

47. Bob Kerrey and Jeffrey Leeds, "A Federal Anti-Education Plan," *Wall Street Journal*, November 19, 2013.

48. Fall enrollment in two year public degree granting institutions fell from 7.22 million in 2010 to 6.4 million in 2014. National Center for Education Statistics, *Digest of Educational Statistics*, Table 303.70. Although the NCES projected a recovery to 6.76 million in 2015, the National Student Clearinghouse estimates that enrollments actually continued to fall substantially. https://nscresearchcenter.org/currenttermenrollmentestimate-fall2015/.

49. National Center for Education Statistics, *Digest of Educational Statistics*, Table 3.

50. Emma Brown, "College Enrollment Rates Are Dropping, Especially Among Low Income Students," *Washington Post*, November 24, 2015.

51. Aline van Duyn, "Thomson Sells Education Unit for $7.75bn," *Financial Times*, May 11, 2007.

52. David Schick and Mary Beth Marklein, "College Students Say No to Costly Textbooks," *USA Today*, August 20, 2013.

53. Rip Empson, "Blackboard: With Both Co-founders Now Gone, It's The End of an Era for the Education Software Giant," *TechCrunch*, October 18, 2012.

54. Scott Jaschik, "Blackboard Buys Angel," *Inside Higher Ed*, May 7, 2009.

55. Michael J. De La Merced, "Providence to Buy Blackboard for $1.64 Billion," *New York Times*, July 1, 2011.

56. Christopher Dawson, "Blackboard Founder and CEO Resigns—What It Means for the LMS Industry," *ZDNet Education*, October 17, 2012.

57. Jacob Bogage, "Blackboard Loses High-profile Clients as Its Rivals School It in Innovation," *Washington Post*, August 22, 2015.

6. Lessons from Clown School

1. The phrase is attributed to Benjamin Franklin.

2. "Houghton Mifflin Harcourt Secures New $650 Million Cash Investment and Recapitalizes Balance Sheet in Historic Restructuring," *Business Wire*, February 22, 2010.

3. Joshua Margolis and Hillary Elfenbein, "Doing Well by Doing Good? Don't Count on It," *Harvard Business Review*, January 2008.

4. A wide variety of surveys seek to rank universities domestically and globally. What these mostly have in common is how persistent the names at the top of the lists are. One recent study concluded that moving into the top 20 institutions ranked by the much-cited *U.S. News & World Report* survey would be wildly expensive and nearly impossible. Shari Gnolek, Vincenzo Falciano, and Ralph Kuncl, "Modeling Change and Variation in *U.S. News & World Report* College Ranking: What Would It Really Take to Be in the Top 20?," *Research in Higher Education* 55, no. 8: 761–79, December 2014.

5. Although the company lost money in 2015 and is projected to do so in 2016, it believes that it will achieve positive EBITDA in 2016. As discussed in chapter 2, EBITDA has a very tenuous connection to operating cash flow. In the case of 2U, the company had originally stated that cash flow breakeven would trail EBITDA by one year. In a recent earnings call, the CFO both rescinded that previous estimate and refused to establish a new one. "We're not ready to put a stake in the sand as to how much longer" it will take to generate cash flow, she said. Comments of Cathy Graham, Edited Transcript,

TWOU—Q1 2016 2U, Inc Earnings Call, Thomson Reuters Streetevents, May 5, 2016. Research analysts at Credit Suisse, which rates 2U as an "outperform," project that the company will finally generate operating cash flow in 2019. Michael Nemeroff, Kyle Chen, Alexander Hu, and Christopher Rochester, "2U, Inc: 1Q16 Results/Guidance Above; A Front Row View of Profitability," Credit Suisse Equity Research, May 5, 2016.

6. Jess Hempel, "A Different Kind of Tall Tale," *Fortune*, February 11, 2013.

7. Christina Passariello, "Startup University's Disruption Plan: An Old-School Master's Degree," *Wall Street Journal*, December 9, 2015.

8. Graeme Wood, "The Future of College?" *The Atlantic*, September 2014.

9. Jordan Weissmann, "This For-Profit College Wants to Compete with the Ivies. And It's a Brilliant Business Idea," *Slate*, August 15, 2012. http://www.slate.com/blogs/moneybox/2014/08/15/the_minerva_project_this _for_profit_elite_college_is_a_brilliant_business.html.

10. Jo Johnson, "Return of the Prodigal Son," *Financial Times*, February 7, 2009.

11. Carol Loomis, "The Wit and Wisdom of Warren Buffett," *Fortune*, November 19, 2012.

12. Devin Banerjee and David Carey, "Permira Quadruples Its Money Selling Renaissance Learning," *Bloomberg*, March 13, 2014.

13. To manage the sale process, McGraw appointed as CEO a seasoned, long-time IBM operating executive, Buzz Waterhouse, who had previously managed the sale process of Harcourt for Reed.

14. Anya Kamenetz, "Amplify Unveils New Digital Curriculum," *The Hechinger Report Digital/Edu blog*, March 3, 2014. http://digital.hechinger-report.org/content/amplify-unveils-new-digital-curriculum_1297/.

15. Interview with senior Amplify executive.

16. Molly Hensley-Clancy, "How Rupert Murdoch Suffered a Rare Defeat in American Classrooms," *Buzzfeed*, August 24, 2015.

17. Brooks Barnes and Amy Chozick, "Media Companies, Seeing Profit Slip, Push into Education," *New York Times*, August 19, 2012.

18. See Discoveryeducation.com webpage, "Explore Your Community," http://www.discoveryeducation.com/what-we-offer/community/explore-your -community.cfm.

19. Jonathan A. Knee, "The Melting of Mark Zuckerberg's Donation to Newark Schools," *New York Times DealBook*, August 25, 2015 (review of Dale Russakoff, *The Prize: Who's in Charge of America's School* (New York: Houghton Mifflin Harcourt, 2015)).

20. Neera Tanden and Paul Reville, "Taking a Page from the Bay State's Education Playbook," *US News & World Report*, December 4, 2013.

21. Kenneth Chang, "Expecting the Best Yields Results in Massachusetts," *New York Times*, September 2, 2013.

22. Cambridge Associates, Private Equity Index and Benchmark Statistics, December 31, 2015.

23. Betty Corcoran, "Can Investors Make Money and Do Good in Education'" Edsurge, November 5, 2014.

24. The classic discussion of the importance of local barriers is Bruce Greenwald and Judd Kahn, "All Strategy Is Local," *Harvard Business Review*, September 2005.

25. Deepa Seetharaman, "LinkedIn Slashes Guidance; Shares Plunge," *Wall Street Journal*, May 1, 2015.

26. Saul Hansell, "Once an Acquirer, TMP Worldwide Decides to Divide," *New York Times*, February 18, 2003. On a smaller scale, another precedent in the same sector is the acquisition in 2000 by Dice.com, the leading job site for tech professionals, of MeasureUp and CCPrep, online services to help people prepare for tech-certification programs. Dice.com ultimately abandoned both businesses.

27. Jay Greene, "Microsoft to Acquire LinkedIn for $26.2 Billion," Wall Street Journal, June 4. 2016.

28. Zara Kessler, "Education looms big in shared dreams if LinkedIn Microsoft," Seattle Times, July 2, 2016.

29. Henry Mance, "Pearson to Sell School Software Provider Powerschool for $350m," *Financial Times*, June 17, 2015.

30. Caroline O'Connor and Perry Klebahn, "The Strategic Pivot: Rules for Entrepreneurs and Other Innovators," *Harvard Business Review*, February 28, 2011.

Index

Page references followed by 'f' and 't' indicate figures and tables respectively.
Page references followed by 'n' indicate notes.